GETTING SOMETHING TO EAT IN JACKSON

Getting Something to Eat in Jackson

RACE, CLASS, AND FOOD IN THE AMERICAN SOUTH

Joseph C. Ewoodzie Jr.

PRINCETON UNIVERSITY PRESS

PRINCETON & OXFORD

Published by Princeton University Press
41 William Street, Princeton, New Jersey 08540
6 Oxford Street, Woodstock, Oxfordshire OX20 1TR

press.princeton.edu

All Rights Reserved

Library of Congress Cataloging-in-Publication Data

Names: Ewoodzie, Joseph C., Jr author.
Title: Getting something to eat in Jackson : race, class, and food in the
    American South / Joseph C. Ewoodzie Jr.
Description: Princeton ; Oxford : Princeton University Press, [2021] |
    Includes bibliographical references and index.
Identifiers: LCCN 2021016475 | ISBN 9780691203942 (Hardback :
    acid-free paper) | ISBN 9780691230672 (eBook)
Subjects: LCSH: Food habits—Mississippi—Jackson—History. | Food security—
    Mississippi—Jackson. | African Americans—Food—History. | Cooking, American—
    Southern style—History. | Social classes—Mississippi—Jackson. | African Americans—
    Race identity—Mississippi—Jackson. | African Americans—Mississippi—Jackson—
    Social life and customs. | African Americans—Mississippi—Jackson—Social conditions. |
    Jackson (Miss.)—Social conditions. | Ethnology—Mississippi—Jackson.
Classification: LCC GT2853.U5 E96 2021 | DDC 394.1/20976251—dc23
LC record available at https://lccn.loc.gov/2021016475

British Library Cataloging-in-Publication Data is available

Editorial: Megan Levinson and Jacqueline Delaney
Production Editorial: Ellen Foos
Jacket Design: Karl Spurzem
Production: Erin Suydam
Publicity: Kate Hensley and Kathryn Stevens

Text photos are by the author except for figures 3.1, 3.2, 4.1, 5.1, 7.2, 9.1, 10.2, 10.3, 11.1,11.2, 11.3, and 13.1 which were taken by Ethan L. Caldwell.

Jacket art: Photos by Ethan L. Caldwell; cutlery by Fourleaflover / iStock

This book has been composed in Miller

Printed on acid-free paper. ∞

Printed in the United States of America

10 9 8 7 6 5 4 3 2 1

For my ladies—

Caroline, Jaden, and

Josephine

Every now and then, Grandmama sent these Mason jars of pickles and pear preserves. Or she gave us pounds of government cheese, peanut butter, and crackers near the middle of the month. Grandmama laughed and laughed until she didn't when I called the cheese Gourmet African American cheese. You tried to act too good to eat Gourmet African American cheese, but sometimes I caught you making these buttery grilled Gourmet African American cheese sandwiches with something ultrabougie like pumpernickel bread. I couldn't understand why you were so ashamed of eating like we didn't have much money . . .

—KIESE LAYMON, *HEAVY: AN AMERICAN MEMOIR*

CONTENTS

CHAPTER ONE

Getting Something to Eat

JONATHAN TOLD ME to come dressed up.

He invited me to meet and have lunch with him and a group of men. The men were part of an elite and exclusive organization called The Boulé, the first African American Greek society.[1] To fit in with them, I had to dress in formal attire. When I arrived at his house, he approved of my black suit and white shirt, but suggested a different tie from his collection. Instead of the skinny and black tie I had on, he lent me a regular-sized cream-colored tie with blue stripes. He wore a blue shirt, a matching tie, and a khaki-colored suit jacket with black pants. We drove to the lunch location in separate cars because I was permitted to stay only for the first half of their gathering. They met on the eighteenth floor of The Capital Club on South Congress Street. "This is what's left of some of the old, exclusive places in Jackson," he muttered as we entered the elevator. Referring to Jim Crow laws, his comment was simultaneously an explanation and indignation.

The elevator doors opened to an elegant lobby area through which we walked into a private dining room. Around rectangular tables, a dozen or so older Black men were already eating and enjoying each other's conversations.

"How you doing, Archons?" Jonathan greeted them. Archon, the title for supreme court justices in ancient Athens, is how they referred to one another. He introduced me as the guest for the day and then motioned for us to get something to eat. At the general dining area entrance, an older Black man, a server, stood behind a wooden podium. As we approached him, Jonathan simply said, "Boulé" and gave him a friendly head tilt. In response, the server smiled and invited us to enter. The Capital Club is still a member-only establishment, so this general area was not open to the public. There were round tables covered with beige tablecloths and set with gold-trimmed plates and bowls alongside polished silver utensils in the large, naturally lit dining space. The glass walls were covered with elegant drapes, but behind them was a stunning view of the city. In one corner, a middle-aged white man played solemn classical music on a grand piano.

The room was probably only half full. One Black family of six or so members sat at one table. Another smaller Black family occupied another. The rest of the clientele was white.

"Go ahead and help yourself, man," Jonathan said to me as he went over to greet the larger Black family.

A buffet of food and an omelet station were to our left as we walked into the room. When I dished out a cup of their vegetable soup, one of the servers hurried to me and offered to take it to my table while I went through the rest of the line. All the servers were Black, and most were men. Each wore a white shirt, a black vest, and a bow tie. For my entrée, I passed on the fried chicken, ribs, and steak and decided on black-eyed peas, scalloped potatoes, and fish.

I was on the side of the buffet opposite Jonathan when he finally made his way to the food, so I thought I was going down the wrong side.

"No, no, it's both sides," he assured me. He added, "Oh, make sure you look at the dessert, too. They'll bring it to you." When I walked over to the dessert table, two teenaged white girls came over to see about an Oreo pie. They were so excited about it that they nearly bumped into me. Unfortunately for them, there was none left. I pointed to the bread pudding, and the server at that station dished out a serving and took it to my seat.

As we ate, a few more members of The Boulé walked in. One drew salutations because he had not been around for a while. When the mayor of the city walked in, he received the same warm greeting, including from Jonathan, who I knew would be running to try to unseat him in the upcoming mayoral election. Much of the rest of our eating time, which lasted approximately forty minutes, was filled with cordial conversation and laughter. By the details of their chatter, they seemed to have known each other, including the servers, for a long time. They asked about each other's families and children. The men who were dining had been members of the upper class for as long as the men serving had been in the working class. Despite the clear class divide, members of The Boulé were exceptionally polite to the servers; they always began their requests for service with, "When you get a moment could you please . . ." or, "At your convenience, please . . ." Perhaps, in those moments, their shared racial identity superseded their class distinction.

After the servers cleared our plates, one of the men glanced over to Jonathan and signaled that they were ready to begin the second portion of their meeting. Jonathan gave me a more formal introduction, highlighting my educational background, and mentioned that I was in Jackson to conduct a study for my dissertation. I spoke for about ten minutes about my academic interests, aspirations, and impressions of Jackson. I made sure to mention that W.E.B. Du Bois, a past member of their organization, was among my intellectual heroes. I even read a short passage from a copy of *The Souls of Black Folks* that I brought with me. I then fielded questions, which mostly included specific details about my time in the South. When I finished, Jonathan thanked me for spending time with them and ushered me to the elevators so they could continue with the rest of their meeting.

On the following Tuesday morning, I joined two dozen or so homeless men and women for breakfast at St. Andrew's Episcopal Church. St. Andrew's sits on the same block as The Capital Club. When I arrived, a middle-aged Black man smoking a cigarette greeted me.

"It's cold out here, ain't it?"

"Yeah, man, I didn't expect it to be this cold," I responded.

"You gonna need a bigger coat—one with a hood," he advised.

The lives of Black folks in Mississippi exist prominently in the imaginations of most Americans though not in detail, but in old, blurred pictures. Black folks in Mississippi are often out of focus because popular understandings of their lives are stuck in the past, in the 1960s, and their stories are told with images of protests and sit-ins. These retellings are so ubiquitous that it seems as if life has not been moving forward in Selma, Memphis, or Little Rock since the Civil Rights Movement. But, it has and continues to. This book is one telling of what has been happening on the streets, in the kitchens, and in the living rooms of Black folks in Jackson.

I also got to know the lives of low-income families and middle-income families. I spent months with a young mother and her sisters who lived well below the poverty line, were regularly unemployed or underemployed, and relied on social welfare programs. I spent time with them at their apartments and accompanied them to work, church, funerals, family gatherings, welfare offices, and job interviews. I also became part of the life of a grandmother who worked two jobs—as a school bus driver and as a cook at a day care center—to raise two grandsons and an adopted son. I attended church and funerals with her, rode on the school bus with her, and went with her to her grandsons' football games. Most importantly, for this book, I spent countless hours shopping for food, cooking, and eating with her and her family.

While attending a weekly community forum at a local coffee shop, I met a middle-class couple who had relocated to Jackson from Washington, DC a few years prior to start a BBQ restaurant. They are the return migrants about whom social scientists are beginning to spill so much ink.[2] After patronizing their restaurant a few times, I started volunteering in the kitchen, sweeping floors, and washing dishes. Over time, I became close to their family and took part in the family's social life—I had dinner with them more times than I can remember. At their BBQ restaurant, I also befriended one of their loyal customers. A few months after I met him, he decided to become a vegan in hopes of losing weight and regaining his health. I followed him through this journey, visiting eateries in the city that catered to his new diet and learning how to cook quinoa and tofu at his home.

I followed the lives of these socioeconomically diverse African Americans in Jackson to understand their everyday eating practices. More specifically, I wanted to learn about the foods available to them, how they choose among what is possible, and how they prepare and enjoy their meals. I use what I learned to understand their lives as socioeconomically diverse Black Southerners in contemporary urban Mississippi. *Getting Something to Eat in Jackson* is about the South and, more centrally, about food and race. In the next pages, I zoom into each of these foci.

Sociology of the South

The earliest sociology writings in the late 1800s were responses in favor of and in opposition to slavery.[3] These writings were works about the South that also contributed to national conversations. Similarly, from the time of the Missouri Compromise of 1820 through the Civil War and Reconstruction, social scientific writings (including sociological ones) about race relations in the region were reflections of national concerns.[4] They included some of the discipline's best works. Here, we can think of masterful works like Anna Julia Cooper's *A Voice from the South* (1892), Ida B. Wells's *Southern Horrors: Lynch Law in All Its Phases* (1892), and W.E.B. Du Bois's *Black Reconstruction in America* (1935). A sociologist of the South, Larry J. Griffin, calls these types of works "sociology *in* the South," or "sociology aimed at advancing general knowledge about human affairs by exploiting what the South had to offer." They differed from the sociology *of* the South, "sociology aimed at deepening understanding of the region per se."[5]

At some point, the South's role in illuminating national problems changed, so scholarly exploration of the South became less about the country and more about just the region. Sociology *of* the South became less aligned with sociology *in* the South. When millions of Southern Black folks moved to other regions in the country at the turn of the twentieth century, they took with them the fight for full citizenship in the United States. Their struggles were no longer set in Birmingham, Columbia, or Greensboro; they were also now set in New York, St. Louis, and Denver. So, beginning around 1950, sociological research about the South, including ethnographies, slipped out of the center of the discipline. As the Civil Rights Movement spread to the rest of the country, as Martin Luther King, Jr. moved to Chicago to campaign against housing inequalities, and as the Black Panther Party took hold of the movement in the late 1960s and 1970s, the central domestic conflict, race relations, no longer solely lay in the American South.[6] Large-scale clashes and riots that were ignited by racial animus, dreadful living conditions, torturous state-sponsored and sanctioned brutality, all once equated with the South, also were now part of the social fabric in various other regions in the country.[7] Perhaps, the South disappeared.[8] Or, perhaps, the United States became a Southern nation.[9]

To be clear, sociology's focus away from the South was not just about the movement of Black people in the United States. It also reflected a disciplinary shift. After the Second World War, sociology shifted away from descriptive, ethnographic, and folkloric research, popular among sociologists of the South. It moved toward using sophisticated statistical methods that were often inaccessible to general audiences. The discipline also became interested in making more general universal-like claims, which was at odds with Southern sociologists' focus on particular contexts.[10] So, scholarly exploration of the South became less about the country and more about just the region.

The alignment of the sociology of and in the South has waned over the years, but it is returning. For one thing, fortunately or not, the sun has set on the exclusive dominance of quantitative, large-data research that aims to make claims that can be replicated. Ethnographic and other qualitative methodological approaches are, once again, in fashion. This shift invites scholars like me to evoke and build on the ethnographic (and folkloric) traditions of sociologists of the South from decades past such as Anna Julia Cooper and Howard Odum.[11] This disciplinary turn has already produced path-breaking qualitative Southern sociological work by the likes of Zandria F. Robinson (race, class, and regional identity in Memphis), Vanesa Ribas (race, migration, and labor in rural North Carolina), Sabrina Pendergrass (race, culture, and Black return migration), Karida Brown (the history of racial identity in Appalachia), and B. Brian Foster (race, place, and community development in rural Mississippi).[12]

More critical than transformations in the world of sociology, sociological research about the South is returning to the discipline's center because, once again, the South is central in social and political debates in the United States. Some of the nation's recent provocative issues either are playing out in the South or are old, unresolved national contradictions with deep roots in the organization of Southern life.

For example, Georgia's 2018 gubernatorial election, along with voter ID legislation and other acts of voter suppression especially after the 2020 presidential election, has brought back into focus the history of the battle for the vote. These voter constraining measures are not just being implemented in the South—Midwestern states from the Dakotas to Ohio all have various versions of such laws—but they harken back to struggles in the South, including the symbolic and violent clash on the Edmund Pettus Bridge in Selma, Alabama.[13] During the 2020 presidential elections and in the subsequent US Senate runoff, all eyes were on Georgia. National politics lay in the hands of Southern voters. During the same election cycle, Alabama's abortion law, the most punitive and restrictive in the country, made women's health and reproductive rights even more central in political debates.[14] A few years prior, North Carolina's HB2 statute provided the stage for furthering public conversations about human rights for transgender peoples.[15] Police brutality against unarmed Black American citizens has recalled centuries of government-sanctioned torture and lynching of the Black body. Recent discussions about the causes of deepening economic inequalities begin with slavery and include racially discriminatory New Deal policies engineered by Southern Democrats.[16] For these and many other crucial social problems, the South casts a large shadow over the nation. This book exists in that moment and offers a deep portrait of a Southern city while pointing to pressing national social patterns and problems in research on race and food.

Race (and Blackness)

There once was a time when Black Americans of varying class backgrounds lived in and around the same neighborhoods. Racially discriminatory federal, state, and city housing policies, such as exclusionary Federal Housing Authority practices and racially restrictive deeds and covenants prevented Black folks who had the financial is more, I include in this analysis the experiences of people who are homeless, a population that is often ignored. In what follows, I investigate what types of foods are available to these diverse Black Southerners, how they choose from among what is available, and how they prepare and consume their meals.

Food

Most of us eat every day. We must; we need the energy. But, we also eat because we want to. It makes us feel good. It brings us to the people we love. Eating certain foods makes us happy; it triggers feelings of home, feelings of belonging. What and how we eat reflects how we imagine ourselves, which reflects how we imagine the world.[23] Food helps to delineate the social groups to which we belong. In this book, I use what and how people eat to investigate how race and class overlap in the South. I focus on food availability, choice, and consumption in the lives of people inhabiting different social classes within the same racial category.

Food availability is very much about people's living circumstances. Their encounters (or lack thereof) with various social and economic structures, including institutions, shape what is available for them to eat.[24] Whether someone is poor or affluent, employed or unemployed, or lives in a poor or rich neighborhood all come to matter in what kinds of food they find available. The homeless men I followed had exited or been pushed out of the city economic structures—many did not work. Whatever measly income some might have had came from their piteous relationship with a stringent welfare system. They also had various levels of interactions with the criminal justice system. They lived under constant threat of harassment from the police and parapolice officers. Some had returned back to society after having spent some years in prison—they often returned worse off than when they entered. Most obviously, these men I followed were also unhoused. These sparse encounters with many of the city's social structures left them without much control over their food availability. As such, the shelters and other service-providing institutions essentially determined their food availability. They ate what the service providers decided. On top of this, and perhaps more subtly, the cultural structures in which people are born or choose to participate also influence what foods appear to us as available.[25] In a place like Mississippi, Black and Southern food traditions loom over everyone's options. The meals I ate with the homeless men often included macaroni and cheese, greens, and fried catfish—all foods that most other Mississippians, regardless of race and class, also enjoy. There were some differences as well. Sometimes, the differences were qualitative. More affluent folks ate refined versions of foods that poorer people also ate. Other times, the intersections of race and class swayed their participation in various branches (e.g., slow, organic, or local food) of the modern food movement.[26]

If social and economic structures, including ones that shape employment chances and housing conditions, significantly shape food availability, studying food choices shows how people navigate the structures they encounter. Food choices are about seeing how ordinary Black Americans circumvent constraints and deal with historically (and regionally) rooted oppressive social and cultural structures in the contemporary South.[27] These explorations reveal both the ingenuity and the human costs of deprivation. They display that Black folks in different class groups have different living circumstances and therefore approach their food decisions differently. This, in many ways, disrupts the assumption that soul food and other Black American food traditions of the past are responsible for unhealthy eating behaviors among Black Southerners. Food choices are not motivated just by habits and traditions in their pasts. They are also the result of paradoxes and problems people face in their present context. And, they are reflections of people's outlooks and projections of themselves into the future.[28]

So far, I have suggested that food availability reflects people's living circumstances and that food choices reflect how people navigate their circumstances. Food consumption, what people eat and how they eat, illustrates how people think about themselves. This follows the popular saying that people are what they eat. For the various Black folks I got to know in Jackson, the foods that sit in front of them reflect who they are and where they fit in the world in which they live. When the homeless man stares at the fried chicken that the church is serving him at eight o'clock in the morning, he takes a deep breath before taking a bite. In between his inhale and exhale, he thinks through how and why his life has gotten to a point where he must eat such greasy food early in the morning or risk going hungry. When the mother of a middle-income family watches her child eating a piece of fruit that she purchased from her nearby grocery store that she knows to be bottom-barrel produce, she wonders why members of her family and her community are valued less than those who live in a different zip code. Also, I pay attention to eating as a social activity, one imbued with symbols of class and race performances.[29] I study how people serve their taken-for-granted preferences for certain foods and restaurants (including the plates and utensils they eat with) and how they eat (including the space in which they eat, the people with whom they eat, and the time of day and for how long they eat).

Getting Something to Eat in Jackson, then, is a book set in the contemporary South that shows what we can learn about food by studying Black life in the South and what we can learn about race (and blackness) by studying food in the South. I began the research with a two-week visit in June 2011, returned for most of 2012, and again in the summer of 2016. I focused on distinct class experiences in my fieldwork: homeless, working poor, middle class, and upper-middle class.[30] I thought of class as a subjective location and a relational explanation of economic life chances and accordingly assigned participants to each class group as I came to know their day-to-day living circumstances.[31]

I observed the experience of homelessness among people who, during the time of my fieldwork, had virtually no stable source of income, consistently were without housing, and did not have the capital (cultural, economic, or social) to improve their lives. The working-poor experience was represented by those who frequently had housing, but were at times unemployed or underemployed and relied on social welfare benefits during my time in Jackson. While they had the know-how to navigate the maze that is public assistance, they often lacked the educational background or networks to permanently lift themselves out of poverty. Middle-class people in my research were those who did not need social welfare benefits.

They lived on the wages of their employment. While some financially struggled, they had enough financial resources to squeeze by or relied on their educational backgrounds and networks to permanently survive. I observed the upper-middle-class experience among people who appeared to have significantly more financial resources than they needed to cover their month-to-month expenses. They were also self-employed or held managerial positions at their workplaces and held various leadership positions in the city. In all, I got to know about thirty African American men and women who were living in different corners of Jackson.[32]

The book's four main parts are based on the four class groups I studied and the conceptual components of foodways: availability, choice, and consumption. Part I focuses on the experiences of those who are homeless. In those chapters, I focus on food availability. Part II focuses on the experiences of those who live in poverty and covers food choices. Part III is about the experiences of those who are middle-class and also about food choice. Part IV is about the experiences of those who are upper-middle class and covers food consumption. In each of these parts and with its corresponding component of foodways, I investigate one aspect of Black American life in the contemporary South. Through analyzing food availability, I look into the various structures that Black folks in the South encounter. By exploring food choice, I illustrate how they navigate the structures they encounter. From studying food consumption, I provide a social-psychological analysis of Black folks in the South as they face and navigate today's cultural, social, and economic structures.

In the next chapter, I first provide a historical account of food and Black American life. Then, I review the historical significance of Jackson, Mississippi, in the history of race in the South and why it makes for a suitable place for this study. Finally, I share how I entered my research setting, how I met people and became part of their lives.

CHAPTER TWO

Soul Food and Jackson

AFRICAN AMERICAN FOODWAYS, which are a mixture of the "cooking traditions of West Africans, Western Europeans, and Amerindians," began in the late fifteenth century when Spanish and Portuguese colonizers arrived on the west coast of the African continent for what became the Transatlantic slave trade.[1] The arrival of Europeans on the African continent influenced the diet of some African communities. Communities in present-day Northern Angola and Western Congo began cultivating the crops that Europeans introduced because they proved easier to grow, especially during droughts and flooding, than indigenous crops like sorghum, millet, and couscous.[2] Some of these influences remained on the continent and became part of what the captured and enslaved Africans took with them to the New World. Most of the Africans who became slaves were agriculturalists who had mastered growing what would become significant export crops such as rice and indigo of English North American colonies such as South Carolina and Louisiana.[3]

Captured Africans aboard slave ships did not have a say in what they ate. Whatever was made available to them was a drastic shift from the foods with which they were familiar. In the following passage, Rawley and Behrendt summarize foodways on slave ships, highlighting not only what enslaved people ate but also how and with what utensils they ate:

> It was customary to give two meals a day, placing ten slaves about small tubs containing their victuals. Each slave was provided with a

wooden spoon. A staple on English ships was horse beans, brought from England, and stored in dry vats until they were boiled in lard until they formed a pulp. Slaves were said to have a good stomach for beans, and besides, [as one crewmember put it] "It is a proper fattening food for captives." Rice, available in Europe and Africa, was a second staple; it was sometimes boiled with yams, available in Africa. Meat, whether beef or pork, was rarely offered. Slaves from [West Central Africa] were accustomed to yams; those from [present-day Ivory Coast and Ghana] were accustomed to rice. Palm oil, vegetables, lemons, and limes from time to time appeared in this regimen. . . . North American slavers commonly fed their slaves rice and corn, both of which were available in America and Africa, and black-eyed-peas. The rice was boiled in an iron pot and corn was fried into cakes. Water was the usual beverage, sometimes flavored with molasses by the Americans. Wine and spirits were administered as medicines, and the smoking of tobacco in pipes was often encouraged.[4]

This account highlights the beginnings of an African American food tradition, even pointing to certain foods that would become staples. It also highlights how intimately historical and socioeconomic structures—slavery—shaped African American eating practices, especially what was available to them.

On slave ships, food served as an essential symbolic tool for both the captured and the capturers. To begin with, the success of the journey depended on whether the traders had a sufficient supply of food. Historians estimate that between one-fifth and one-tenth of those transported to the New World did not survive the voyage.[5] According to some scholars, the distance from Africa to the Americas paired with food shortages most significantly explains the high mortality of enslaved Africans during the Middle Passage. More slaves died on voyages that were longer than three months than on voyages lasting a month or less, and this difference was typically due to insufficient food supply on longer journeys.[6] For the capturers, providing enough nourishment for enslaved folks was vital to maximizing profit.[7] However, the slave traders also withheld food, along with various other draconian disciplinary acts, to scare enslaved Africans from thinking about a revolt.[8] Importantly, food was also a tool of resistance for the captured. Protesting their horrendous

maintenance of sharp racial boundaries during the nineteenth century.[20]

Enslaved Africans in America also built their sense of self, including their dignity, belonging, and culture, with food. Holidays such as Christmas, New Year's Day, the Fourth of July; religious revivals; and Sundays were special, symbolic occasions because they were days when those enslaved people defied how their masters viewed them and created who they imagined themselves to be. On these days, which were by civil and religious law days away from the fields or the watchful eyes of their masters, they experienced fleeting freedom. This small taste of liberation was marked by eating and drinking what they wanted.[21] It was during these times that they established and expanded their foodways. It was the beginning of the association of food and African American soulfulness or spirituality. The Swedish feminist Frederika Bremer's account of her visit to a church revival in Macon, Georgia, in May 1850 aptly illustrates this fusion of faith and food.

> At half-past five [in the morning], I was dressed and out. The negroes' hymns were still to be heard on all sides. . . . People were cooking and having breakfast by the fires, and a crowd was already gathering and filling the benches under the tabernacle for the seven o'clock morning worship service and the eleven o'clock sermon that would follow. . . . After the service came the dinner hour, when I visited several tents in the Black camp and saw tables covered with all kinds of meat, puddings, and tarts; there seemed to be a regular superfluity of food and drink. . . . The people appeared gay, happy, and gentle. These religious camp-meetings are the saturnalia of the negro slaves. In these they luxuriate both soul and body, as their natural inclination to do; but on this occasion everything was carried on with decency and befitting reverence.[22]

Similarly, Christmas was a day of feasting, arguably the biggest of them all. Here is Harriet Jacobs's description:

> Slaves, who are lucky enough to have a few shillings, are sure to spend them for good eating; and many a turkey and pig is captured. . . . Those who cannot obtain these, cook a 'possum, or a raccoon, from which savory dishes can be made. My grandmother raised poultry and pigs

for sale; and it was her established custom to have both a turkey and a pig roasted for Christmas.[23]

These passages highlight how foods that were enjoyed on celebratory days became imbued with so much significance.[24] These dishes became an active part of the social construction of what it meant to be Black in America and how Black folks defined themselves even then.

From the bitter depths of slavery through the promise of emancipation and reconstruction, African American foodways changed continuously while simultaneously emerging as a distinctively recognizable cuisine. Throughout the Civil War, both Union and Confederate states used Black people for menial labor, among which cooking skills were vital.[25] Their cooking, an outgrowth of Black food traditions, served both Black and white soldiers. At the dawn of emancipation, Black Southerners continued to subsist on salt pork and cornbread. "Emancipation did give them greater access to poultry, however, resulting for some in the cooking and consumption of fried chicken for breakfast and supper. Fruit cobblers, [adapted from British foodways], biscuits, turnips, sweet potatoes, and pork salad . . . were also familiar foods in Black Southern homes."[26] During the Reconstruction Era, when the free labor on which Southern planters had relied for dozens of decades was no longer available, Southern white people did all they could to resist and reverse all liberties the abolition of slavery might have afforded Black people. "In hundreds of cases," writes historian Eric Foner, "planters evicted from their plantations Blacks too old or infirm to labor, and transformed 'rights' enjoyed by slaves—clothing, housing, access to garden plots—into commodities for which payment was due."

Further, Southern whites detested the very act of negotiating wages with Black people whose labor, in their minds, they outrightly owned.[27] In the decades that followed, what some historians refer to as the nadir of American race relations, Black folks faced violent attacks worse than those in any other period following the US Civil War.[28] As a response to these and other harsh social circumstances, as many as 2.5 million Southern-born Black Americans packed their belongings and headed to Northern states.[29]

Mothers, unsure of how long the northbound trip would take, supplied relocating family members with more than enough provisions. As one story goes, Liza Bowman, a South Carolinian, must have spent days preparing for her son's sojourn. She made "tons of hoecake biscuits, pan after pan of cornbread, fried rice cakes, pickled vegetables, tomatoes, okra, beets, string beans, squash, and jar after jar of cooked beans." Also, she sent along "cured and smoked bacon, slabs of salt pork, hams, and jerk beef; she packed sacks of cornmeal, flour, grits, dried beans, and rice" as well as dried fruit and herbs.[30] As they traveled northward, they brought with them and spread their foodways. Isabel Wilkerson, author of *The Warmth of Other Suns*, attests to this in her writing: "As best as they could, the people brought the Old Country with them—a taste for hominy grits and pole beans cooking in salt pork, the 'sure enough' and 'I reckons' and the superstitions of new moons and itchy palms that had seeped into their very being."[31]

In their new locales, Black migrants did not always have the ingredients they were accustomed to and they did not always have the means to buy what they wanted once the Great Depression hit. Still, they cooked what they knew, adapting their food traditions to their social circumstances. In the following excerpt from *Black Metropolis*, the landmark 1940s study of Black life in Chicago, Drake and Cayton provide a sense of how migrants managed in the 1920s. It shows how Black migrants in the North depended on one another to survive. It also shows how the context of their lives shaped how they fed themselves.

> I arrived at six o'clock, bringing twelve cents' worth of sausage and a ten-cent loaf of bread. Mr. Ben and Slick were both dozing in their chairs. I mentioned that I was tired and sat down. Ben and I passed a few words about the weather. Slick announced that he wanted to listen to "Gang Busters" on the radio at nine o'clock. Finally, Baby Chile called us to the kitchen for supper—a platter of neckbones and cabbage, a saucer with five sausage cakes, a plate of six slices of bread, and a punchbowl of stewed prunes (very cold and delicious). Baby Chile placed some corn fritters on the table, remarking, "This bread ain't got no milk in it. I did put some [egg] in it, but I had to make it without any milk."[32]

In the thick of the Depression, a growing number of people relied on federal surplus distribution of food and the coordinated efforts of neighbors, but many suffered. For most Black people who were not so lucky, food insecurity ran rampant. In *Deep South*, another cross-class study of Black Americans, the authors report that many Black folks lived in semi-starvation during two 2-month stretches in the year when they had neither money from selling their produce, credit from their sharecropping landowner nor stored food from their garden.[33] In the North, in places such as Harlem and Philadelphia, people attended "rent parties," where the host charged a small amount for food, drinks, and entertainment. These events raised funds for the hosts to cover their housing, but they also put certain foods, the ones Black migrants took with them from the South, closer to the struggles of blackness.

During the Jim Crow Era, caste-like race relations endured, particularly in the South. Social divisions became more pronounced as segregation emerged as the law of the land. Public places, including schools, transportation, restrooms, and drinking fountains, were all legally segregated. To meet popular (i.e., white) demand, restaurants were also segregated. Again, food became part of the process of racialization. In response, Black-owned restaurants popped up all over. In a sense, according to Opie, "many of the eateries owed their success to the Jim Crow laws."[34] The food at Black restaurants was not significantly different from what white Southerners were eating, but it began taking on additional symbolic value. These foods became a form of resistance because they were eaten in spaces that rebuffed the laws of the day. In the South, Black restaurants became safe havens from harassment. In the North, The Bon Goo Barbecue and The Red Rooster (the original one) in Harlem became places where those who had migrated could get a taste of "down-home cooking," a cultural marker that became a comforting memory of the life they had left behind in the South.[35]

Entertainers and musicians also helped to crystallize poor Black Southern food as a symbol of Black racial identity. Before Black musicians like James Brown, B.B. King, Ray Charles, and Aretha Franklin became part of American popular culture, they were refused services in white restaurants and instead ate at Black-owned mom-and-pop restaurants. The music they played, soul

ordinance of secession, still stands in Jackson and operates as a museum. Along with other members of the newly created Confederate nation, young white Mississippians fought and died to defend the institution of slavery and the way of life it required. Some of the fights took place in Jackson.

In the postbellum South, white Mississippians, through paramilitary organizations, most notably the Ku Klux Klan, continued fighting to uphold racist social structures. The end of the nineteenth century saw white supremacy reincarnated as Jim Crow laws. Signs on water fountains and stores and restaurants became a way to guard racial boundaries.[42] As the twentieth century turned and through the spoils of the World Wars, Black Americans in Jackson, Mississippi, and in other regions of the South endured a subtle war in an enduring South where so much stayed the same even as the world was changing so rapidly.[43] Nine students at Tougaloo College, who, like the author Richard Wright, hungered for words, challenged the new racial order by insisting on being able to read in the white-only public library downtown. Trained NAACP nonviolent protesters, their resistance became part of a nationwide movement and a significant part of what became the cornerstone of the Civil Rights Movement.[44] In May 1961, a few hundred Freedom Riders arrived in Jackson to challenge segregation laws.[45]

The history of Jackson, a racialized one, is still painfully obvious today. During my time there, I saw and felt it in politics, if not from city hall, then from the State Capitol on High Street, where lawmakers repeated some of the ideas of the city's namesake. It was in the tiredness of those who were just scraping by, in how they carried their burdens, some of which had been passed down on to them from previous generations, some of which they will surely pass down to the next. I saw it in the hopelessness of those who lived next to abandoned houses and on neglected streets and were forced to numb their pain with a bottle or a blunt. This racial history was also in the survivor's remorse of those Black folks who are, by some measures, doing economically well and in the class-based tensions that structured their relationships with cousins still stuck in poverty.

Well-meaning progressive white folks also wrestled with the racial histories in their newspaper articles, in their conversations and prayers, in their politics, and in their cross-race friendships. Some wished that things could be better, that it could all be undone, that there was a finite price so that they could once and for all pay the burden of racism and no longer deal with their guilt. The history of Jackson was their agony when they fought with racist white folks, of which there are still plenty, to do and be better and with Black folks whose trust they seem never to be able to secure. Perhaps more than anything, the racialized history of Jackson laid in the back of everyone's mind. It was like the thickness in the humidity of a Mississippi summer breeze—quiet, ever-present, and, at times, suffocating.

Jackson spans 106.8 square miles (smaller than Omaha, Nebraska, and Salt Lake City, Utah, but bigger than Sacramento, California, and Milwaukee, Wisconsin) and has about 175,000 residents (smaller than Providence, Rhode Island but bigger than Fort Lauderdale, Florida). Nearly 80 percent of the city's population is Black; only 18 percent is white. As a metropolitan area, Jackson has the highest percentage of Black people (45 percent) in the United States.[46]

Jackson is what Zandria Robinson would call a "soul city."[47] Like other historical urban Southern cities, soul cities are resisting the tri-racialization of many American cities with the continuous growth of Latino populations. Jackson is holding firm to the Black-white binary, unlike Southern cities like Charlotte that are receiving Latino immigrants. Some cities, like Atlanta, are retaining the Black-white binary because of sizable growth in Black populations. Jackson remains as such because of the out-migration of many of its white residents. On the heels of the modern Civil Rights Movement, Black families moved from West Jackson to the more affluent North Jackson. With the arrival of Black people, wealthy whites moved farther north, outside of city limits. As whites moved out, middle- and upper-class Black families flowed to the areas that whites vacated. According to one lifelong resident, "The city went from 40–60 Black-white to 80–20 Black-white in a decade. And that's where we're at now."

Between 1970 and 2010, the city's population significantly decreased, from about 202,000 to 173,000. According to a member of the city's chamber of commerce, any increases in the Black residents most likely came from surrounding rural towns. For Robinson, this rural connection is another feature of soul cities. Finally, soul cities also often maintain old Southern power dynamics, as reflected in local electoral politics. Despite becoming majority-Black in the 1980s, and despite a bourgeoning middle- and upper-class Black population, white folks continued to have a stronghold on political capital in the city until 1997, when Harvey Johnson Jr. defeated J. Kane Ditto to become the city's first Black mayor.[48] African Americans have since held most of the city's highest offices, but economic power is still in the hands of old white elites. These attributes—a stagnant Black population, ties to surrounding rural communities, and old Southern power relations—fit Robinson's characterization of soul cities.[49]

Almost all of Jackson's white residents live in the northeastern corner of the city, north of Fortification Street and east of US Highway 51. Half of the 42,000 residents in this part of the town are white. In a few of the neighborhoods, more than 90 percent of residents are white. This area in the city also contains the most affluent residents of Jackson. Their average household income is nearly $73,000 (compared to $50,000 for the city) and the median household income is $48,000 (compared to $35,000 for the city).[50]

The liveliest neighborhood on the northeastern side of town is Fondren, between Northside Drive and Woodrow Wilson Avenue, where some of the upper-middle class participants of this study lived. It is the center for most of the city's art galleries, trendiest fashion boutiques, and some of its most popular eateries. Rainbow Natural Foods and Co-op is in Fondren, which was the only place to buy natural and organic foods until Whole Foods Market came into town. *Jackson Free Press*, the state's only alternative newspaper, used to sit just down the street from Rainbow. A block or so over are Sal and Mookie's New York Pizza and Ice Cream Joint, the historical Brent's Drug Store, and Babalu Tacos and Tapas, all popular places in the city.

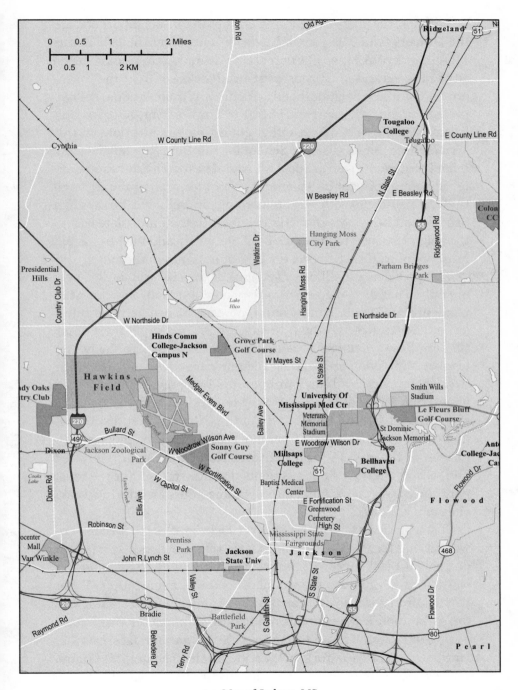

2.1. Map of Jackson, MS

Perhaps, the biggest anchoring entities in this neighborhood are the University of Mississippi Medical Center and the G.V. Sonny Montgomery VA Medical Center, which employ thousands of the city's most educated citizens. Just two blocks south of the southern border of the neighborhood (Woodrow Wilson Avenue) are two predominantly white, private liberal arts institutions, Millsaps College and Belhaven College. Other educational institutions in this area include the Mississippi School for the Deaf (the official state school of students who are deaf or hard of hearing), Education Center School (a private independent school for grades one through twelve for students with various learning disabilities), Murray High School, and Bailey Magnet High School. To the immediate east of the neighborhood are LeFleur's Bluff State Park and the Mississippi Museum of Natural Science, the largest museum in the state.

Most residents in all other sections of the city are Black. There are only a handful of census tracks where less than 85 percent of residents are Black. Ninety-three percent of residents who live around downtown and the west side are Black. I spent most of my time in these portions of the city. They are also where the homeless, working poor, and middle-income participants of this study live. The average and median household income in this area are about $32,000 and $24,000.[51] Very few residents live downtown around West Capitol Street and South Gallatin Street. Establishments like Parlor Market, a perennial contender for the best restaurant in the city, and King Edward Hotel, a recently renovated Hilton hotel, attract some residents downtown. But, for the most part, the area remains quiet after working hours and during weekends and holidays.

Just a block away from Downtown Jackson, close to East Greenwood Cemetery, is the Farish Street Neighborhood. It is about 90 percent Black. According to the civil-rights activist and journalist Charles E. Cobb Jr., the neighborhood was named after Walter Farish, a freed slave who was the first to settle in the area. It was the social, political, economic, and cultural mecca for Black folks during the 1950s, 60s, and 70s. Farish Street was for Jackson what Harlem was for New York.[52] Like the Apollo Theater, the Alamo Theatre was where big names in soul, including Nat King Cole, performed in Jackson. On this same street were the offices of Carsie

Hall, Jack Young, and R. Jess Brown, the only three Black lawyers in Mississippi in the 1960s.[53] The civil-rights activist Medgar Evers, then serving as the NAACP's first field secretary in Mississippi, had an office on this street. After his assassination, thousands of mourners followed his casket down Farish Street.

Since its glory days, the Farish Street Neighborhood has become run-down—it is now one of the city's poorest neighborhoods. A few well-known establishments remain on Farish Street and await the decade-long plans for revitalization. F. Jones Corner is a beloved late-night spot that draws a massive crowd after two in the morning when other bars close. Just a few doors down, Peaches Cafe has been on the street since the 60s and continues to serve Southern staples throughout the day—it was my first stop when I arrived in Jackson. A block down, the Big Apple Inn still serves tamales and their famous pig-ear sandwiches.

Less than a mile southwest of the Farish Street Neighborhood is Poindexter Park, close to where West Capitol Street and Robinson Street intersect. It is an entirely Black neighborhood and even more impoverished and more dilapidated than Farish Street. In its census block, 98 percent of residents are Black, the median household income is $14,459, and nearly 70 percent of residents live below the poverty line.[54] Jackson State University is the most prominent entity in this neighborhood. Several establishments serve the university clientele, and there are a handful of other entities, like Koinonia Coffee Shop. But, most of the areas around Jackson State are filled with tens of corner stores and fast-food restaurants, hundreds of abandoned buildings, and thousands of people enduring harsh poverty. It is where the homeless men I got to know spend most of their time.

Part I

CHAPTER THREE

Smack—Late Afternoons

I BEGAN VOLUNTEERING at Stewpot, Jackson's biggest soup kitchen, in June 2011. On my first day, I worked alongside a group whose employer had given them the day off to volunteer and a handful of others who seemed to be regular volunteers. We were assigned to put food on lunch trays. Following the regulars' lead, we formed an assembly line beside a long table. One person scooped macaroni and cheese onto the lunch tray; another added green beans and passed the tray down for a cookie, some fruit, and utensils. After we fixed about one hundred or so servings, we switched to other duties. I worked with one Black man on filling cups with ice and water.

The people whom we came to serve began to pour in shortly after noon. They were mostly men.[1] Some came by themselves; others came with friends. Some of the men came with women, maybe their girlfriends or wives. A few couples came with children. I fixed my attention on one Black male who looked to be in his mid-thirties. He wore blue jeans, a white undershirt, and old tennis shoes. He walked in with a woman and four children. I do not know if he was the father of these children, but it looked like he was the man in their lives from the way they surrounded him.

A man with a booming voice—one of Stewpot's staff members—began his introductory remarks as everyone settled in their seats. "God loves you!" he loudly exclaimed, pointing at the crowd. "Did you hear that?" he asked.

"He loves everybody," someone interjected.

3.1. Lunch trays at Stewpot

"He loves everybody," the speaker repeated. "And, as we enjoy this meal, that is the testimony of God's love for you, God's expression of love is in his mercy, his forgiveness, and his grace toward anyone that will ask, and his commitment to build and change communities."

As he talked, I looked at the crowd that stared back at him. They looked exhausted. The skin on their faces sagged. Their eyelids dropped, and for most of them, the whites of their eyes were not entirely white; they were soiled. Life had been unkind to them.

After a prayer and an announcement that mental health professionals and lawyers were available to provide one-on-one counseling, we started serving. My job was to hand out cups and soda. When we were being trained how to serve, we were instructed not to let the people choose their drinks because it would take too long. Instead, we were to give them whichever soda we grabbed from the cart. But, when I went around with the sodas, they did the grabbing. Some were happy with whatever they got; others were dissatisfied. One guy got upset that we did not have any more Sprite.

3.2. Lunch crowd at Stewpot

The younger men refused to drink diet soda. They kept their hands
raised until they got a tray of food and something to drink. Some
ate everything on the plate; some ate all but the bread; others took
a few bites and, perhaps unsatisfied with the taste, threw everything away, returned the trays, and left. Those who wanted more
food stood in line for it—that line wrapped around the room. Those
who arrived late for lunch, "first-timers" they were called, could go
to the front of the food line. Those who wanted to speak to the
lawyer or the mental health professional waited for their turn. After
a while, the bearded man with the bold voice announced that the
lunch was nearing its end, a nudge for people to finish up and leave.
Within thirty-five minutes, they had all trickled out.

I returned to Stewpot to volunteer a dozen or so times. The more
time I spent there, the more curious I became about the lives of the
clients. From brief conversations with them, I started to remember their names and faces. I also started to recognize the different cliques and their various preferences, but I wanted to know
more. I wanted to know more about who they were, how they fell

into homelessness, what it meant to them to be in homelessness, and how they coped with it. I was especially curious about how they managed getting something to eat every day. Besides Stewpot, where else could they go? If there were several options, how did they choose?

I quickly realized that I would not find answers to these types of questions from volunteering at Stewpot. To learn how they led their lives and sustained themselves, I had to become a part of their lives. So, that is what I did.

After a few more weeks of volunteering at Stewpot, I acquainted myself with a handful of the men and started spending time with them outside the soup kitchen. From January through March 2012 and in June 2016, I spent nearly all my waking hours as they did, and from April through November 2012 and again in July and August 2016, I spent about ten hours a week with them. During this time, I learned about the life circumstances that brought these men into homelessness; I witnessed the physical, social, and psychological struggles of homelessness. I became a part of the social ties that helped ease these challenges. Through all this, I paid attention to their foodways, especially their food availability.

Existing research about people who are homeless covers a wide range of topics. Most commonly, scholars have focused on defining homelessness, obtaining an accurate count of the homeless, identifying the causes of homelessness, and understanding various strategies for coping with the plight of homelessness.[2] Interestingly, getting something to eat, a core aspect of their lives, has been consistently overlooked. *Sidewalk,* sociologist Mitchell Duneier's classic work on the lives of book vendors on the streets of Greenwich Village, mentions the eating habits of the men on the streets, but only in passing.[3] Here and there, it recounts how the men get food from churches or restaurants at the end of the day. Elijah Anderson, in his book *Streetwise*, distinguishes "regulars" and "hoodlums" from "wineheads" in part by whether they purchase something to eat or beg for it. Still, he provides no analysis of their food habits.[4] In another well-regarded book about homelessness, *Down on Their Luck*, David Snow and Leon Anderson offer a detailed ethnographic account of various aspects of homeless people's daily lives, but how they get food is not featured in their otherwise exhaustive analyses.[5] They intermittently sprinkle in discussions about access to food with descriptions about access to other services. Research on *how* and *where* the homeless get something to eat is not entirely forgotten, but unlike other major concerns they face—employment, shelter, or salvaging the self—there is no detailed analysis of food matters in the lives of people who experience homelessness.[6] I provide one here.

Quantitative research on homelessness tells us that while food insecurity is prevalent among the homeless population, access to food does not register high on their list of most pressing needs. When nearly three thousand nationally representative homeless survey respondents were asked to identify the one thing they needed most, food ranked sixth among other needs mentioned; employment, affordable housing, and assistance with rent, mortgage, and utility costs ranked higher. When asked to choose their single most pressing need from a predetermined list, food dropped to ninth place.[7]

Yet, food is a problem for many people who are homeless. In the same study, 57 percent of those surveyed reported that they did not have enough to eat, 39 percent reported going without food for full days at a time, and 12 percent said that they turned to trash cans or handouts as food sources.[8] Access to food among the homeless has been related to various factors; demographic background (Black or Hispanic race/ethnicity), individual deficits (health problems, prison record, history of child abuse), and prior episodes of homelessness are all associated with greater food insecurity for homeless people.[9]

Differences in food insecurity by types of homelessness exposure (transitional, episodic, or chronic) suggest that there are two potential ways to understand food access and homelessness: the *street wisdom* and the *desperation* hypotheses.[10] The street wisdom hypothesis predicts that those who are chronically homeless will experience less food insecurity than those who find themselves in homelessness irregularly because the chronically homeless become more knowledgeable about navigating the world of social services. By contrast, the desperation thesis predicts that the chronically homeless will experience more food insecurity because they are less connected to the domiciled world and tend to have fewer economic and social resources that enhance food access. One set of researchers found support for the desperation thesis.[11] Compared to those who were chronically homeless, people who were transitionally homeless faced specific kinds of food insecurity. They ate fewer meals per day (71 percent versus 46 percent, respectively), went without food for several hours (47 percent versus 36 percent), had inadequate access to food (73 percent versus 52 percent), turned to trash or handouts as a food source (12 percent versus 3 percent), and lacked access to affordable food (45 percent versus 34 percent).

In my fieldwork, I observed consistent access to food among the homeless men I followed. Most were chronically homeless, meaning that they had been homeless for at least two years when I met them and had experienced two or more spells of homelessness during their lifetime.[12] Their experiences seemed to support the street wisdom hypothesis. They did not consider finding something to eat to be their most pressing need. It was common for these homeless men to eat one or two meals a day. I add that, for those experiencing homelessness, regular access to food comes at a price. To regularly get something to eat, they had to do three things. They had to learn and abide by an already established set of daily routines. They had to accept and tolerate the rules of service providers. They had to understand and conform to their place in the world—specifically, they had to accept that they were indeed down-and-out. Any efforts toward trying to get out of homelessness often conflicted with their efforts toward making ends meet. In various practical ways, which I discuss below, *surviving* homelessness was incompatible with *escaping* homelessness.

These insights suggest that the two main perspectives on food access among the homeless, the streetwise and desperation theses, represent coexistent processes rather than competing ones. The longer people remain homeless, the more they learn about the routines of homelessness, and the more they come to know and abide by the rules of service providers—this makes them streetwise. Becoming streetwise can prove detrimental because the practice and habits of becoming streetwise hinder their efforts to escape homelessness. Extended exposure to homelessness can have an institutionalizing impact on individuals, similar to exposures to mental hospitals or prisons. Like in those other institutions, surviving homelessness requires a set of skills that might not be useful outside of it.[13]

The subsequent chapters, Chapters 4 and 5, illustrate how the homeless structure their lives into a routine that survival requires. I begin in this chapter with a late afternoon and, in the ones that follow, describe different portions of the day for the homeless men I met. With each portion of the day, I demonstrate how the homeless organize their lives around the schedules of food and other service providers. I show the consequences of any disruptions to their daily routine. And, I highlight how the men I followed responded to the rules of service providers and the implications for not obeying them.

Late Afternoon

I was driving to Stewpot to volunteer when I passed by a guy who looked like he was hurrying to the same place for lunch. I recognized him from the day before. He stood out because, while most people dove right into their food when we handed them their trays, he took time to say his own rather long prayer, which consisted of bowing his head and raising both hands. He also ate only half his food and packed the rest in a container to take with him. When I saw him walking, I slowed down and asked if he was heading to Stewpot. He nodded, smiled, and hopped in my car. He introduced himself to me as Smack. After I parked, he thanked me for the ride and began walking away, but before going too far, he turned and said, "I gave you mine [referring to his name], but you didn't give me yours." So, I told him my nickname: Piko. Signaling our difference in status, I went through the building's side entrance after I greeted the security guard who stood by it to make sure I was either an employee or a volunteer. Smack went toward the front entrance and joined the rest of the people waiting to get inside.

After a few more interactions, Smack became my first introduction to the homelessness world in Jackson. He is a small guy, standing at just four and a half feet or so, but he commands attention with his voice, charisma, and Baptist preacher-like mannerisms. Most people at The Opportunity Center (a day shelter for homeless men and women) were tired of his preaching. Being new at the center and wanting a way in, I listened.

In the middle of one of his long sermon-like monologues, he exclaimed, "We live in a day and times where parables have got to be done away with. Everybody can't understand the words of the wise." He quoted a few Bible verses about Jesus's order to his disciples to go into the inner-city and spread his word. Then, as if to interpret what the scripture says, he continued, "Where is the inner city? The inner city is the hood, the ghetto. It wasn't suburbia; it wasn't goddamn Ridgeland; it wasn't goddamn Eastover; it wasn't Deep South Jackson; it wasn't Clinton. He said, 'Come in the hood.'" As he mentioned the names of each of these more affluent sections of Jackson and its surroundings, his voice got progressively louder.

"I gots to bring it to you so that you can understand. . . . We live in a day and time when parables have got to be done away with." He repeated himself, more solemnly this time and with the same cadence as a preacher repeating their sermon theme. "If you can't get it with the *'thees,'* and *'thys,'* I got to bring it to you where *thou* can get it."

I busted into laughter. "Where *thou* can get it?"

"Yea, where *thou,*" he repeated with more emphasis, "can get it."

Knowing that he had me right where he wanted me, he continued, "I am the word according to Smackavelli. . . . I am Smack, Smacko, Smackavelli."

Around 4 p.m. on another January weekday, I walked with Smack and with Lee, another man who is homeless, to The Men's Shelter. Smack knew I was researching homelessness and agreed to show me the "real deal." Lee thought I was homeless. They had both slept outside—or "camped out," as they put it—the night before, but they were determined to get a bed that night. The main arguments in this first part of the book began to form in my mind that day as I observed their lives at the shelter. It was my first encounter with how they patterned their days and the stock of skills and behaviors they developed to navigate homelessness, especially to get a place to sleep and something to eat.

As we walked the mile-and-a-half from West Capitol down toward South Gallatin Street, Smack and Lee explained how they decide between staying outside and accessing support services.

"You can stay with Mother Nature, baby," Smack began to explain. "See that field right there? If it was summertime, and it wasn't no rain, I'd have me some blankets out there right now, posted up."

"The city don't care?" I asked.

"Shiiit, I don't give a fuck about the city," Smack loudly called out.

"They ain't gonna take you to jail," Lee responded.

"What they gonna do? Take me to the Wathall [Hotel], mother-fucker?" The Wathall Hotel was a well-known hotel in Downtown Jackson.

"If they take you to jail, they gonna have to feed ya," Lee added.

"They know you homeless, so they gonna let you out." Smack explained why, in his experience, the police have stopped arresting the homeless. "They see it as a waste of taxpayer money. They don't want you in there," he chuckled. "What they want you in there for? The [man in charge of the jails] already said they don't want you, and Sheriff Tyrone Lewis don't want you either. Messing with you and all that paperwork, ha!"

We all started laughing again. And then, in a serious tone, Lee added, "They got too many people out here to take care of," hinting that the homeless folks are not among the people about whom the city cared. "They ain't gonna fuck with you."

"See you can sleep right there," Smack commented as he pointed to what looked like leftover concrete from a torn-down build-ing. "Salvation Army used to be here. You can make this shit easy on you, or you can make it hard. That's on any aspect of life." He explained that shelters provide good services, but they come at a cost. For instance, the shelters' operating hours make it hard for those trying to maintain a job.

"See, you got a person who's a hard sleeper, and his job start at 9. But here, he gotta be up at 4:30 a.m. . . . He ain't done no drugs. I'm just talking anybody. So, if you got somebody who gotta be up at 4:30, but ain't got to be there at work till 9 a.m., you fucking his body up. So, he says, 'Fuck it. I'm gonna be out here, sleep all the way till daylight, and get my ass up when I know I got nothing but an hour to go to work.'"

I met some of the people to whom Smack was referring. Not only did the waking hours make it difficult for those who work but the hours for getting in the shelters also posed a challenge. To get a bed, they had to line up around 4 p.m. They were on their way to get in line.

For the rest of our walk, through Clifton Street, Hooker Street, and then down South Gallatin, they told me stories about what it used to be like to live on the streets. Smack and Lee are two long-time homeless men, so they have lived through the city's changing homelessness policies. According to them, the portion of West Jackson, where we walked, was where homeless folks lived during the 1970s and 1980s. It was Jackson's Skid Row.[14] They remembered it fondly. Those who wanted to stayed in the Salvation Army shelter close by, where, according to Smack, "we did whatever the hell we wanted to." Others camped out around Hooker Street, which was, as the name may suggest, the place for rampant drugs and prostitution.

Smack pointed to a red brick house down the street that he used to "own"—where he sold drugs. Lee pointed to a spot where he used to smoke crack. "Man, ain't a spot out here I ain't smoked dope in. This is Hooker Street," Smack exclaimed. They both remembered a Ms. Deborah and a Ms. Cooper, who used to sell drugs and rent rooms. Smack got his nickname from Ms. Deborah. Things started to change around the time Smack got locked up in the early 1990s when the city decided to reclaim that space because of its proximity to downtown.[15] It was when the police started locking up homeless people "like it was nobody's business." And, they "beat the mother-fucking shit out of homeless people" when they started clearing it out. "Everybody in this bitch went to the pen[itentiary]."

Their story is part of a broader history of African Americans and homelessness that is usually absent from studies about US homelessness.[16] That history begins with runaway slaves and formerly enslaved persons who, during the Civil War, sought refuge among Union soldiers.[17] They heroically contributed to winning the war, but after it, they had nowhere to go. All other freed Black persons in the immediate aftermath of the war were also essentially homeless.[18] By some estimates, there were between one and four million Black Americans scattered across the South without roofs over their heads. Even using the lowest estimates, that is twice the US homeless population in 2018. If they had places to stay, they were meager facilities, according to Du Bois's analysis of the Seventh Ward in Philadelphia.[19]

When millions of Black folks moved north during the Great Migration, overcrowded and overpriced housing forced many into homelessness.[20] The Great Depression decimated the economic well-being of all Americans, but it hit African Americans "earliest and most severely," and New Deal policies that were meant to ease these hardships were drawn up with the help of Southern Democrats to exclude Black folks, especially Black tenant farmers. These policies also expanded the rolls of Black homelessness.[21] And then, there was urban renewal and slum clearance, the deindustrialization of the economy, and the impacts of crack cocaine.[22] I heard in the biographies of the men who I got to know how these latter historical moments shaped their journeys in homelessness. Today, the homeless population in the South is less than it is in other parts of the country. In fact, 0.25 percent of Mississippi's population are experiencing homelessness—only seven states have lower rates. The rates of homelessness have been decreasing since 2010, but the racial disparity remains relatively the same. In 2018, Black Americans made up 55 percent of Mississippi's homeless population when they are 38 percent of the state's population.[23]

About eight people were waiting in the driveway when Smack, Lee, and I approached The Men's Shelter. They all knew each other and were chatting and joking with one another. Shortly after our arrival, a tall man popped out of the front door and sat down on a chair he brought out with him. He did not engage with anyone, and the people waiting knew not to speak to him. The power dynamics between them made it a faux pas. After a little while, the man brought out an orange Gatorade cooler filled with water. On the white handles of the cooler, he shoved a few Styrofoam cups. Then, he brought out an aluminum foil container with what looked like day-old doughnuts. He did not say anything to anyone, but people knew to get some water and some doughnuts. They drank with one of the cups and shoved it back by the handle for the next person to use. It was one of two instances when people would get something to eat. The second instance would not come until three or so hours later. Though they would have two chances to eat within five hours, they would have virtually no say in what they ate. Moreover, their access to food was so determined by the shelter that rejecting any of its rules and regulations would mean giving up the chance to eat.

Smack assumed that I would stay at the shelter, so he notified those in charge that I was a first-timer and, on top of that, a volunteer at Stewpot, both of which unbeknownst to me bought me some privileges. After me, the first-timer, priority was extended to those who did not stay at the shelter the previous night, followed by people who showed up late the day before and slept on the floor in a sleeping bag, people who slept on the couch, and then people who got beds. After we arranged ourselves in line, the man in charge motioned for me to go inside to fill out intake forms. I did not plan to stay at the shelter for the night—it was ethically indefensible, but I wanted to see what a first-timer would have to do to get a bed. My experience of the process is nowhere near that of someone who had suffered the economic and social losses that bring people into homelessness. I was not, in any sense, homeless—I had an apartment in which I stayed throughout my research. I went through the intake process because I wanted to at least understand its logic and observe how these men spend their time at the shelter. It was the start of my witnessing the rules that homeless men in Jackson had to abide by.

I was interviewed by a large Black man who sat on the other side of a long table. He first asked for my ID and then for my social security number, home address, and an emergency contact's phone number. He noticed my last name and guessed that I am African. I confirmed and told him that I am from Ghana. Then he asked for my education level.

I told him I had some college.

"How many years?"

"Four," I foolishly blurted out.

For the first time, he looked up. I was nervous at his glance because my answer was inaccurate. He looked back down. He handed me my license. I thought it was over, but I was wrong.

He gave me a double-sided form. "Fill all of this out except for the part about the names of your children."

It was the same information that I had provided him. "Why would they have me fill out this form myself when I had just told him everything?" I thought to myself. My nervousness was now mixed with frustration, which was familiar to poor people seeking different kinds of social welfare benefits. Under the guise of preventing fraud, service providers inundate their clients, who are often already mentally exhausted, with paperwork. Some experts believe that policymakers are using paperwork as a deterrent for those looking for assistance.[24] After I filled out the first page, I tried to hand it back to him.

"Did you fill out both sides?" he asked without looking at me. I did not even respond; I just flipped it over and kept writing.

As soon as I handed him the paper, I admitted to him that I was a researcher learning about the experiences of homelessness in Jackson. He gave me an expressionless stare; he was not upset, maybe just confused. I apologized for wasting his time and asked his permission to hang around a bit and see how the evening went for the men. After checking with his supervisor, he agreed to my request and told me that he would reassign the bed that would have been given to me. He also agreed to treat me like all the other guys and motioned for me to go back outside and wait. Those in the front of the line asked if I had been given a bed. I nodded. Earl, a former doorman at Stewpot, who knew about me and my work, came out fifteen minutes later to assure me he had informed the staff about my research, that they would all treat me as one of the regulars, and that I could stay for as long as I wanted. I thanked him for his help.

Shortly afterward, it was time to check-in. First in line, I walked toward Earl, who instructed me to spread out my arms for a pat-down. In my pockets, he found a pencil and took it away. "You ain't supposed to have this." (He gave it back to me later.)

After the pat-down, another guy checked and took IDs—I gave him my driver's license. He was in on my arrangement. He handed me a towel and a face towel.

"Are you taking a shower here? Because everyone is supposed to shower before you make your bed and sit on the couch," he asked.

I shook my head no.

"Well, just take the towel and washcloth anyway."

I expected the room to be filled with bunk beds, but it was not. It was, instead, furnished with beds that were made from benches. The beds were lengthened dining booths, booths like those at any diner. There were some sheets on the bed for us. As I started to make my bed, Bed #1, the guy who had Bed #2 rushed in and headed for the bathroom.

"Come on, man, you gotta get in the shower, or they gonna cut you."

"I'll wait for you to go first." I started to stall and started to make my bed.

"Man, you can make that bed later. You better come on." He said again, more emphatically this time.

He grabbed his stuff and went straight to the bathroom. I did not understand the rush. I kept stalling. After five minutes or so, when I went into the bathroom, I realized that he was rushing because there is only one shower stall for the thirty or so men staying at the place. What is more, as I was told earlier, everyone is required to shower before they do anything, even before they could sit on the couch. So, until their turn came to shower, they had to remain standing. When I went into the bathroom, there were five people already ahead of me. I tried to urinate in the one toilet available for everyone. It was not covered at all, so everyone in the bathroom could see anyone who was using it. After a few seconds of unsuccessfully trying (stage fright, I guess), I left.

By this time, most of the people who had a bed had been checked in. Bed #1 had already been reassigned. To confirm what I was observing, I went by Smack's bed and asked him to explain the order of things.

"Shower, then you can sit on the couches and watch TV. Watch the news, and then dinner will be served. Then you come back and watch TV till they turn off the lights."

I hovered around the sleeping area a little longer, chitchatting with others who were making their beds and waiting on their turn to shower, then I returned my towel. When I went to the TV seating area, which had couch space for about eight persons, a handful of people were already seated, watching TV. Lee, the man I had walked with, asked me if I had already taken a shower. I nodded, even though I looked the same, with the same clothes on and everything. Others also asked, perhaps to ensure that, as a newcomer, I knew the rules of the place.

We watched the 5 p.m. local news, in silence. It mainly covered the city's commemoration of Martin Luther King Jr. Day. The coverage included excerpts of Mayor Harvey Johnson's speech, clips of community marches, and highlights of events at Freedom Corner (the intersection of Medgar Evers Boulevard and Martin Luther King Jr. Drive). At the end, the news anchor, a Black woman,

"Well, the store is rock-bottom bare," he said, referring to his stash of food. For Smack, having his food stash was vital because it temporarily relieved him of having to depend entirely on service providers for food. For example, on the day when he missed going to lunch at Stewpot because he went to the clinic to check on aches in his arm, he resorted to his stash of food. Without his surplus, it was difficult to run these errands. If he goes to see a lawyer about his appeal, he has to fit it around the operating hours of soup kitchens or risk missing a meal.

"You ain't got nothin'?"

"Nothin', man."

"I see that's why ol' Smacko carrying meals around," the man responded, referring to the pieces of bread that were wrapped in the paper towel in his hand.

"You know that ain't my style, man."

"Aight, come by tomorrow. I'll get you something."

"I ain't got a damn noodle in my bag, man."

"Just drop by tomorrow."

"Okay."

We started walking toward the bus station. "So, did you get something to eat last night before you left?" he asked me.

"No." For ethical reasons, at that point, I was ambivalent about eating at the shelter. I explained to him I did not feel right taking food that others needed more than I did.

"Man, fuck feeling bad. Feeling bad and full are two different things."

When I realized that no one was turned away because of a shortage of food, I changed my mind. I decided to eat at the shelters also because of something that Smack said that morning:

"Bro, you say you wanna get this shit down, and you wanna get this shit down real, so you gonna have to, goddamn it, get it how we live it. I told your ass the uncut things. Ain't no better way to get this goddamn information that you seek until you get it hands-on."

I nodded in agreement. It was sage advice. As we dodged oncoming traffic from the morning rush, my mind drifted to the cars that blew past us. I wondered what the people who were driving by thought of us who were on foot.

"And," Smack continued, still thinking about how I can maintain the integrity of my project, "you about to blow your cover. You better believe motherfuckers are observant out here, bro. They observant. They the most observant motherfuckers on the planet."

I was not worried about blowing my cover because I was not being secretive. I revealed myself to anyone interested in my project, but I appreciated his advice to fit into their lives as completely as possible.

When we got to the bus station, we sat on the bench with our backs to the bus stop. We were facing the tall buildings, which for Smack represented the city government. He said he likes to come there to watch the government. If I were not there with him, I imagine he would have just sat and stared at the building or, more likely, struck up a conversation with someone else. Because he had a captive audience in me, he preached nonstop, covering topics as diverse as why capitalism was destined to fail and why America would go down with it; why Americans were not real Christians (especially because they embraced Halloween, a pagan holiday); why it was terrible to lie to children about Santa Claus, a homosexual; why God "fucked Virgin Mary" to have a son; how he came to believe in Islam; how he knows that the FBI has a file on him; and why Tupac was better than Biggie. I did not question his theories on the various topics, but as a hip-hop head, I argued with him on the last one. I thought we were just sitting around, shooting the shit, but when he asked someone for the time, I realized that coming to the bus station was intentional. We were waiting for The Opportunity Center (the day shelter for homeless men and women) to open. At "The OC," as it was affectionately called, he and other clients can shower, wash their clothes, watch TV (mainly to stay informed about the weather), make phone calls, and network with other homeless men.

While we were walking up West Amite Street to The OC, he told me about wanting to get in touch with his brother for some money, something to eat, or a place to stay, especially on cold nights. He had called his brother at his job and home, but his brother did not call back. He told me he was the next-to-youngest child, what

Southerners call the "knee-baby," and that he has an older brother in Miami, whom he had not seen in a while.

Smack's contacts with his siblings reflect the complicated relationships that homeless folks often have with their domiciled relatives. People who are homeless are not as disconnected as we once believed. While sporadic, they do stay in touch with their housed kin.[2] Unfortunately, often their relatives are impoverished and lack the resources to lend any significant material support. Their relationships are also often marred by conflict.[3] Likewise, based on meeting the family members of other homeless men, I learned about their tumultuous relationships. For example, I met Smack's brother and, by all indications, he did not have disposable resources to provide the kind of support Smack imagined. When I went with one man to see his nephew, we were received warmly. His nephew invited me back to his home to explain that he reduced his contact with his homeless uncle because all the financial support he had given him had been squandered.

"Do you have any kids, man?" I asked Smack.

"Yea, I told you I adopt everywhere I go," he responded.

"No, but I mean do you . . ."

"You mean biological? Hell yeah."

"Where?"

"Somewhere around this goddamn town, and I ain't gonna go look for them motherfuckers either. Little badasses, they worse than they daddy."

I chuckled and then probed further.

"You for real? You got kids, but you don't know where they . . . ?"

He cut me off. "I know where they at. I just ain't going."

A few silent steps later, he added, "I live a corrupting life bro, and ain't no way in hell I'm gonna traumatize my goddam kids and have my kids come out worse than me. . . . No, sir." His comment was a small window into how he thinks of himself—as someone unfit to father his children—and how he manages what some might call a "spoiled identity."[4] He added, "Every once in a while, I give a shout-out to my brothers and sisters, their aunties and uncles, to go over there and check on them. As long as they among the motherfucking living, that's all I need to know." Nearing the parking lot of

The Opportunity Center, he repeated himself, a bit slower this time. "As long as they among the motherfucking living . . ."

It opens around 6:30 a.m., so by 7 a.m. The Opportunity Center is a busy place. When I arrived there at 7:30 one morning, the place was already buzzing. I checked in with Billy and Ray at the front desk and headed straight to the back area—a large room with benches and tables, a microwave, and a television. Checking in for me was just a matter of saying hello to people at the front desk since I was a pseudo-volunteer there. For all others, Ray, Billy, or whoever was in charge of the door checked for a TB card to ensure that the people entering had been screened for tuberculosis. They checked pockets and bags to ensure that they did not have drugs. Using a metal detector, they checked for weapons; all pocket knives were confiscated at the front door. Most people hated the check-in process, especially the use of metal detectors, but to use the resources at The OC, they had to put up with it. It was the price they paid.

There are usually about two dozen people at The OC, mostly men, in the back area on most mornings. On this morning, I observed a few clusters of people. One cluster, about five or so, sat on foldable chairs near the entrance. Some leaned their heads on the wall and dozed off, but most talked with one another. Another set of people sat on foldable chairs by a long table in the middle of the room. They were not as huddled together as those who sat by the entrance, but they conversed with each other just as much, though a few of them also hung their heads to sleep. Sleeping at The OC was common since most woke up before dawn. A third set of people sat on a long picnic-style table with benches attached near the television. Half of them put their heads on the table and slept, and the other half attentively watched the twenty-inch television hanging above their heads; conversation in this area was sparse. Places like The OC are essential for the newly homeless because it is where they learn about the routine for survival; it is where they get to know the names and operating hours of all the service providers in town. Building these networks is a critical way path toward surviving.[5]

4.2. The Opportunity Center

4.3. Check in at The Opportunity Center

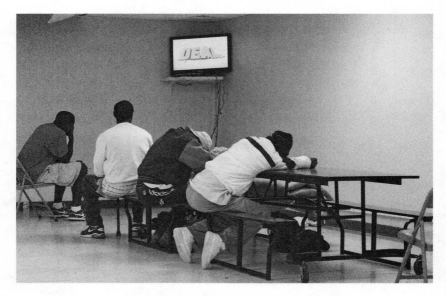

4.4. Sleeping at The Opportunity Center

If people were not talking, watching television, or sleeping, they were looking to get something to eat. For those who did not make it to the 5 a.m. breakfast at Gateway, it meant that they had not eaten since 5 p.m. the day before, except for whatever ready-to-eat snacks they might be carrying with them. On one of my first days, I saw a man near the television eat Banquet spaghetti and meatballs with his hands. A few others waited for their turn to use the microwave to warm up noodles or water for instant coffee. There was a large box of doughnuts by the microwave.

"When did these get here?" one person asked.

"Some white folks brought them in this morning," another responded.

"Man, that shit look like something nobody supposed to be eating. That look like shit."

His condemnation did not stop people who desperately needed something to eat from warming up the doughnuts to have with their coffee.

According to the weatherman on the local morning news, there was a 70 percent chance of rain that day. He assured his viewers that it would be harmless rain that would pass quickly as the day progressed. Sure enough, when I stepped out to get some air, it was raining. Everyone had hoped that the rain would not start so early; they had hoped it would hold out until about 10 a.m. so that they could make it to breakfast at Galloway United Methodist Church and back. Smack had planned on making the mile-and-a-half walk down to the church, but he changed his mind because of the rain. Several others made the same decision. One guy wondered if he could just brace the rain. "It's just a matter of making it down there," he commented. On second thought, he decided against it because he did not want to worsen the cold he already had.

It rained for about an hour. Because of the rain, many of the men I was around did not have breakfast that morning.

On weekdays, most people at The OC usually leave to go to breakfast around 8 a.m. They head to Galloway United Methodist Church, except on Tuesdays, when they typically go to St. Andrew's Episcopal Cathedral. Once they got to the right place at the right time, they also had to do as they were told or risk being punished by the service providers.

While following a few men to Galloway United Methodist Church for breakfast one day, we ran into a man everyone calls "Black." He is handsome, dark-skinned, and physically fit—he later told me that he had been a boxer in his youth. He was walking in the opposite direction to everyone else; he had been turned away from breakfast that morning. He was barred from The OC, which, when his ban was communicated to the other service providers, meant that he would be turned away from soup kitchens as well. Billy, who works at the door at The OC, explained to me the day before that Black was barred because he had "acted out." Apparently, he attempted to change the channel on the television at The OC, which was against the rules. When Billy confronted him about it, he got agitated, slammed his hands on the desk, and then ripped the office phone from its jack when Billy tried to call the police.

There is a fickle and tumultuous relationship between clients and service providers. Client and staff interaction is steeped in negotiations for power and respect and frequently results in conflicts that lead to clients being barred for some time or banned indefinitely. Elliot Liebow, in *Tell Them Who I Am,* explains that fear of the homeless, both by the service providers and by the homeless themselves, often breeds this destructive relationship. To temper their concerns, service providers tend to over-exert power over the homeless. "Given the power of the staff and the other providers to set the terms under which life-supporting goods and services will be doled out, it is not surprising that the world of shelters and service providers takes on, from the homeless [person's] perspective, an abusive, authoritarian coloration."[6]

When Black saw me at Galloway that morning, he attempted to explain what had happened. He was not trying to change the channel but instead was trying to fix the television's video quality. He got upset because Billy tried to get the police involved. For lashing out and not accepting his place, the consequence for him, as for others who got in trouble, was losing food access. At Galloway, I overheard Ray, another employee at The OC, say while referring to Black, "That boy gonna starve to death. Don't nobody want him— he can't go nowhere for food."

About fifty people sat around eight large round tables, waiting to be served in the church's basement fellowship hall. The woman in charge, a slender white woman with a kind and long face, stood in the front of the room with a couple of other volunteers. With them were a couple of Black men in blue shirts, hired to serve as security guards. Most of the people who came to be served were already seated when I arrived. A few others stood in line at the back of the room to get a cup of coffee. I wanted to sit by Smack, but his table was full. The lady in charge saw me looking for a seat and directed me to the overflow room, a section reserved for latecomers. A few more people, including Ray, joined me at the overflow room. For breakfast, they served macaroni and cheese, beans, green beans, salad (consisting mainly of lettuce), and stale cookies and cake.

After eating, I went into a lounge space where people congregated to watch TV. Galloway also has a clothing service. So, as people hung out in the lounge, they listened for their names to be called to receive various clothing items that they had requested. I met William Montgomery in the lounge. He introduced himself as "Minister Montgomery" and insisted I refer to him by that title. We had refilled our coffee cups and were reaching for a sugar spoon at the same time.

"Go ahead, brotha," he said, in his crisp, baritone voice (think Ving Rhames).

"Oh, my bad. Thanks," I responded.

"How you been? I've noticed you around."

As we sipped our coffee, we started talking, casually at first, and then more seriously about his relatively new life on the streets. Minister Montgomery was born and raised in Jackson, but had been living in California since 1996.[7] "I went to California—well, a lot of people from Mississippi go to California—because Mississippi ain't got no income, no economy. Your cost of living is higher out there, but you get an opportunity to get a good-paying job, you know." He is a homebuilder. While he was in California, he worked as a subcontractor. "I used to be making $9,000 a month, no taxes, no nothing, straight money. But, you know, houses quit going up, self-contracting failed, they squeezed the middleman out. See, I was the middleman. They laid all kinds of people off. [The contractor] lay all his people off, he prolly working by hisself now. So, I left my car and my truck out there and just came back." He had been back for seven months.[8]

Around 10:30 a.m., it was time for all of us to go. Galloway was closing its doors. I walked with Minister Montgomery and one of his friends, Toni, back to The Opportunity Center.

"You walking today, huh?" Minister Montgomery asked.

"Yea, I'mma walk up with you guys," I responded.

"Where did you leave your car at?" I guess he had noticed me in my car, despite my efforts to keep my car out of sight.

"Up there by The OC," I responded.

"Imma get that name right, but tell me what it is one more time?"

"It's Piko."

"And what's your major again?"

"Sociology."

"Sociology. Good. The mind is a terrible thing to waste, I tell ya. Living in the last days, we goin' need it."

Walking past Smith Park and the Cathedral of St. Peter, through the pleasantly cool Mississippi winter breeze, the sounds of the church bells and chirping birds filled our soundscape. I walked between the two men. To my left, Toni is a lanky man who wears glasses and walks with a slightly hunched back. To my right, Minister Montgomery is a well-built, immaculately well-kept man, from his shoes and socks to his facial hair. He is one of those black-don't-crack men who looked forty even though he was probably in his mid-fifties. Before I knew his name, I referred to him in my notes as "Mr. Smooth." Observing him disabused my image of homelessness. Yes, some people were unkept, but there were also people like Minister Montgomery.

While nibbling on the cookies they had carried out from our "breakfast" meal, Minister Montgomery and Toni started to think about where they would go for lunch.

"Where do y'all like to go? Gateway or Stewpot?" I asked. Their responses revealed how, within their limited choices, they decided between two shelters.

"I stay away from Stewpot through the week," Toni responded. He thought the food at Gateway is, most of the time, better than the food at Stewpot. Minister Montgomery agreed, but in his view, the difference was how the food was served, rather than the actual taste of the food.

"See, Gateway be hot, but Stewpot don't. That's the only difference. Cuz Stewpot, they already have the plates ready, and they . . ."

"Yea, and they pray . . ." Toni interjected.

"Naw, he goin' talk before they pray. That's the problem," he concluded, and then proceeded to impersonate the chaplain who leads the lunch program at Stewpot, the man with the bold voice. We all laughed at his stellar impersonation.

Down the street from us, on Capitol Street, we noticed a Channel 12 News truck that was parked on the side of the road.

"That's the newsman; I need to get on the news. I got something to tell 'em," Minister Montgomery commented.

"What you gonna tell 'em?" I asked.

"I need to get on the news and announce to the city that I need a job." We all started laughing again. "It's growing. Mississippi is growing, but it's these Mexicans taking all the jobs. I mean, I got clientele. I just gotta be patient and wait on them to get the money. While I'm waiting, I can't just sit and wait. I'm doing my cousin's shop over there now. I'm putting an addition on his shop. So, that's what I've been working on. I was there yesterday."

I could not help but think of the sociologist Edna Bonacich's split labor market theory, the idea that antagonism between racial groups results from one group driving down the cost of labor and reducing the chances of employment.[9] Latinos make up only 2.9 percent of the state's population, but perhaps going along with the popular narrative, Minister Montgomery has come to believe that he is losing jobs to Latinos.[10]

Toni was quiet through much of this conversation, but he seemed to be paying attention to what we were talking about.

"So, sociology is what? What kind of business is that? What do you do to make money?" Minister Montgomery asked.

I explained that most sociologists teach at colleges and universities and write.

"Well, that's good. We all got a calling—whatever you got is a calling. This is me: I'm a carpenter and a carpenter's son, the way Jesus was. I'm right in there with him. I minister." He told us that he learned carpentry from his father and his sixth-grade woodworking class. He had a teacher who used to put $100 on everybody's desk to show how much money they could make from being a carpenter, which is what did it for him.

He would like to work more than he does now, but the schedule at the shelters where he stays constrains his hours. "My cousin want me to come over there and build on these two walls. . . . I could do that today. Only thing is time don't permit me now. See, once I get over there, I gotta be thinking about watching the clock, know what I mean? I gotta get back in time to check-in and get a bed and stuff like that."

The shelter's operating hours affected job opportunities, especially for transitionally homeless people like Minister Montgomery, someone who was still trying to return to his previous life. He had not fully come to terms with his homelessness, so he attempted to organize his days in ways that might lift him out of it. Unfortunately, his efforts conflicted with the routine required to survive homelessness; they were disruptions to the routine, so they made life more difficult. This tension is most significant and noticeable with people who are new to homelessness.

When our conversation turned to shelters, we spoke about the rules. At the time, the two main shelters for men allowed each client fourteen days a month. "You can break 'em down and stay at one place for maybe a week or a couple of days and then go to the other place, but you have to deal with both of 'em," Minister Montgomery explained.

"So, which of the shelters do you stay in?"

He explained that he prefers Gateway over The Men's Shelter. "Gateway is okay. You can sit in the chapel and eat. You can't eat in the back, but you can still eat in the chapel. And you can come out and take breaks. You don't get nothing down there [the Men's Shelter]. They treat you like you in prison. Be there at six o'clock—that's it. Go to bed—watch TV. That's The Men's Shelter now. You can't even take your stuff back there with you. You gotta put all your stuff in a cubbyhole. You gotta turn your cell phone off and everything." After a few more steps, he prompted Toni, who had not said much, to share his experience about the consequences of not abiding by the rules. "He can tell you about his experience—he got experience. Tell him about the cookies," he said, laughing.

"I don't wanna talk about it," Toni mumbled, looking straight ahead. He was not laughing.

"Sixty days," Minister Montgomery added.

"Sixty days? What happened?" I probed, but Toni was reluctant.

Apparently, for taking three cookies from the dining area into the sleeping area, Toni was barred from The Men's Shelter for sixty days.

"Man, he so pissed off about it that he don't even wanna talk about it." Minister Montgomery kept on. "Might as well laugh about it. He can't go back there until his sixty days is up."

Toni finally gave in. "Can't get no bed or nothing. . . . After my days are up at Gateway, I gotta figure what to do—sleep under the bridge or something." He told us that he had the cookies, but he was not going to eat them in bed at night. He was going to eat them on his walk to The OC the next morning. "Can't win, man," he added. We had reached The OC. "It's the same here too. They'll put you out for less."

In addition to following routines dictated by the service providers' operating hours and abiding by the service providers' rules, the men were also better able to survive by accepting their social status in homelessness. On the one hand, acceptance makes establishing routines easier. On the other hand, acceptance creates distance from resources that might be useful for life outside homelessness. Beyond continuing to lose touch with family members and others in the domiciled world, they also lose whatever skills they may have had. Becoming streetwise makes it easier to *survive* homelessness, but more challenging to *escape* it.

Further, surviving homelessness requires the homeless to employ various strategies to justify and accept their state of extreme deprivation, what scholars have termed "identity talk."[11] I saw this during one afternoon with a middle-aged homeless man named Charles. He organizes his day strictly by the terms of the survival routine. Through the stories he tells me, especially the long monologue at the end of this section, he clarifies how difficult it is to come to terms with homelessness. As Charles expresses, the chronically homeless do not become so socialized into homelessness that they view it as a satisfactory alternative to being housed. Instead, they come to accept the terms of homelessness because, sadly, it becomes less challenging to maintain it than to try to get out of it.

We were sitting on a bench outside of The Opportunity Center, watching trucks pulling up to pick up people for work. When one red Ford F-150 pulled up, he asked me if anyone got in.

"Yeah, a couple of people did," I responded.

"They going [to] be making . . . just $5 or $6," he commented in a tone of disgust.

"So how does it work? They just come and take people?"

"Yeah, pretty much."

I asked him how much they were going to get paid.

"Some of them make $20. [The employers] keep they asses out there till dark."

In their search for work, the homeless face many barriers since most have little education, poor job skills, and spotty employment history. Beyond these constraints, transportation, clothing, and access to job announcements also make seeking and gaining employment difficult. If, despite these setbacks, they find work, it is mostly day jobs that are handled "off the books" and with little protection from employer abuse. These employers, who are aware of their backgrounds and desperation to work, often take advantage of them, offering low wages, irregular hours, and poor work conditions.[12] In one study, workers reported that employers often quote higher pay, but after deducting various costs (such as transportation fees), they pay measly wages. Some reported earning $30 a day for working fourteen hours, a mere $2.15 an hour.[13] For these reasons, many prefer informal ways of making money including panhandling, recycling, or plasma donation.

"My man missed me yesterday," Charles commented, referring to a man he works with. "He say he might come get me on Sunday, and he know for sure he gonna come get me on Monday, get back to my little job."

The morning rush for jobs was dying down around late morning. Those who would work that day were already gone. The ones left were those who did not want to work that day and those who were stood up by their employer. If they were not out there working, many were doing identity work; they were engaged in a "range of activities individuals engage in to create, present, and sustain personal identities that are congruent with and supportive of the self-concept."[14] Among these strategies, I am most concerned with identity talk.[15] From other researchers who capture the day-to-day lives of people who are homeless, we have learned that the homeless talk a good amount about their lives, especially about their lives before homelessness and how they make sense of being in their social position. This talk ranges from distancing themselves from other homeless people to voluntarily embracing the status and often includes fictive and embellished storytelling about one's past.[16]

Charles's identity talk was often folded in with his commentary on whatever was passing through our panoramic view. Some of it, both praise and criticism, was directed at those who run The Opportunity Center. Some of it was about people who passed by. He knew all the gossip about who received money from their social security benefits or who had gone home to spend a day or two with family members. Because we appeared to be stationary, a few people dropped off their bags with us as they ventured to a nearby corner store to buy cigarettes. In one instance, Charles saw a white woman walking with a man across the sidewalk in front of us. We knew they were both among the homeless population because we had seen them at various soup kitchens. Pointing with his head, he began his commentary about the white woman. He seemed both appalled and disgusted to see her on the streets. I did not understand his reaction, but he explained before I asked.

"You see a white woman like that, especially down south like Mississippi here. Man, when you see a white girl with a nigga like that, man—her folks don't want shit to do with her, man. She a low-class bitch." His tone toward her was not about inter-racial dating; it was about how he made sense of seeing white folks who are in homelessness. He shared a quick story about a white man who asked him about where to find an abandoned house where he could stay. He was equally appalled about that.

"Them low class. I'm first-degree low class, and they second-degree low class." I laughed at his categorization.

"They first-degree, too. Low. Low as you can get. You white? And you out here like this? Shiiit! White folks got money. I mean, niggas got money too. Very few niggas got money. But one thing about a white person—man, they'll stick together. You ever heard of that?"

"Yup."

"The majority of white folks got money. But a nigga man, very few. [White folks] don't look after you, they look after themselves. But, thems low class. She on the shipwreck like I'm on a shipwreck—very, very low class. What I call 'trailer trash.' You ain't never been to the penitentiary or prison or locked up or behind bars, right?"

I shook my head.

He lowered his voice to make sure it was not in earshot of anyone. "Any time you see a white muhfucker in prison, that's a trailer trash, low-class white folk." He paused for a few seconds then added, "I'd take a spray can and paint 'em black."

I laughed again, more nervously this time, unsure of what to make of his commentary. He had already moved on and began talking about a speeding car that passed by the road we were looking at. But, in my head, I stayed on his comments about white folks and homelessness—there were at least two ways to interpret them. I took it to mean that white people did not belong on the streets as he did. Part of this, I imagined, was simply a claiming of the streets. Most of the people in homelessness were Black, so the spaces they inhabited were racialized as such.[17] They were like other survival spaces in Black American life, like barbershops and beauty shops or churches, where white folks' presence in these spaces would be viewed as an intrusion.

Another read of his comment, a haunting one that reflects racism's psychoemotional trauma, is that white folks ought to fare better in life. They should certainly do better than Black folks. In Charles's mind, if white people have all the privileges, how or why would their lives end up the same as his, a Black person in Mississippi? For him, there was a melancholic congruence between his racial identity (blackness) and his lot in life (homelessness). He recognized that and, in some ways, accepted it, so what was the white person's excuse? They did not belong in homelessness, so if they were there, it must be because they are "first-degree low class."

There were other recognitions of how race mattered in the world of homelessness in Jackson. Besides Charles's observations, I saw other Black folks observe that white people who are homeless are often arrogant. On one morning, Billy stood in the middle of a half-dozen people who were either sharing what they knew about an incident or were listening in to get caught up on all the details. Black, one of the men who seemed to always be in the know, said he witnessed the incident and recounted it. According to him, Wanda, a middle-aged white woman, got into a fight with Reena, a younger Black woman. The fight was over which sleeping space on the concrete outside The Opportunity Center belonged to whom. Reena had the upper hand and, on top of it, she had the help of her boyfriend. According to Black, Wanda was beaten up for "no real reason" other than because she was "just an old white lady." "That wasn't right cuz she just an old white lady," he repeated.

Those listening on agreed with him, but hesitatingly. The violence toward her was not right. They all agreed, but they also knew that Wanda often moved about The Opportunity Center with an air of superiority. From their observations, Wanda and the few white folks among the homeless population continued to choose to believe in their whiteness even when they were down-and-out.[18] And for doing so, they get more sympathy from service providers. Though the incident in question occurred at 11 p.m. the night before, the consequences were playing out that morning during check-in. Wanda, who looked worn-out and bruised, earned the pity of Billy and was let into the center. Reena was refused entrance and had to wait for the director to arrive to see about her fate. So, even though Charles viewed white people who were homeless as "first-degree low class," they were still white.

When I tuned back into Charles's commentary, he was talking about getting something to eat. The morning was turning into afternoon.

"It's almost eleven," he announced. "It's almost slop time."

"You gonna go up there?" I asked, referring to Stewpot.

"Yeah, I might." He had not yet decided if he would go to Stewpot or Gateway. There was a third option that day, too: a church on Bailey Avenue was serving lunch. When he realized that it was Friday and that Stewpot would be serving fried catfish, the decision became an easy one. It was the only day when he and others who go there to eat knew what would be served.

After the meal, Charles and I went back to where we had been sitting. One guy, whom we both knew, came by where we were sitting. We asked why he was not at Stewpot for lunch. He explained that he had gone to Gateway instead and, as often happened, we wondered what was served at the other place.

"Gateway had red beans and rice," he said.

Charles grinned, knowing he had made the better choice that day. We told him that Stewpot had fried catfish.

"Goddamn it," he exclaimed. To make him feel even worse, we exaggerated that they had good-sized nuggets of catfish and generous portions too.

"Even the beans was kinda good today," I mentioned.

Charles agreed. "Yeah, them baked beans were good. Baked beans and salad."

After the guy walked away, Charles launched into a story about what he used to do before coming to Jackson.

"I used to be a chef, a vegetable chef, studying to be a master chef. I used to cook thirty-five things a day, working in a cafeteria. I went to Job Corps for that, and they shipped me to Atlanta." He was in Job Corps at Morganfield, Kentucky. One guy who was sitting nearby us joined the conversation—he also went to Job Corps. And a third guy, who had been at the same campus (Morganfield) as Charles, joined when he heard talk of Job Corps.

These kinds of reflections, often embellished, are a common strategy of identity talk.

"Man, I loved to that place. Man, I hate that I fucked that shit up. I'm talking about nice. Inside swimming pool, outside swimming pool, a bunch of pool halls, tennis courts, golf courses. It was like an army base." His speaking pace picked up, a sign of how fondly he remembered the place. One of the other guys enthusiastically nodded, confirming Charles's descriptions of the place, and shared that he was there for two years and learned how to be a brick mason, a skill he has been using for twenty years. He spoke about Job Corps with a sense of appreciation. Charles talked about it with fondness and a sense of regret.

"I did welding at first. Got out of welding and got into mechanics. Got out of mechanics and got into culinary arts. That's when they sent me to Atlanta, then I got home-sick and came back home. I loved to that motherfucker though. That was a big place, ain't it?" They both agreed. "I was staying in 13–40. I still remember my zone. I was in the B zone. There was fifty guys in there with me. Man, I loved to that place. I wish I was in there right now."

The three of them carried on for a while about how they spent their allowances, how they spent their time off, and some of the regulations of the place. It was clear that the details about how much money they spent and the number of women they courted were all exaggerated, but we, the listeners, went along with the stories anyway.

"And when you graduate," Charles added, "[they] do the ceremony and everything, man. You throw your cap and everything when you finish. I love that place, man. I fucked up. I fucked up." Coming to this conclusion was part of reconciling with his past and also accepting his current place in life.

Taking a step even further back, he explained that he left home at sixteen because he wanted to go to Job Corps. He thought it was a faster way to adulthood.

"Everybody wanna hurry up and grow up. Ain't a person on this earth, with human sense, that never said, like I said, 'I'll be glad when I get grown.' I quit school in eleventh fucking grade. I didn't wanna be home anymore. I dropped out, took the GED class, didn't get it, didn't give a damn. I just gave up—just gave up, man. I said,

'Fuck it.' All I was after was money. I just wanted new clothes, had a bunch of new clothes."

It was somewhat embarrassing for him to talk about his regrets, but he kept on. Whenever he started getting emotional, he threw in something funny, usually a sexual comment, to keep it light and keep us laughing. The following monologue, which he delivered with little probing, ignored attempts at any interruptions.

"See, I always ran the streets. Really, I like city life. I'm just on the wrong end of this fucking shit. I need to be behind a desk. When I came from prison when I did that work for restitution, I used to make $442 every two weeks. I used to sell everything that goes up with a light post: cables, light bulbs, whatever. I used to work at a spot on South State Street. They hired me temporarily, [but] I came up hot and lost that job. I learned how to do the job too, how to do receiving, taking the shit from the truck, stocking. Then they sent me to shipping. When the computer came back with my [drug test] results, it was redder than that fucking truck. They said, 'Man, we give you thirty minutes to leave our premises.' It was a pretty day like this here, and it started—man, I'll never fucking forget it, a beautiful day like this—and it started pouring as soon as I stepped out on the street. On my momma. I'll never forget it. I was hot; I was hot on Beirut. I was drinking and smoking that shit. I was smoking crack. What I'mma lie to you for? I'm a crack head. I smoke crack. I ain't lying. I need a blunt right now. Can you help me? That's what I went to prison for—selling cocaine. You know I had to taste it, sample it. I ain't lying. I ain't ashamed of my game. What I'mma lie to you for? Charles smokes crack, you goddamn right. My momma know I do it. My sister and brothers do too, and that's why I can't face them. You know, shame and disgrace, disgrace to the family."

He continued: "I tried too many times to make a change. I reckon, the only way I'll make a damn change is die—serious, man. It's gotta be something really deeper than that. I mean a lot, lot, lot, looot, loooot—a whole fucking garbage can full of money. Other than that, I think I'm stuck. It's like I'm in a basketball game, and I'm fouled out, so I gotta just watch the game come to an end. That's how my life is right now. I'm fouled out. I think Satan just pulling me. He got my baby fucking toe, you feel me, one of my baby toes, and just holding it. I can't see it, man. I can't see it. I can't see it. I'm just telling you the damn blank truth. I just can't see it. It's really, really hard man, just eat some rat poison and call it a day."

When people who are experiencing homelessness get to where Charles is, when they come to accept that they are indeed down-and-out, they are both streetwise and desperate.

CHAPTER FIVE

Carl and Ray—
Afternoons and Evenings

WHEN CHARLES SAW ME in The Opportunity Center's parking lot toward the end of one day, he asked where I had been.

"I've been around, man. You was asleep when I came in earlier," I responded.

He came outside to throw away some garbage. He was helping the workers clean up The Opportunity Center. If he helps them clean up, they give him a few dollars when they get paid. "What you doing later on?" I asked.

"Going to my cave." That is what he calls the abandoned buildings where he sleeps. He does not like to sleep at shelters.

"Where you going?" he asked.

I said I was going to hang with him that night.

"Well, I'm going to eat at Gateway, then just hang out, man." He added that he was going to some dangerous places where people drink and smoke.

"You think I'm afraid to go to those places?"

He did not respond. He just smiled. I sensed he was reluctant for me to follow him around. I said I was going to come along anyway.

The Opportunity Center director announced at 4:30 p.m. that it was time for people to leave the premises. I walked away with Charles. I mentioned that I had noticed he did not sleep at the shelters and asked why. He explained he did not like the rules and structure of the place and thought those in charge there were rude. So, to relieve himself from their harassment, he slept in different locations. As we walked by one business building, he pointed out that he used to sleep on its veranda but had stopped because the police accosted him. So now he spends most of his nights in abandoned and boarded-up buildings.

Charles and the other homeless men I got to know were not always docile followers of the rules; at times, they refused the services; at other times, they knowingly broke the rules. They lived with the tension of, on the one hand, accepting the routines and regulations and surviving and, on the other hand, challenging them and risking the consequences. It was a dance they had to master: doing what they had to do to survive and resisting the mandates of service providers to retain bits of their dignity. Even with someone like Charles, whom I have characterized as having accepted homelessness, there were still instances of rebuffing the service providers.

We were going to go hang out at the bus station, where I had spent time with Smack, to wait for dinner at Gateway. The bus station was a popular place to pass the time. When we got there, we ran into a couple of guys from The Opportunity Center: Larry and L.J. Larry asked where I was staying for the night. He had forgotten that I was a researcher. I went along with it and said I was thinking about The Men's Shelter.

"[It] is just up the street from Gateway, so come eat with us," L.J. offered. I agreed.

They expressed their frustration about a new policy at The Opportunity Center. Those like Larry, L.J., and Charles, who refused the rules and rejected the services of the shelter had previously slept on a concrete slab right outside The Opportunity Center. But, a new policy prevented them from doing so. The new policy was the result of the incident involving Wanda and Reena. They were less bothered by the gendered physical abuse and more annoyed by the fact that the incident had ruined their stable sleeping arrangement.

While we were talking, a light green van illegally drove into the bus station. Charles, Larry, and L.J. got up and walked toward it because they knew the woman in the van. She came to give away bags of food. They knew that car—and that of others who just drive around and pass out food to homeless folks. These do-gooders know where to find homeless people during certain times of the day. Learning to recognize these vehicles was part of the socialization into homelessness. In the small brown paper bag that she handed out, there was a sandwich, a bag of chips, cookies, and a bottle of water. Charles was the first to take out his sandwich. He quickly unwrapped it and peeked between the two pieces of white bread.

"Bologna! Always fucking bologna," he disappointedly exclaimed. He exhaled, reminding himself how little a choice he had in getting something to eat. But, the limited selection did not mean a complete absence of agency.

He slapped the pieces of bread back together and took a big bite, then opened the bottle of water. I unwrapped the cookies first. Like Charles sitting on the bench next to me, I placed the contents of the bag on my lap as I ate. Larry and L.J., who were standing, held on to their bags as they ate their sandwiches. Larry did not want his cookies, so he gave them to me. In return, I gave him my bologna sandwich. Charles took L.J.'s chips. He did not want any more of his sandwich after his first bite, so he broke the rest into small pieces and threw them to the birds.

Besides shelters and random do-gooders, organized groups (especially churches) also feed people who are homeless on a somewhat regular basis, weekly usually, say on a Tuesday evening or Saturday afternoon. On Sundays, a couple of church groups come to pick up people from The Opportunity Center, take them to Sunday school or church services, and then feed them. These various groups' efforts are often uncoordinated. So, at times, two or three groups may serve on some days and none on other days. When this occurs, people eat as much as possible and carry some of the food with them. Such was the case on one September day.

When I arrived at The Opportunity Center around 3 p.m., no one was there except for Heather, the director, and a couple of her staff members. They talked to three white women who were there to donate some supplies—soaps, shampoos, and toothpaste—and

5.1. Volunteers deliver water at The Opportunity Center

help launder clothes. After they left, Heather expressed her annoyance. She always graciously welcomed donations to the center, but Heather also frequently expressed her frustration that people donated more for self-edification than for doing good. This group rubbed her the wrong way because they seemed too keen to take photos with the donations they brought. Her staff added that one of the women was rude and did not greet anyone as she walked. The donors were white. They coveted the image of themselves in front of Black folks who are homeless.

"I just wanted to punch her in the face," said one staff member.

"And I would have held her head for you," said the other.

"Oh, come on, guys. Y'all being crazy now," Heather said. "Come on, let's go to the park."

It was the second day of the Sixth Annual Project Homeless Connect Week, and there was a concert at the park. We ran into Matthew, a man who is homeless, as soon as we got to Poindexter Park, which was just across the street. I did not know Matthew very well, but we were acquainted. He immediately launched into an explanation of some incident when he saw Heather.

"I didn't hit him. He ain't got no marks on him, but he told him that I jumped on him every time. He ain't even got no bumps on him."

Heather knew what Matthew was talking about. I did not.

"He's talking about the white man that always carries his stuff with him. He usually dresses decent, works for the TV station, or used to work for the TV station," Heather explained to me.

"Big guy, with a big stomach?" I clarified.

"Yeah, the asshole who think he better than everyone?" Matthew added. We all laughed, but it was not at all funny to Matthew.

"He has an attitude problem," Heather agreed with Matthew. "He thinks he's better than everybody. He'll come in The Center with an attitude. 'Let me in; why is this taking so long?' kind of thing." That attitude was the air of white privilege that followed the white man even into homelessness. "Some time ago, down at Stewpot, he did that, and Matthew got mad at him, and he shoved him. It was in front of everybody, and [the CEO of Stewpot Operations] banned him. Not only can he not come to eat there, he can't come to any Stewpot-owned place." His ban meant he was banned from Stewpot, The Men's Shelter, and The OC. Matthew listened along. He did not argue with any of Heather's characterizations of what happened. His shoving the white man was an act of resistance, a challenging of whiteness.

"And, of course, Matthew was drunk at the time, so when they told him to either stop or go away, he did his usual I'm-drunk-I-can-do-what-I-wanna-do thing and made it worse."

"Oh man, so how have you been eating?" I asked. I knew part of the consequences for breaking the service providers' rules would be a restriction on his access to food.

"You know, I go to Galloway in the morning and Gateway for lunch. I survive."

"He's been doing a lot of drinking, actually." Heather had built a warm relationship with most of the people who come to The Opportunity Center, so she was able to talk about all their involvements. Most respected her and her efforts to help the homeless. Some (especially those who were often in trouble with her) disliked her, asserting that she is just another racist white woman.

"He got a windfall check. He doesn't know I know this," Heather went on to me about Matthew, who stood by, listening. "He got a windfall check, and he and his buddy were out all weekend getting high and getting drunk to the point that he was at the bus station yesterday morning and could hardly stand up because they were throwing up so much. So, he's been living off alcohol lately."

"See, Matthew, Ms. Heather knows everything," I interjected.

He stood in an embarrassed silence because all that Heather was saying might have been true.

"I love you, Matthew," Heather said, perhaps realizing she had put too much of his business out.

"I love you too, Ms. Heather," Matthew responded to her subtle apology. "How's you and that baby?" he asked.

"I'm good, we good. That check is gone now, isn't it? Wasn't it for six thousand or something?"

"I wish it was that much. If it was, I'd come get you, and we'd go to dinner."

"How much was it, then?" Heather asked.

"I didn't have any money. I don't need money to drink. Someone told a lie on me. See, that's why you guys believe everything people say."

"I don't believe what a lot of people say," she jabbed back.

"You believed that I had $6,000," Matthew responded.

"But that's too bad, though, about your ban," I contributed.

"You pushed a white man," Heather mentioned. She understood the world not to be color-blind—it was part of how she, as a white woman, kept the trust of the people for whom she advocated. She understands that, per the racial grammar in their Mississippi, pushing a man was one thing; pushing a white man in front of another white man with power was quite another—it was a more egregious offense. "He's out indefinitely. I've told Matthew if he would get really sober, we would go down there together and let him apologize and be done with that." Matthew shook his head, disapproving of the suggestion. He refused to bow to the structure, both that of the service providers' and the structures of racism and was happy to bear the consequences. He walked away.

There was music coming from the pavilion in the center of Poindexter Park, so we went by to see the performances, mostly gospel music, by a few men and women who are homeless. When it ended, those who put on the program packed up to leave. A good amount of the homeless folks stuck around. The park is for them another place, besides day shelters, where they could kill time in between meals.[1] It is also where, I was told, people drink and smoke during the day, as long as they properly hide it from the police who occupy a nearby office.

Carl was at the park because he had been barred from The Opportunity Center for two weeks. He got in trouble for ignoring the policy that prohibited sleeping on the veranda. He knew of the policy, but as he explained, "There were a lot of mosquitoes where I was staying," an abandoned building close by, "so I just went and slept out there." He deliberately broke the rule. In his view, the worse part was that the other person who slept out there with him did not get barred. He was in the middle of his two-week suspension when I ran into him that day.

We sat on the bench where Carl had been spending his time with a few other folks. Carl loaned two cigarettes to one guy. His new "hustle" was to buy a pack of cigarettes and sell each for fifty cents. His business venture is but one example, a rather creative one, of shadow work some of the homeless men engage in to earn meager spending money.[2] Another guy came by to bargain for some cigarettes. He did not have any money, so he offered one bus pass for two cigarettes. He knew, as did Carl, that the bus pass was worth more than one dollar, but he was desperate for a smoke.

Carl and those around him were waiting for college students who come to the park with food. It was around four, so a few people debated between waiting for the food and getting to the shelters to stand in line for a bed. They would be fed at the shelters, but the students' food would be a nice break from whatever they would be fed at the shelter. Two chose to stay; the other two left. Those who waited spent most of the rest of the time joking and laughing with each other—laughter was often plentiful even amid the hardships they faced. Most of the jokes were toward another man, Leroy. He was in the thick of a disagreement with his girlfriend, who sat on the other side of the park. The two of them, to our amusement, yelled all kinds of profanities back and forth at each other.

By 4:30 p.m., the people they were waiting for, students from Mississippi College, drove up in a pickup truck. They brought leftovers from their cafeteria. Mississippi College is a conservative Christian college, so coming to the park was, I imagined, part of practicing their faith, part of their proselytizing and living out Matthew 25:40 and carrying for "the least of these." Those who came to eat had to listen to a short sermon and a prayer before they could eat. This is a common trade-off. At first, there were just a dozen of us at the park, but about fifteen minutes after the students arrived, the number of people tripled. And, the newcomers were not all people who are homeless. Young mothers, grandmothers, and several children poured in from the surrounding neighborhoods to get something to eat. The area around the park was perhaps the most impoverished in the city. In its census block, a total population of 501 persons (98 percent Black or African American), the median household income is $14,459, and nearly 70 percent live below the poverty line.[3]

The students who came to serve us, two college-aged white women and one white man, unloaded their food from their truck and began getting ready while everyone lined up. "Ladies first," they instructed. Before serving, the young man, who appeared to be the leader, got into his sermon. He was a handsome and charismatic man—think Justin Timberlake—who seemed comfortable with being around and interacting with poor people of color. He, J.T., had been to the park several times before, so he knew some of the people. He asked them about their well-being and their families, to which most responded positively.

"I got something for y'all to think about," J.T. began, standing on the bed of their truck, looking down on us. He spoke with a faint Southern accent.

"Don't give us nothing hard to think about now," someone jovially yelled out.

"I won't; I won't," he joked back. "How many people want peace in their life?" His audience grudgingly responded. They knew it was a rhetorical start to his preaching.

"We all want peace, lots of folks. They want peace, but they don't know how to get it. For example, there is this verse that says, 'The eyes of man are never satisfied.' So, lots of people, though they want peace, they kinda reach for stuff to fill a void. It could be people; it could be substances, drugs, alcohol." I tuned him out to pay attention to the murmurs around me. Everyone was listening, but seeing and hearing their eye-rolling and the comments under their breaths, I could sense people were getting annoyed. But to get the food, they listened on.

"It could be like, I don't know, there's a number of things people do to get peace, cuz the Bible says, 'The eyes of man are never satisfied,' so it seems like nothing on this earth can satisfy my soul. It's a bad predicament that we're in. But there's some good news though, cuz there's this one verse that says, 'The minds on the flesh is death, so our own ability is death, but the mindset on the spirit is life and peace.' Okay, so now there's a way for me to have peace through the spirit of God. Jesus says if anyone thirsts, let him come to me and drink. How many of y'all crave something to drink?"

No one responded. A lady in front of me started talking under her breath, just loud enough for me to hear. "What is he talking about? If you ain't' got no money, you ain't got no peace. So, what the fuck you talking about?" It was not loud enough for the speaker to hear and it did not disturb the proceeding, but it was her subtle form of resistance.

"You want alcohol, it makes you feel good, and then what happens?" the young man asked.

Carl responded, "It makes you feel bad." He once told me that when these folks come with their food, they just had to do what they had to do to get it. It is one of the ways of appeasing the service providers—one part of the dance.

"So, the alcohol makes you feel bad again," the young man continued. "You go back to it, and you go back and forth, but what did Jesus say? He said, 'Anyone who thirsts, let them come and drink.'" The murmuring grew a little louder. He sensed that people were getting impatient, so he brought it to an end.

"We're here to have a relationship with God, so until we have a relationship with Jesus, we'll keep up digging these wells that can never fix our hearts. Only when we seek in the Lord can we finally have peace. And I'm so glad I found it." He probably expected applause, but he got none. Instead, everyone secured their position in line for food.

Faith-based organizations have long provided services to people who are homeless.[4] For some, these services are accommodative, meaning they seek to meet the clients' immediate needs. For others, services are restorative, meaning they aim to transform the life circumstances of their clients.[5] For service providers in each of these two categories, how does faith affect the services they provide, especially if providing social services is part of accomplishing their faith mission? And, how do clients perceive and respond to the faith that is part of the services they receive from faith-based organizations? One study that sought answers to these questions found that for many of the service providers, especially those who had restorative aims, feeding people who are homeless was a means to a more important end. They believe that bringing people who are homeless to Jesus is what is really going to save them, that "the love of Jesus is what's really going to do the trick." The clients, who are often more focused on meeting their accommodative needs, found the religious incorporation as a hindrance to the services provided and, at times, an invasion of their faith preferences.[6] The college students who served in the park that day exemplified these research findings. After the sermon, they prayed and started dishing out the food they brought.

They served grilled chicken, rice, and green beans. The two white girls were the ones serving us, and they did so warmly, greeting everyone who came through the line, gregariously and enthusiastically going out of their way to meet everyone's needs. The women in front of me got plates for themselves and for each of the children they brought with them. Some even got extra plates for family members who could not make it to the park. The men behind them moaned and complained about it, but the volunteers assured them there would be enough food for everyone. The guy in front politely asked if he could get extra green beans instead of the rice. I did the same. We ate on paper plates with plastic forks and knives while sitting on the benches. We held the plates in our laps and hurriedly scarfed down the food. Eating was not a social activity; in fact, it was a break from socializing.

The young white man who had preached, J.T., was making his rounds greeting and chatting with people. He was evangelizing. When he finally made it to the bench that Carl and I were sitting on, he sat between us. He asked me where I was from, since I did not have a Southern accent, and what I was doing in Jackson. I tried to pull Carl into our conversation in my responses to him, but Carl had turned his attention to someone else. He did not jump in as I had hoped. I read his disengagement with the young man as intentional. He had to listen to the sermon to get the food, but he did not have to listen to the rest of it. He probably knew that he was going to be preached at again.

After a few more introductory questions, the young man asked me, rather abruptly, what I wanted to do with my life.

"I'm not really sure, man," I answered, still reluctant to engage with him. "What do you wanna do with your life?"

Carl was now listening in to our conversation.

"Follow Christ," J.T. responded.

"That's a good answer. That's a good thing. That'll lead you to a good place," Carl chimed in. He was not mocking J.T. He was giving a response he knew J.T. would have wanted to hear.

"What do you think happens to you after you die?" J.T. asked.

I did not anticipate the question. "What do I think happens to me after I die?" I repeated, somewhat in shock at the question.

"I have no idea, man. I'm just trynna figure out what happens to me here. What do *you* think happens after you die?" I asked again, turning the question back to him.

"I'll tell you what happens . . ." It was the beginning of his rehearsed spiel that he gives people to inspire or motivate them to turn to Christianity. He turned to a Bible verse on his phone and handed it to me for me to read. After I got done, he turned to another one, and another, and another. I read about ten verses. As he went through each of the verses, I simply asked him more questions about what he believed. After my failed attempt at not engaging with him, I shifted my efforts now to trying to understand why he came to the park to feed the homeless, what he thought he was accomplishing, and if, in his evaluation, he did accomplish his goal. My probing questioning probably came off as rude (and, I'll admit, self-righteous), but my objective was to understand the underlying logic of service providers who had restorative aims.

"So, what does it mean to live a different life through Christ?"

"Good question, Piko. Let me show you. I'm gonna show you what he did and what it means to be through him."

"Nah, just show me what it means to be through him."

"Okay." He scrolled to another verse that simply said that faith without action is worthless.

"See, so it's not just an intellectual thing. Faith by itself does not mean anything. Believing gives me the spirit to get me to live differently."

"So yeah, that's what I'm trying to get you to explain. What does living differently look like?" I asked.

"Another good question. Okay. Let me know if I lose you, Piko." He opened to another verse that said Christ is a new creation and gives the spirit to live differently. I repeated my question, he pulled out another verse, and for a third time, I repeated my question. Carl was not in the conversation, but at this point he was paying attention to it. He had a half-smile on his face that I took to mean he was supportive of my questioning. It was something that he and others who came for food probably could not do, lest they risk being potentially denied of the services they needed.

Most of the others had finished their food and were dispersing. As Carl had done, they dodged further conversations with the service providers. In their minds, they had already paid the price with their initial attention for the food they came for. Still, the college students found a few to engage with. From the corner of my eye, I saw the other college students, the young women, talking to some of the people they had served, presumably proselytizing to them as well. These college students' feeding strategy fit that of other groups who were more focused on restoring lives by bringing people to Christ. It included a higher level of one-on-one interactions with their clients than service providers who aim to provide accommodative services.[7] My conversation with the young man was one such interaction.

"Living a different life means helping people and telling people about Jesus. Like coming out here to the park, feeding people, and telling them about Jesus."

"It seems like y'all just wanna keep feeding people. Like y'all want people to stay out here so that when you come the next time, they will be out here, but people don't really wanna be out here."

"I wanna be out here, that's why I come out here," he responded.

"Yeah, you wanna be out here to give food to people. You want them to stay out here so that when you feel like doing good, you can come and give them some food." This was what Heather and her staff had been upset about with the volunteers at The Opportunity Center. It made me think of Herbert Gans's article about the functions of poverty, especially the tenth function: "[it] helps to keep the aristocracy [and some Christians] busy as providers of charity."[8]

"Nobody wants to live out here," I continued. "You know what would be ideal? If you came here one week and no one was out here for you all to feed. Isn't that what we should want? Shouldn't that be our bottom line? Or do we even want that?"

"We do," he calmly responded.

"You sure?" I asked, more playfully this time to make sure I did not worsen the mood. He agreed, but admitted that he did not know how to do that.

"Yeah, we do, we do."

"So how do we do that?"

"I don't know, man, and I don't have the power to do that. I can only do what I can do." He meant that he had the power to help them survive homelessness, but not to help them get out of homelessness. He was not alone.

"Oh, come on, man," I exclaimed. "You follow Jesus Christ, man, and all things are possible through him. He is all-encompassing and powerful, is he not? And you're saying you don't have the power to do that?" I was not mocking his faith because the tenets of my faith are similar, even if our interpretations of the Bible are different.

"That's something to think about," Carl interjected. His comment sounded supportive of my line of thinking. I was not saying anything profound; I said something that he and others in homelessness were already thinking. When one researcher asked homeless folks about how they viewed the religious components of the service they received, a third of the respondents commented that the religious efforts of restorative organizations were hypocritical. They cited that many of the organizations that claimed to be Christian also had unreasonably strict rules, the consequences to which were the denial of survival services. That, to them, was not very Christian. Others believed that it violated their religious privacy. Half of the people interviewed in this study also saw religious content as coercive and forced.

5.2. A sandwich and a Bible verse

J.T. and I ended with polite pleasantries. He thanked me for the conversation, and I thanked him for the food.

After they left, I followed Carl and a few others to The Opportunity Center parking lot. Another church, a Black church, had also come to provide food. As soon as we sat down on the raised concrete slab, the place that Carl had been penalized for sleeping, the preacher that accompanied the group started preaching. He spoke for about thirty minutes, after which they handed out the bags of snacks they brought.

For those who do not stay in the shelters, what are the late nights like? After the soup kitchens and shelters close and after volunteers leave, how do people manage the rest of their evening?

These after-hour times are the portion of homeless men's lives to which I got the least amount of access. These are the moments when the drinkers drank and the smokers smoked. It was when, under the security of darkness, they roamed the streets and did as they pleased. It was when, as one man described, the devil took the strongest hold on them and forced them to resort to the bad habits they were trying to kick, when they spent their resources to chase the fleeting highs of life. I heard plenty of stories about what happened away from the watchful eye of the sun—stories about their sexual escapades and parties in the park that lasted till the wee hours of the morning. I tried to stick around for some of it, but many expressed their unwillingness to share that part of their lives with me.

I got to see a small amount of late-night life from hanging with Ray, Eric, and Willie. Ray, who worked at The Opportunity Center, had adopted Eric and Willie as his mentees. I met Ray when I first started at The Opportunity Center and got to know Eric through him. Eric and Willie were not big fans of The Opportunity Center; they refused to subject themselves to the rules of the place, so they spent most of their time at Eudora Welty Library. At least at the library, the rules to which they had to abide were for the general public and not targeted at people who are homeless. After Ray finished his shift at The OC, he would walk to the library, hang with them for an hour or so, then head to Gateway for dinner. (They were constant patrons at Gateway.) They would spend the rest of their waking hours at the bus station or Smith Park following their dinner. On days that Ray had money, they would go to a bar to play pool.

A few weeks after I got to know Ray, I became part of this routine. When I arrived with Ray at the library one day, after we had dinner, he introduced me to the security guard, a stubby, friendly, middle-aged Black man, as someone writing a book about Jackson.

"I tell him if his book become a bestseller, he taking all of us to a Knicks or a Giants game," he joked.

We sat in comfortable couches in the lounging section of the library. Ray read the Bible. I read *Ebony* magazine. Willie read the newspapers. Eric was in the computer room, playing games. The library was, for them, a safe and comfortable place to pass the time. An hour or so later, around 8:45 p.m.—the library closes at 9 p.m.— we left. We walked down State Street, heading toward the bus station.

"Is eh, whatmecallit open tonight?" Ray asked.

"What?" Eric responded.

"The Locker Room."

"Yeah, it's open. I think it is. They stay open till 2 a.m. every morning. Do you shoot pool?" Ray asked me.

back to the upbeat mood we were in, he added, "You should write in your book, 'I met three happy homeless people in Jackson, Mississippi.'" We started laughing again.

"These are my friends, the only two."

"Y'all see that?" I responded, "Y'all see how he didn't count me in?"

"Eh, I mean, I'm just starting to get to know you. You aight with me, though, Piko. You a mutherfucker," he said in laughter, "but you aight."

Part II

CHAPTER SIX

Zenani—Younger Days

ONE OF THE MEN who checked people in at The Opportunity Center and kept order at the place, Billy, was transitioning out of homelessness after spending nearly a year of sleeping outdoors and in shelters. He worked most weekdays and at least one day during the weekend, so while I focused on understanding the lives of homeless men, I spent much of my days around him when I was at The OC. On one occasion, I invited myself to hang out with Billy after work. I wanted to see how he spent his time away from The OC—word was that he drank a lot and became a different person when he got drunk. Spending time with him outside of work was also a way for me to begin building contacts away from The OC. When I met him, he was staying with a daughter. I was curious to see if his four daughters, about whom he often spoke, might be appropriate and willing participants in my study.

On the day Billy and I were to hang out, we cashed his check at one of the many predatory financial institutions that littered West Jackson. We went to one on South Gallatin Street. They took 5 percent of his income. Right next door, conveniently, there was a liquor store, where he purchased three twenty-four-ounce Budweiser cans and a pint of Taaka vodka before heading to the house where he had been staying. Zenani, his youngest daughter, was there, playing with her children in the living room when we entered. The room, dimly lit with worn and stained carpet, had two old black leather couches perpendicularly arranged along two of the walls and an ancient fireplace that looked like it had not been used in decades. A mixture of marijuana and cigarette smoke filled the air. On the floor were small, filled ashtrays. I sat on one couch and Billy on the other. He handed me one of the beers. Zenani sat directly across from me in an armchair as her children continued to play on the floor.

As soon as we settled into our seats, Zenani asked her father to take the children to the store to get them something to eat. This request was my first observation of their foodways; several hundred other instances followed.[1] I spent numerous hours with them and paid attention to how food popped into their lives and competed with whatever else might be demanding their attention. I noted what foods were available to them. Compared to Smack, Charles, Ray, and the other homeless men I spent time with, they had a little more choice even in their constant precarity, so I also paid attention to how they chose among whatever options were available.

Billy reluctantly agreed to take the children and motioned for them to head outside with him. I followed. He held his grand-children's hands tightly as we crossed the busy street, first to the median and then to the corner store, across from their house. The store was a brightly painted wooden structure. The store owner, who appeared to be of Indian descent, sat behind two thick fiber-glass panels with a small hole at the bottom for transactions. In front of the counter were three large coolers filled with an assort-ment of beer and sugary drinks. The children seemed to know what they wanted, immediately running to one aisle for Cheetos—they both preferred the flaming hot flavor—and then back up-front for a Faygo soda. It appeared that getting something to eat from there was a frequent occurrence given the ease with which they navigated the convenience store.

Back at the house, the children played in the middle of the liv-ing room and were warned to leave the grown folks alone. We, the grown folks, talked initially about me and why I was in Jackson—answering their questions marked my first attempt to recruit them to participate in my study and ask for their consent. I explained my project to them, saying I had come to learn about life in Jackson and was open to whatever they could teach me.

"So, why don't you have a tape recorder?" Billy asked as he took a swig of his vodka.

"I do. I've been recording some things."

"So, you been recording me?" he asked, now gulping down his beer.

"I will after I get your permission."

He burst into laughter and then confirmed that he did not mind at all. I asked him to show me around town to learn about the city beyond what I saw at The Opportunity Center. He agreed.[2] I asked the same of Zenani, and she also agreed. Even with their verbal commitment, it would take several more conversations to really "get in" with them to gain access to the inner logic of their lives. And, consent was ongoing.[3] I did not assume that having permission on that day meant that I had permission for all other days, so as frequently as once a week, I checked with them to ensure that my presence in their lives was with their permission.

Jamila, Billy's oldest daughter, whose apartment we were in, came out of an adjacent room and joined us in the living room. She wore a long pink bathrobe that flowed down to her ankles. She appeared not to be feeling well. I could tell that she was on some sort of medication from her droopy eyelids and hazy eyes. Later, I found out that she had become dependent on prescription pills since returning from her last tour with the military. She exchanged pleasantries with me when she sat down by her father, but except for occasional laughter, she remained quiet through most of our conversation.

Seemingly more comfortable with my presence, Zenani took over the conversation. She asked me about my relationship status, commented on my Northern accent, asked if I had any children or wanted any, and even offered to make me some. We all laughed at how forward she was with her questioning. Her family members punctuated our laughter with comments like, "Zenani, you a fool," or "Girl, you too crazy." She was mostly joking. But to avoid further sexual advances, I constructed my relationship with Zenani and her sisters to be that of brother and sister. Over time, they introduced me as their adopted brother. They deemed me the second smartest sibling in their family—Jamila was the smartest. When Zenani exhausted her questions, I turned the focus onto her. She shared that she was in a relationship and wanted to get married in a couple of years; she could not get married any sooner because her boyfriend was in jail. At this last admission, the room exploded into laughter once again. "Don't y'all be laughing at my man like that," she jovially yelled out to her family members.

As I sipped my beer, Billy kept throwing back the vodka and used the beer as a chaser. Only an hour into our drinking, he was on to his second pint of vodka. Zenani continued talking about her relationship. She remarked that she had been in many bad relationships in the past, but this one was different.

"What makes it different?" I asked.

"I can't really say." She fumbled around with her hands. "Um," she looked up at the ceiling, searching for the right words. "It's like T.I. and Tiny." She compared her relationship to that of the famous hip-hop artist who had been in and out of jail and remained married to his wife. And, again, the family laughed at her and with her.

Our conversation kept on like that for two hours. We laughed a lot, but most of it was about tragedies—incarceration, heartbreak, poverty, addiction—that had become the norm for them. They were glimpses into the socioeconomic structures that shape their lives. As I spent time with them, I observed how these structures allowed for certain foods to be available to them. How they chose among what was available to them, their food choices, showed me how they navigated through and around what they encountered.

How do people living in poverty choose what they eat?

Even without a focus on poor people, scholars of food choice make it clear that a wide range of factors shape what people choose to eat. Some argue that one's life course influences the elements that come to matter in food choices.[4] Another set of researchers say that different factors come to matter more than others in certain circumstances and with certain populations. Some of the factors include visual appeals or pleasurable taste, need and hunger, sociability, social norms or image, weight control or health, price and convenience, and habits or tradition.[5]

Those who focus on the eating habits of people in poverty often believe that poor people have limited choices in what they eat and, among what they have, they often make choices that are bad for their health. This lack of choices results from poor folks living in food deserts, "areas characterized by poor access to healthy and affordable food."[6] There is sufficient evidence that areas with low-income populations and high proportions of African Americans have fewer supermarkets or chain stores and fewer midsized or large stores than advantaged areas. Also, African Americans and Latinos need to travel farther than their middle-class and non-Latino white counterparts to access supermarkets.[7] These findings are significant because supermarkets and larger retailers offer greater variety and healthier food at lower prices than small retailers.[8] For these reasons, some researchers link food deserts with poor eating habits that result in poor health.

Another explanation for how poor people, especially African Americans, eat points to past food traditions. Food scholars, particularly anthropologists, long ago established the importance of food to family relations and the importance of familial food habits and customs to one's foodways.[9] Others have illustrated that tastes and distinctions between good and bad food, what is to be valued and rejected, develop over time around family traditions and shape lifelong eating habits.[10] In many ways, past food traditions form the food habits of all people, but the food habits of African Americans, especially those who are poor, are thought to be particularly important. As anthropologists and historians have painstakingly documented, some of which I have presented in Chapter 2, foodways have defined how they have navigated systematic oppression and even defined themselves.[11]

Works about present-day African American eating habits often debate the role of soul food in poor health among African Americans. In a 2012 documentary, *Soul Food Junkies*, filmmaker Byron Hurt frames his discussion of poor diet among Black people around his father's "addiction" to soul food. He acknowledges that the proliferation of fast foods in poor Black neighborhoods is part of the problem, but concludes that "we are a nation of soul food junkies" and that soul food is the real culprit for poor diet among African Americans.[12] Further, many believe that soul food continues to be a mainstay because of its cultural significance for Black Americans. In a series of articles for various news outlets, political commentator John McWhorter has called food deserts a myth and has pointed to soul food as the real source of an unhealthy diet.[13]

These two are not alone. They simply articulate a popular sentiment about a static South. The presumptions in these types of arguments are that poor Black folks are still regularly eating soul food and that soul food, as it is prepared today, is unhealthy food. I interrogate both of these assumptions below.

The three chapters in this section take up the question about the food choices of poor Black folks. I draw on sociological theories about why people do what they do in general—what various theorists and philosophers have termed motivation, will, purposiveness, intentionality, choice, initiative, or agency. More specifically, I use and expand upon an innovative approach, presented by sociologists Mustafa Emirbayer and Ann Mische, that aims to explain people's tendency toward certain decisions. In this context, I will be trying to understand how people like Zenani approach their food decisions.[14]

Emirbayer and Mische argue that there are three elements to decision-making: considering and selectively incorporating *past* patterns; evaluating the limitations and possibilities of *present* circumstances, and imaging and planning for desired *future* possibilities. According to the theorists, all three components (past, present, future) are always present, but one dominates. The question they leave us with is this: under what circumstances does one element come to matter more than the others? So, how do people (specifically Black folks) in poverty make decisions about what they eat? Do past patterns determine their food choices? Those who write about soul food's continuous role, like Byron Hurt and John McWhorter, make this argument. Do their present circumstances dictate their food choices? Those who insist on the importance of food deserts lean toward this line of thinking. Or are people in poverty influenced by desired imagined future (i.e., health) outcomes? Very few scholars argue for the latter.

In this chapter and the next chapter, I'll make the case that poor Black folks in Mississippi today make their food choices within the limits and demands of their present circumstances. Their eating habits are dictated by the poverty in which they currently live, but not necessarily how those concerned with food deserts argue. For poor Black folks in Jackson, food decisions anchored in the present are driven by convenience and affordability. The conditions of contemporary poverty, its constant stress and instability, is incompatible with past food traditions. Relying on small family farms and practices of curing meats and canning and pickling vegetables are now replaced by buying foods from corner stores, dollar stores, and fast-food restaurants and cooking out of boxes and packets. Soul food is not their everyday food as we presume it to be. Some of these traditions were not fully passed down because of rapid changes in Black life in Mississippi—the assumption of an unchanging South could not be more erroneous. Even older Black folks whose lives were steeped in these older Black food traditions cannot recreate the foods they once knew.

Zenani's (Food) Past

Billy was born in 1955 and raised in Newton, Mississippi, a small rural town about sixty-five miles east of Jackson. Both his mother and father had children from previous marriages, but he grew up with the five that his parents, Andy and Mary, had together. "Momma" worked as a domestic worker for white families while "Daddy" was up north, working at a steel mill during winters. When his father stopped doing seasonal work and stayed with the family year-round, his mother took on their household labor full-time.

He had fond but different memories of his parents. He described his father as a "tough motherfucker" and a "strange person" with "two sides"—a tough side and a kind side.

"A lot of people didn't like him, because they say he was mean, and you see the way I talk? That's where I got that from. He was a tough-talking motherfucker, but Daddy always kept a pistol in his back pocket to back his talk up."

Billy's father was also physically abusive, which he justified by his ability to provide for his family. "He was a kind person. If you look at it like that, because he was going to take care of his children, and he was going to help his children. He wasn't going to help nobody outside that. You could forget that."

He beamed with pride when he talked about how his father cared for him and his siblings. They might not have always had all they wanted, but they had what they needed. Most importantly, they had more than enough to eat.

every Friday, and even people out of the community. They knew [my mother] was going to cook that fish, and she wasn't turning down nobody."

He went on. "Mama was so kind, and you're talking about can cook. You ain't never ate no biscuits from scratch. When we didn't have food, all we had [was] flour, lard, and sugar, and a little bacon. She could take that flour, lard, and that little bit of bacon and make everybody in the community full."

He remembered when his mother passed away.

"She [was] so close to the Bible that it scared me. I didn't think she would never die, she was so good. Then she died, just like that."

Her death was shocking because it occurred so unexpectedly.

"It pissed me off. I just seen her alive and well. She wasn't sick or nothing, and I couldn't understand it for a long [time] . . . That's when I really, really, started drinking heavily."

On the day his mother died, Billy found out his wife, Ms. Deborah, was pregnant with their third daughter. When she was born, they named her Mary, after his mother.

"But, you know, shit happens. Mama wasn't going to live forever. I found that out. And I just kept drinking, and drinking, and drinking, and drinking, until it got to the point I am now. But that's life. Fucked up! There ain't never going to be no fair hand here, not to no poor-ass motherfucker from Mississippi." The way he told his life stories reminded me of how the novelist Ralph Ellison defined the blues: "an impulse to keep the painful details and episodes of a brutal experience alive in one's aching consciousness, to finger its jagged grain, and to transcend it, not by the consolation of philosophy but by squeezing from it a near-tragic, near-comic lyricism."[19]

Around the time of his mother's death, Billy had been married to Ms. Deborah for several years and had lived in Los Angeles, her hometown. Ms. Deborah brought a different (food) history to their union: Her father is from Arkansas and her mother is from Lawrence, Mississippi, just a few miles from Newton. Ms. Deborah's parents found each other in Las Vegas, to where they both moved in their teens. Their families were part of the second Great Migration when the American West increasingly became a destination for Black Southerners.[20] A few years after her parents married, they moved to Los Angeles and had children. Unfortunately, their marriage didn't last. Her father was not as ambitious a man as her mother had hoped, and perhaps more importantly, Ms. Deborah's mother came out as a lesbian and found a supportive queer community to which she could belong. Her father, a bit heartbroken, a bit embarrassed, and a lot homophobic, expressed his disapproval of her mother. In one instance, her father attacked her mother, breaking her jaw. On that same day, under threats for his life from her community, Ms. Deborah's father left and moved back to Vegas. He remarried and started a new life and family there. So, Ms. Deborah and her brother were raised by her mother, with her mother's partners in and out of their lives.

Ms. Deborah's mother did not cook much. "The only time she would cook was Fourth of July. And she'd cook Thanksgiving and Christmas. . . . She was the sweet potato queen. Oh my God, it would melt in your mouth." On those holidays, they would be with other family members who also lived in L.A. Big Momma, her auntie, would make the dressing, Auntie Fannie would do the greens. Uncle Will would make the fruit salad. But, on the day-to-day, they ate at fast-food restaurants, Jack in the Box, Taco Bell, or at whatever local fish and ribs spots around them.

"Basically, that's how we functioned every day. So, when I met my husband, I couldn't boil water."

Ms. Deborah and I were having this conversation in front of Zenani's apartment in West Jackson. It was the summer of 2016. Billy had been dead for six months from cancer. Grief hung in the air—all my conversations with their family began with reflections about him. For Ms. Deborah, it was emotionally confusing. She mourned him, the man with whom she had shared her life, with whom she had shared the joys of it, and from whom she had endured the most profound pain, including abusive physical pain. On a different occasion, when she and I made the hour drive to Newton, when marijuana had blunted her caution, she unleashed her blues: her rants and insults filled with painful details of brutal experiences that still ached her consciousness and included all its tragic moments which too frequently were near-fatal. But, on that day, in front of Zenani's house, under mature trees that protected us from the summer sun, she was measured. Death sanctified Billy, and she resented that. She wished to not take anything from him, but she wished that her pain, the one she still felt, would not be buried with him.

Growing up, Ms. Deborah frequented Mississippi, especially during the summers, to visit her grandparents in Lawrence. On one of these trips, she met Billy. "He was very attractive, very suave, and he had a job. He gave me money all the time. He spoiled me, so I didn't have a problem with it," she recalled. Their fling continued the following summer and the one after that until, one day, Billy showed up in Los Angeles ready to be with Ms. Deborah. Against her mother's wishes to marry a man from small-town Mississippi, Ms. Deborah moved in with Billy in an apartment down the street from her mother's. They got married and, shortly after, had their first child, Jamila. He supported the family on menial jobs and she cared for the family.

Billy spoke positively about living in California, except that he missed his mother's cooking.

"When I told Mama that, because I used to always call Mama every day, she said, 'That girl going to starve you to death.' She said, 'I'll tell you what you do. When you get a chance, y'all come down here, and I'm going to show her how to cook.' We flew down there that same summer. When Deborah seen Mama, she was so impressed with her because Mama could sew too. She started showing her how to sew, but we didn't have no child but Jamila, and when everybody seen Jamila, they went haywire over her, little red baby with curly hair. I told Mama, 'Show her how to cook something.'"

After having their second child in California, they moved back to Newton, Mississippi. During this time, in Billy's account, their marriage began to fall apart. For Ms. Deborah, the beginning of the end was much earlier, in California, three days after their first child's birth, when she found herself on the floor being kicked by Billy. It was the start of beatings at Billy's hands, which intensified when they moved into Billy's family house in Newton.

"His father died in that house beating up his mother up in that very same house. It was like a karma or aura or something because he loved his father so much. When his father died in that house, it's truly my belief that he got in Bill. I don't believe his father wanted to leave here. Because when I met [Billy], he was so much like his mother. That was the sweetest man I knew. And when I moved back in that house, he'd beat me up like that was breakfast, lunch, and dinner, don't you worry about nothing."

Ms. Deborah found solace in domestic abuse shelters and her occasional returns to California, but Billy's mother was her biggest comfort. "She was my only rock when I left [California]. Her and my grandmother. She was the kind of mother that was always an abused wife and mother. And every time he beat me up, she would, like Celie in *The Color Purple*, tell me that it was going to be alright." They commiserated over their cooking, sharing meals, and feeding the family.[21]

Billy also had affairs, which led to conflicts at home and more physical abuse. After one episode, which resulted in a fight between Deborah and the other woman, Commandeer, the family moved to Jackson. They tried counseling and other efforts to repair their marriage, but they eventually separated, though the fighting continued. The worst of it was one incident that involved an iron, a lot of blood, and a visit to the emergency room for stitches.

After that incident, the judge ignored the need for Billy's signature and granted Ms. Deborah the divorce from Billy that she had been seeking. Also, he was instructed to make monthly child-support payments. After the first few months, Billy stopped paying and skipped town, first to Newton, then to Louisiana, where he lived for nearly ten years. He returned to Jackson in 2010, eighteen months before I met him.

This biographical account of Zenani's parents, especially the portions about their food past, is commonplace in writings about Black folks' foods. A large part of food scholarship that focuses on African Americans provides beautiful historical accounts of the eating and cooking habits of African Americans in prior decades. In these works, there is a great deal of attention to the ingenuity of how they fed themselves in the face of constant oppressive conditions. Using the foodways of Black Americans as its object of analysis, food scholars excavate the hidden histories of Black life in the South.[22] They also use their focus on food to talk about the changing social, economic, and racial dynamics of the South, especially the tri-racialization of the South.[23] Oddly, there has been little attention on how today's poor Black Americans eat.

John T. Edge's recent book, *The Potlikker Papers*, illustrates this omission. The arc of this masterful book covers from the 1950s to the 2010s. The first few chapters of the book, especially the third chapter, "Poor Power," squarely deal with the cooking and eating habits of poor Black Americans. As the book chronologically progresses, the experiences of poor Black people fade and eventually disappear. The chapters that cover the 2010s are about high-end restaurants that pay homage to poor Southern Black folks and the organic farmers and pitmasters who source these restaurants. And, it focuses on the experiences and foods of migrants arriving in the South. Unfortunately, it tells us nothing about what poor Black Southerners are cooking and eating today. The omission in this otherwise impressive text is glaring. It is also instructive. In its efforts to celebrate and reconcile a problematic past and anticipate a hopeful future, this book, and others like it, forget about a still-challenging present. This omission is not just recognizable in food scholarship on Black Americans. It can also be seen in Southern studies's obsession with a "New" or "Nuevo" South, an obsession that has existed since the end of the Civil War.[24]

Zenani's Younger Days

When Billy left, it brought welcomed calmness in their household, but it also dragged the family into poverty—urban poverty. On top of Ms. Deborah becoming the sole parent, she also became the only breadwinner. Around this time, Zenani, their fourth daughter, drifted away from home and wound up getting pregnant in her mid-teens. Two days after my interview with Billy, I sat down to talk to Zenani about her life. We sat near a glass window at a sandwich shop in Downtown Jackson.

I began our conversation by asking her about her parents' marriage. "It was a bitch," she responded in between bites. "That's all he fucking did was beat my mom." Without prompting, she brought up the incident with the iron. Despite their abusive relationship, Zenani characterized her childhood positively. "The younger years, they were damn good, you know, even though my mom and dad went through problems, but they were good. We didn't want for anything else. No matter how much they fought, we still had what we needed. Might didn't come as fast as it would if he were there, [but] we never went without. And we always were taught that family, if I got it, you got it. What can I say? My mama did her best."

She said she loved going to school. "I knew all the kids, and the kids knew me. When we came home from school, Mama always had a meal ready. Soul food, you know, anything—fried chicken and green beans—you know, basic food." What was "basic food" for her would not be the same when her father left. Her mother had to work more and parent all her daughters by herself, so as would be expected, the number of home-cooked meals decreased. Single motherhood and the challenges of feeding the family took their toll.[25]

Sometime after her father left, Zenani moved away from home. It was when she met Tracy, whom she refers to as her first real love.

"I was standing out on the corner one day, and he saw me," she recalls. "We started talking. We exchanged numbers, and we hooked up from there. . . . He was good to me. I mean, we went through our ups and downs. I mean, he was a whore, but that was Tracy being Tracy, you know what I'm saying? He was much older than me, so he's got much more experience than me. So, you could imagine what a fifteen-year-old and a twenty-three-year-old's relationship would be like." I could not.

She moved out and lived with Tracy. He provided for her needs, anything from school supplies to clothes and jewelry. She took care of herself, including doing her cooking and cleaning. She relied on whatever home training she had prematurely learned from her parents during her "younger years." Tracy worked in the informal economy on the streets. By Zenani's estimation, he was making several thousand dollars a month. Those were the "ups" in their relationship. The "downs" came when she confronted him about other women, especially on nights when he would stay out until five or six in the morning. On those days, her questions would lead to an argument and, on some occasions, physical abuse.

"I mean, I never was scared of him. We spoke, you know. I was fifteen—he was twenty-three, twenty-four. You can imagine a twenty-four-year-old man beating a fifteen-year-old up. Yeah, it got physical, but he didn't like hit up on me and black my eye or anything like that, you know? Never was that. I got jealous once, and I was thinking, like, it gets better da, da, daa, da, daa, da, daa. It only got worse from there."

Before she turned sixteen, she found out that she was pregnant. It was unexpected, but her family was not in total shock because two of her three older sisters also had given birth during their mid-teens.

"How did getting pregnant change you?"

"The responsibility, the reality of, 'This is forever going to be your child. You are forever going to have to care for this child, be a mother.' I didn't have a free life like I used to have. I used to get up and go when I felt like it, you know what I'm saying? All that was over with."

"Were you ready for it?"

"No, not really, but I got prepared for it." Going to school was too stressful, so she dropped out. Tracy, her boyfriend, was there and was supportive through most of her pregnancy, but got arrested before their daughter was born. She moved back home when the baby came, but they maintained their relationship while he was locked up. She visited as frequently as every other week.[26] Through financial contributions from his friends, he supported their child. When he returned from jail, they resumed as they were before. Tracy's father had died in prison and his mother, a crack addict, was doing a five-year bid. So, in some sense, his relationship with Zenani was all he had—at least that is how Zenani made sense of what kept them together.

Less than two years later, they conceived their second child. This time, a son.

"[I wanted my son,] but I wasn't planning for him. I wasn't planning for [my daughter] Tracey, or [my son] Trayveon, but they came. I vowed after Trayveon that I would never, well, I'm not going to say never, have any more children." Just like the first time around, Tracy was locked up when their son was born.

"I was trying to be a mom and go to school, and it was hard. Like, I had support as far as family, but it's hard being a kid and being a mother. . . . 2008, that's when I dropped out of school. 2010, December 12, I got my GED. . . . [After that], I didn't work. I was just trying to figure out my life and figure out where I need to start at, and then I had my GED. Year after that [2011], I went to Hines

6.2. Zenani in 2012

[Community College]. I did a year. I didn't finish that up. Now here we go into 2012. Been looking for a job. I've been having ups and downs, but you know, I'm getting through it."

How Zenani, and others like her, are getting through, primarily how they feed themselves and their families, is the subject of the next two chapters. Their ways of feeding themselves are not celebrated in books, magazines, and podcasts. There are no conference panels about the way poor Black folks in Mississippi feed themselves today. If they appear at all, they are not seen as part of a Black food tradition but as derelicts of the food industry. But, they are part of a Black American food tradition, not in content but in spirit. If soul food was, as the historian Fred Opie once described, "the survival food of Black Southerners [that] became the revolutionary high cuisine of bourgeoisie African Americans," then in this same food tradition belongs flaming hot Cheetos, Jiffy cornbread, and Happy Meals, which are survival food of poor Black Southerners today.[27]

Like thousands of others across the country, Zenani felt the squeeze of the shortage of rental housing, the consequences of the economic downturn that led to rampant foreclosures, especially among small-time rental property owners.[4] Since 2009, rents have risen faster than minimum wage—there are not enough affordable units. [5] According to a 2014 report by the Urban Institute, for every one hundred extremely low-income renters, there are twenty-nine affordable and available rental units.[6] No counties in the country have an even balance of low-income renters and affordable housing. The ratio in Mississippi's Hinds County, where Jackson is located, is slightly better: there are thirty-three units for every one hundred extremely low-income renters.[7] Any smear on a tenant's record would mean refusal in such a housing climate—it is a landlord's market. What is more, families with children are frequently turned away. An audit study based in Mississippi Gulf Coast found that seven out of ten families with children face discrimination in housing searches.[8] All these factors—rental market squeeze, increases in rent, rental market as a seller's market, discrimination against families—negatively affect Zenani.

Zenani resolved that she would get an apartment near both her mother and her sister so that she could rely on them if she needed extra help. A week or so later, she invited me to her new place. It was a white two-bedroom house on Rose Street with a front yard, a porch, a large living room, and a kitchen. The wooden floors inside were painted red. The two stained red couches were the same from her last place. The kitchen, which was down the hallway from the living room, was a decent size. It also had a refrigerator and a stove. Unfortunately, neither was functioning. Despite this, Zenani chose the apartment because she already knew the owner and manager, Mr. Davis (a family friend), which meant that her rent history would not haunt her and she could afford it. Also, it was only a five-minute walk from her mother, who lived on Melba Street. She was willing to forgo the essential amenities because she assumed that she could use her mother's refrigerator to store food and her stove to cook.

Her decision is not unlike what several others in her situation make. Beyond the structural constraints, low-income families often remain in high-poverty neighborhoods because, according to one Baltimore study, they offer coping strategies that help them deal with the perils of poverty.[9] Unfortunately, what the neighborhoods offer do not cover all the consequences of living in poor neighborhoods. Zenani's plan to use her mother's kitchen proved unfeasible over time and it significantly affected how she fed herself and her children.

Ms. Deborah had been living by herself for quite some time. Around the time Zenani moved close by, she had transplanted her ailing brother from California to live with her. Zenani's father, Billy, had quit or been fired, depending on who you ask, from his job at The Opportunity Center and had moved into Ms. Deborah's house to help take care of the ailing brother. Because of this, Ms. Deborah's one-bedroom apartment, which she had enjoyed by herself, was now the main living quarters for three adults. With Zenani and her children moving nearby, her space, especially the kitchen, served six people, not counting other family members who routinely stopped by.

For as long as sociologists have paid attention, we have known that kin support has been one of the ways the urban poor people make do with inadequate resources. Carol Stack's *All Our Kin* masterfully showed how African American residents of The Flats relied on "swapping," what she called "a profoundly creative adaptation to poverty," to make ends meet.[10] More recent research tells us that these support networks now take a different shape. Instead of the consistent ties developed over time, today's urban poor form and rely on disposable ties.[11]

I saw a good amount of kin support in Jackson. Zenani could not survive without the help of her family, neighbors, and friends. From what I observed, their ties to one another were not as disposable as much as they were untenable.[12] There was only so much they could do for one another because they had only so many resources. Zenani did not always know the extent to which her family members could stretch their support and vice versa, so she was unsure if they were as helpful as they could be. This constant feeling of being unsupported, even when family members were doing all they possibly could, brewed a great deal of distrust and conflict. I saw this especially in Zenani's efforts to feed herself and her children.

When I pulled up to Ms. Deborah's house on one occasion, Zenani's sister Mary was at home. She was sitting with her children on the concrete stoop in front of her mother's door. They were each enjoying a snow cone. Billy and Uncle Perry (Ms. Deborah's ailing brother) watched old Westerns in the living room. Ms. Deborah was in the dining room area, working on her laptop. She had graduated with a bachelor's degree in business from nearby Jackson State University within the last three years and was now busily looking for a job.

When Ms. Deborah saw me come in, she moved some things off the table to make room for me to sit down. Zenani followed me in a few minutes later. She announced that she was going to go to Church's Chicken, a fast-food restaurant, but decided to make her own instead. Her mother applauded her decision and added that she also wanted some fried chicken wings. "Can you also make some rolls? I want some rolls." Zenani agreed and made enough for everyone, including the children who rushed inside when they smelled the food. In addition to the rolls and chicken wings, she fried some chicken livers and had me try them. We ate together, but not at the same time or at the same table. We each took bits and pieces of different things as they came off the stove. Everyone got a kick out of watching me taste fried liver for the first time.

The scene at Ms. Deborah's was similar the next day. Billy was switching back and forth between *Bonanza* on the Westerns Channel and Animal Planet. Ms. Deborah was at the dining hall table, looking for jobs again. She had made it through the first set of interviews with an investment firm, but found out that she did not make it to the next round. She was back at square one. Ms. Deborah and everybody else who frequented the house—Billy, Zenani, and Mary—were all jobless and actively looking for employment

"No kids or grandbabies today, Ms. Deborah?" I asked as I made my way to a seat at her table.

"No, I kicked them all out so I can have my peace of mind."

She was snacking on something before I arrived, but decided to make a burger for herself.

"We ain't got no bread because Zenani took a whole loaf of bread with her. She can't be doing that," she complained. Billy chuckled, trying to stay out of it.

"So, all we got to eat is hamburger patty," she continued. "Y'all want some?"

7.1. Ms. Deborah with her daughter (Chotcie) and some of her grandchildren

Perry wanted some. Billy did not.

"You want some?" she asked me.

"No, ma'am, I'm good."

"Don't be shy now."

"I'm not. I ate here yesterday. I'll eat if I'm hungry, you know that." I did eat with them, but only enough to maintain my relationship with them. Too much, and it would be burdensome. Too little, and it would be insulting.

Not long after Ms. Deborah warmed up some oil to fry some frozen cut-up potatoes to go along with the hamburger patty, Zenani and Mary, along with their four children, walked through the door. They all wondered what their mother was cooking and asked if they could have some.

"I don't appreciate all y'all coming here to eat up all my food," she shot back at their request. "I ain't got a job just like most of y'all, but I been feeding you and your kids." Not wanting to hear her mother complain, Zenani stepped outside to smoke. I stepped out with her.

"All that damn talking makes my nerves bad. I come here cuz I can't cook at my place." Zenani talked about her nerves a lot—it was the constant stress of having to think about making ends meet. And any attempt to ease her nerves—smoking, drinking, going out—at best provided temporary relief and at worse worsened her situation.

It was one of the many costs of the affordable housing crisis. Not having the option to cook at her place was the price Zenani paid. We could hear that her children were fighting over something inside. Fed up with the noise, Ms. Deborah ordered Zenani and Mary to take their children back to their respective places so she could have her peace of mind. When she returned to her apartment, Zenani made her children some tuna sandwiches.

When I arrived unannounced at her apartment one day, Zenani jumped in my car and asked me to take her to her sister's apartment even before I could park. We headed to her sister's house and she went straight to her fridge in search of food. Jamila heard the commotion in the place and appeared from her bedroom. She looked like she had not left her bedroom the whole day. Her eyes looked hollowed. She rubbed them as she approached us.

"What y'all doing? I didn't even know y'all was in here."

Zenani responded that she was grabbing something for her kids to eat.

"Uh uh. Absolutely not. You can't just come and take my food. I have just enough to last me till the end of the month." It was the nineteenth day of the month. Zenani kept on as if she did not hear her.

"Zenani, I'm serious. I need what's in there."

Abruptly, Zenani stopped searching and signaled for me to take her to her mother's place. She knew her sister would help her if she could, so she was not upset. Maybe just disappointed. On several occasions, I had seen Jamila help her sisters by giving them money, sharing her food stamps card, and even offering groceries that she had at the house. I had learned from Zenani as well that, while Jamila was in the military, Jamila had spent most of her salary on her sisters when they were unable to work during their pregnancies. If she was unwilling to share that day, it was for good reasons.

Zenani decided to try her luck at her mother's place, but the door was locked when we got there. She knocked, but no one answered. Frustrated, she shook the door handle for a moment, but it did not open. She was distraught. As we made the short drive back to her place, she turned her head away from me and simply stared out the window. Back at her apartment, she found two pieces of frozen chicken in the back corner of her freezer. Her landlord fixed the fridge a month after she moved in. She put some oil in a pan and fried the chicken for her children. On days when she could not find anything in her house, she counted her change to get her children chips and soda from the nearby corner store.

Finding a Job

Zenani became a mother when Bill Clinton made good on his promise to end welfare as we knew it. Before she had children, Aid to Families with Dependent Children (AFDC) became Temporary Assistance for Needy Families (TANF), a grant from the federal government that, along with contributing state dollars, provides cash assistance for families in need. Unlike its predecessor, TANF has broader objectives than simply providing assistance for families in need. In fact, among its four objectives is ending "dependence of needy parents on government benefits by promoting job preparation, work, and marriage."[13] Because the program is run entirely by states and states interpret these objectives as they see fit, there are large variations in financial benefits for families.

What is clear is that TANF has weakened as a safety net for low-income families. In 1996, for every one hundred families with children living in poverty, TANF provided cash aid to sixty-eight families. By 2010, it provided cash assistance to only twenty-seven of such families for every one hundred in poverty. Although the 1996 welfare reforms spurred many welfare-to-work transitions, their time limits and, especially, sanctions have deepened poverty among some families. In 1995, AFDC lifted 62 percent of the children out of deep poverty who otherwise would have been in the lower half of those in poverty; by 2005, this figure for TANF was just 21 percent.[14] These rates also differ by state and have deepened racial disparities—states that provide the lowest TANF benefits have larger Black populations.[15] Southern states are among the ones who provide the least. Mississippi gives the lowest TANF financial benefits to families.[16]

Zenani also lives in a time when minimum wage and low-wage labor meet only a portion of how much is needed to *live* in poverty. The Pew Research Center has shown that annual minimum wage earnings yield $15,080, but an adult with two children needs $18,769 to live just above the poverty threshold.[17] And, as a young Black woman from Mississippi, Zenani accurately represents the ranks of low-wage workers: low-wage is defined as "the wage that a full-time, full-year worker would have to earn to live above the federally defined poverty threshold for a family of four."[18] When Zenani was unemployed, which was during most of the time of my fieldwork—she worked before I arrived in Jackson and has secured employment since my departure—she was among the 66 percent of single parents who lived in poverty when they were unemployed for twenty-six weeks or more.[19]

Without a job, Zenani made ends meet by relying on various sources of income. During my time in Jackson in 2012, she received about $500 a month from TANF and about $400 a month from Supplemental Security Income, a benefit she receives for one of her children. For some months, she received another $200 from her boyfriend, who was locked up and worked at a cafeteria in jail. In total, she had between $900 and $1,100 a month to spend. She paid $500 a month in rent and utilities and spent about $100 on other bills (e.g., cellphone). She put the rest toward her and her children's basic needs and food. At the beginning of the month, she hurried to pay her bills, debts, and favors. To express her gratitude for my help with transportation, she insisted on treating me to dinner at a Mexican restaurant. To thank another woman for a favor, she bought her dog some dog food. By the middle of the month, things got tough again.

When Zenani's finances were low, she would go out on the town, to Memphis or another nearby city, with a handful of her female friends and dance to make extra money. Most of the time, she and her friends were hired to perform for someone's event—a bachelor party, for instance. At other times, she danced at clubs. On one weekday night, after putting her children to bed, she explained this part of her life to me.

"Me and my friend girl was talking about this last night. The hardest thing is you staying up all-night, you staying up all these hours, to make like $500."

"But, I thought you said you could make a few hundred in just a few hours?" I asked.

"It depends on who you with, you know what I'm saying?" She explained that they usually charge the club $150 for each dancer and then rely on any additional tips, which is what might make or break the night.

"What if you get there and they don't wanna spend no money? And that's hard work. It might not seem like it, but it is. And so, shit, [that's why we charge] $150 upfront, and you make your money off the floor." And then she subtly added, "Or, you know, you ask a dude if they wanna do something."

I presumed she performed some sexual acts with some of the men for money. The awkward silence that followed confirmed my suspicion.

After a few seconds, she added, "I mean, it ain't something I'm proud of, but I know if I run into the right somebody, with the right type of money, I'mma get up there."

"Are [the guys you dance for] ever disrespectful?" I asked.

"Sometimes, you have to tell them to calm down cuz they disrespecting me, like 'If you don't stop, I'mma leave.' But majority of the time, they cool. Sometimes, they cheap. When I say cheap, I mean cheap. Like, 'You just got $150, so I'm probably gonna have $20 worth of ones.' That ain't shit. When the sun go up, I probably made just $40 worth of tips. So roughly, I'm walking out with something like $200. That ain't shit for me to come back home with [after] being up all-night."

Her father was lying on a nearby couch watching a Celtics basketball game as we talked. We knew he was listening in on our conversation because occasionally, he would interject something like, "Zenani, don't nobody gonna believe none of that shit!" Perhaps out of embarrassment, all his interjections were accusations that Zenani was lying.

She ignored her father. "Some girls do it for the tuition. Some girls do it to pay for their mortgage. Some girls do it because they have real live pimps." She assured me that she did not have a pimp. "Pimps can be very mean. Like, if you tired, they don't give a fuck."

She spoke more about emotional labor.[20] "You have to really take you a drink and get into another mindset. Get out of your normal body. You be like, 'Okay, I'm this person now.' Like, I'mma sit my normal body down right here and get into this other body." Getting in this state of mind was especially important if she found the men unattractive. "With ugly men, you just gotta swallow your pride." She quickly added, "Some ugly men are sweet. Some ugly men are good men. The money don't even matter to them."

"I ain't gonna make a career out of it, though," she continued. I don't know if she was trying to convince herself or me. "I ain't gonna do it forever because my man don't even know about it." She had told her boyfriend that she used to dance, but he did not know that she was still dancing. "I'll look like a damn fool if he find out. He think I got a regular job. In the fall, I'mma have three fucking jobs. I'mma stop." She lamented that part of her life, but she justified it. "I don't care what people think, [but] I just don't want nobody to believe that that's all I want. I got friends that hate that I do this shit. But, you know, this is the only way we got to survive. Like, I can't go back home to my mom. I can't depend on my sisters. They barely wanna get me now, so I'm like shit, I'm just trying to save up for a car. . . . If I had some support, I wouldn't have to go there. I wanna get settled down with one person and live life and not have to put yourself out there to get certain things in life, and it's gonna come."

Her wish to find a job was not just talk. During my time with Zenani, I watched and helped her look and apply for jobs. When she was lucky enough to land an interview, I accompanied her. In one of our first instances of our job search, we went to the Department of Human Services. Zenani's SNAP (Supplemental Nutrition Assistance Program) benefits were rescinded because the office found out that she was selling them—she sold some to pay her cellphone bill. She had an appointment to petition to be reinstated and to sign up for a job through TANF. Looking for employment is one of the requirements for continuing to receive TANF benefits. In fact, a core tenet of the program is to move families out of poverty through its work programs. Unfortunately, this promise is seldom realized.

We did not wait for long when we arrived at the DHS office before Zenani was called to go into the back area to meet with a caseworker. She motioned for me to come in with her. She was meeting with a short and round Black woman who appeared to be in her mid-thirties. The woman was polite, but she hardly said a word to us during the first half of the thirty-minute meeting. She just kept working on her computer. Every once in a while, she would ask Zenani for a particular document, like a birth certificate, which Zenani would produce from her portfolio. Zenani also interrupted her to ask some questions about how she might be able to get a job through DHS or how getting a job might affect some of the benefits she was receiving.

While the woman worked, Zenani whispered that she needed to get a job, even if it is through the TANF program. She wanted to get the day care voucher for her children, as one of her older sisters had done. Her children do not go to day care because she could not afford the $80 a day per child fee. She mentioned that it was not her first time on the program—she had worked at a day care center, but she did not want to get stuck on the TANF program. She aspired to achieve the program's objectives. But, like it was for so many others on the program, a job was hard to come by. By the end of our time, we found out that she was still disqualified for food stamps for herself for three more months, but she would receive them for her children. So, instead of receiving about $378 for a household of three, she would receive $257. She also signed up for the TANF job program and was to report the next day for orientation before they sent her out for jobs.

From there, we went to see Jamila, her older sister, at the VA hospital. Jamila worked in the hospital's cafeteria. She shared that there might be some job openings, but Zenani would have to look and apply for them online.

"Do Mom still have the Internet?" Jamila asked.

"Mmm-hmm," Zenani responded. "Come over there when you get off work so we can do it." Jamila agreed but lamented having to put up with complaints from her mother.

When I ran into Zenani the following day, she told me that she put in the application at the VA hospital, but did not find transportation to DHS for the orientation to the TANF job program. Lack of transportation was another difficulty that compounded the other problems she faced. She asked for my help with filling out an application for Walmart after she begged for her mother's permission

7.2. Discussing a job application with Zenani

to use her laptop and Internet. What I thought would take thirty minutes or so turned into a two-hour affair when we signed onto the application page. After the general information about work history, she had to fill out a four-part, sixty-five question, multiple-choice questionnaire to gauge her moral character even before she could submit her application. The first section consisted of questions about customer and employee relations; the second section asked about the effectiveness and efficiencies of different work-related situations; the third section included self-analysis questions about work ethic, personal decisions, behaviors, and morality; and the final set of questions asked about past work experiences. It was mentally draining, to the point that it invited the applicants to give up. And, it felt like that was done on purpose.

A few days later, we went to Flowood, eight miles from Jackson, to fill out an application at an assisted living center. Then one at the Winn Job Center. And, then another at Embassy Suites in Ridgeland. The day after that, I helped her apply for another position at the Dollar Store, along with a couple of other retail chains. Every few days, she applied for jobs: at a security company, a cafeteria at Jackson State University, the airport, a day care center, hotels in Downtown Jackson and North Jackson as well as housekeeping jobs at University Hospital. We also attended a job fair where she put in several applications. After submitting each application, we called and visited the places to see if they had received the applications. And then, when she was lucky enough to receive callbacks, I took her to the interviews. In one instance, while we waited at a lobby, she remained uncharacteristically quiet. She was tired, stressed, and very nervous. She asked me how I was able to stay calm in these settings. I think the question was about herself. Why did her vibrant personality fail her in job interviews? Why did her performative charisma flatten in these settings? I could not give her an answer. We sat in an awkward silence until I found a silly joke that made her laugh.

I looked for jobs with Zenani while her children were at school. If we began in the morning, we would both get so lost in the task at hand that we would forget to eat something in the morning or the afternoon. When our hunger was no longer tolerable for either of us, we made our way to the closest food vendor. After filling out applications in Flowood, for example, we rushed to the McDonald's on Lakeland Drive for quarter-pound burgers—her treat. A week or so later, when we went to the Winn Job Center, we stopped at a nearby Captain D's, a fast-food seafood restaurant, on Interstate 55 for lunch—my treat.

Feeding her children when she got home from these job searches proved to be a more significant challenge. For one thing, Zenani gave most of her attention to what she viewed as more pressing and more immediate problems like finding decent housing or finding a job. She often organized her days and weeks around those problems. She never treated her difficulties around feeding herself and her family with the same urgency. That is, I never observed her organize her day around what they were going to eat.

This is, perhaps, a reflection of how food matters compared to other needs. Feeding ourselves appears to be an easier problem to solve than other issues, even though it is not. Food is cheap and convenient, especially unhealthy food. The food industry has made it so, for the good and the bad.[21] Americans spend less of their

7.3. Zenani and her youngest child

monthly income on food, especially meals prepared at home, than most other countries. And, over the last few decades, the cost of food has taken up less and less of people's monthly incomes, though the drop is steeper for the middle and the top 20 percent of families than it is for the lowest 20 percent of families.[22] But, the ease of feeding oneself is only in appearance. Feeding oneself is, in fact, a never-ending problem that is never really solved. It remains and accompanies all the other problems like housing, transportation, day care, and employment that come and go. And, if it is not solved, it inhibits one's ability to solve any of the other problems.

How does Zenani manage her food choices in this context? The details about her life I have provided above make it clear that, for Zenani, and perhaps other folks in poverty, food choices were dominated by the demands of her present circumstances. It was clear that her food choices were made in the context and limitations of her present circumstances. That is to say that they were made "in the face of considerable ambiguity, uncertainty, and conflict; [where] means and ends sometimes contradict each other, and unintended consequences require changes in strategy and direction."[23]

Returning to how social theorists think about different approaches to decisions, Emirbayer and Mische propose that when present circumstances dominate people's decision-making, it includes problematizing the situation, characterizing it to see if a previous repertoire might resolve the situation, or determining if a new strategy might be more worthwhile. Then, one must deliberate, decide, and execute.[24] Zenani can problematize the situation quickly. No matter how much she tries to ignore it, being hungry becomes self-evidently a problem at some point, one that cannot be ignored or dodged. It is not a particularly problematic situation for Zenani either when she has money—the first half of the month. Beyond that, when she depletes her financial resources, getting hungry becomes a situation that cannot be quickly resolved. When it arises, and when she cannot deal with it by herself, she often attempts to fix it by drawing on her previous routines: she goes to her mother's or sister's place to find food. If this strategy does not render the situation resolved, she goes on to the next plan: looking for any extra food she might have in her cupboards. If that does not work, she looks to use all resources that might be within her reach. And then to the next, and the next, until the problem is resolved, only for it to return just a few hours later.

Rarely were Zenani's food decisions dictated by her wish to adhere to past food traditions. Rarely did feeding herself and her family include a wish to serve her family soul food or abide by past Black food traditions. Part of this is because after her parents split and after she got pregnant, all during her teenage years, these foods were no longer regularly part of her life. This is not to say that she does not enjoy those foods. It is to say that soul food is no longer survival food; it is ceremonial food. As a Black person in Mississippi, cooking and enjoying soul food is part of her racial identity. But, it is no longer "basic food" for her and her children as it had been for her when she was a child. What she and her children eat today is no longer a marker of blackness, even though it is survival food, as soul food once had been. Today's survival foods are not the creative ingenuity of Black folks; multinational food companies engineer them so they bear no symbolic value.

When various health advocates attempt to encourage poor folks to improve their eating habits, they often miss this insight into how present conditions shape food decisions. They presume that those in poverty can, with the right coaching and the right willpower, pivot their decisions toward health considerations. And, that they can do so without a change in their conditions. In other words, they presume that, within the same situations, they can switch from a decision dominated by the limitations of their present circumstances to decisions dominated by the promise of their future (health) desires. Their assumption often is that if low-income families are taught how to cook, how to shop, or how to meal-plan, they will make better decisions about what they eat. Or worse, it is that if poor mothers cared more about their health, they would make better decisions. Zenani cared about her health and her children's future well-being as much as any parent, but her circumstances made it challenging to make food choices in that vein. This makes sense if we consider research on how living in poverty negatively affects thinking and planning for the future, especially research on scarcity.

The basic premise of the psychology of scarcity is that people obsess over things they lack. And, "if you face scarcity, you may end up in a kind of psychological tunnel."[25] Zenani's scarcity was economic resources, so her tunnel vision was directed toward finding a job. This tunnel vision may have benefits, but it has even more dire negative consequences. When people focus on what they lack, they tend to perform poorly on other tasks. Why might this be? The proponents of this work argue that scarcity limits or distorts our brain's "bandwidth"—the mental capacity available at any given time.[26] When people face extreme scarcity, their brain's bandwidth is impeded by as much as one night's worth of sleep or thirteen IQ points, which leaves them with little mental energy to take on other tasks.[27] These findings are as true for poor people, who lack money, as they are for CEOs, who lack time. In Zenani's circumstances, she cannot abide by all the nutrition recommendations that health advocates make while also looking for employment and dealing with other stresses of living in poverty. Her bandwidth is often exhausted by it all, and it brews constant stress and frustration. It makes her nerves bad. I saw many instances of this, but one evening stands out.

After filling out job applications at the library, Mary, Zenani's sister, was by the washing machine, doing some laundry when we returned to her house. During this time, Mary and Zenani, along with their children, were living with Jamila. Precious, Mary's oldest daughter, and the rest of the kids were playing in the dining room area. The kids were running after and petting a dog they had found. After a while, Precious got the idea to put some sausages in the microwave; it was a generic Hillshire Polish sausage. Tout, Zenani's daughter, followed along and did the same. They probably had not eaten anything since they came home from school. It was around 5 p.m. After they warmed up the sausage, they gathered around the dining room table, where I was sitting, to eat. They overcooked the sausage, so it was steaming hot and had hardened and they could not cut it with their plastic forks.

The smaller kids, Trayveon (Zenani's son) and Iris (Mary's daughter), were standing by, begging for a piece. The older kids did not want to share, so the smaller kids started crying loud enough to get their mothers' attention. "Give her some, Precious!" Mary yelled. Precious was struggling to eat the sausage because it was still hot. She had unsuccessfully attempted to cut the sausage into smaller pieces, so she picked up the whole thing and tried to bite it. After a third trial, she managed to break off a piece. She tried to do the same for Trayveon, but she was not able.

"Just let him bite it himself," I advised, after watching the boy sorrowfully stare at the sausage. She held it out to him, and with all his might, he took a big bite and broke off a piece. Almost immediately, he spat it back out and blew the steam out to quench his burning mouth. He then took a small bite and chewed. His face shriveled.

"You don't like it?" Precious asked.

He shook his head. But, I watched him eat the entire piece he had bitten. He was hungry. Earlier, he had cornered me and asked me to take him to the store to get something to eat. "I ain't ate noth-ing all-day," he said. I knew he was lying, but it wasn't too far from the truth.

"I didn't eat no brea'fast," Trayveon said.

"You ate at school, though, didn't you?" I asked.

"Yea, I did," he admitted

"What did you have?"

"Pizza." Then he squarely faced me and in as serious a tone as the six-year-old could muster up, he pleaded, "Please, take me to the store."

Not wanting to tell him that I could not, I simply turned away from him. He followed me. I had fallen to the will of my pity in pre-vious instances, but this time, I was determined to withstand it and see how the family dealt with not having enough food at the house.

Resisting to assist with immediate needs was one of the moral problems I faced in my research. It seemed insensitive to look on as young children went hungry, but as an ethnographer, my job was to observe and understand the inner working of their lives. So, step-ping in, pulling out my credit card, and taking them to the store, which I had done before, was ultimately limiting how much I could learn. Even with these justifications in mind, the more comfortable, more gratifying response to the hungry little boy was for me to put him in my car and take him to get something to eat at a place where he can order whatever he wants and eat as much of it as he wants.

Around 6 p.m., Billy (Zenani's father) and Painter (a family friend) walked in. They worked as day laborers on a construction site. They had just come from working on a church in a small town between Durant and Kosciusko. Painter, known as such because of his expertise in painting buildings, had been staying at Jamila's apartment because the $60 a week that she charges is less than the $80 a week that he would have to pay at a rooming house. He did not mind staying in homeless shelters, which are free, but the shelters are often full and closed by the time he returns from work. Billy was also staying at the house at that time. When he walked in that day, he smelled like alcohol.

"What you got in that cup, Dad?" Jamila playfully asked.

"It's just um . . . uh . . ." he looked in the cup, then back at her. Everyone got quiet and awaited his response. "Orange juice," he blurted out. In unison, the room erupted in laughter at his answer because we all knew he was lying.

Guessing that Painter and Billy might have gotten paid, Zenani tried to get some money for food from Painter. She ignored her father because she knew that he had probably spent his money on liquor.

"Now, you know I don't get paid every day," Painter responded to Jamila. "I got some money saved up. I'll pull that up to get them chill'en something to eat. I won't let them starve now." He is a native of Indianola, Mississippi, so he has a distinct Delta accent. He offered $5 to get the kids something to eat. It was not enough, but it was a start. It was an invitation for others to pitch in.

"If you can come up with the money, I'll take you where you need to go," I offered transportation.

While Zenani was trying her luck with people at the house, Mary had gone out to find something for their children to eat. When she came back, she announced that she had gotten them some noodles. She got it from from the place of another one of their sisters.

"Why you gonna feed them kids some damn noodles, Mary?" Zenani blew up at her announcement. None of us understood her anger.

"What the hell you talking about? I just got them kids something to eat, and you mad about that. At least they ain't gonna go to bed hungry."

"They need some meat!" The angrier they got at each other, the quicker the words flew out of their mouths.

"They don't need some meat that bad. At least they got something to eat, Zenani! Damn!" She was just as confused as we were about Zenani's outburst.

"They don't need to go to bed on them noodles either before they go to school and tell someone that tells DHS!" Zenani responded more angrily. The surveillance of DHS and Child Protective Services constantly hung over their heads. Being poor and Black, they appeared hyper-visible to the state.[28]

"Don't give your kids them noodles, then!" Mary cut her off and went into the back room. She was still talking, but it was barely audible from where I was sitting. Iris, Mary's daughter, was crying on the floor that she did not want any noodles.

Zenani must have heard what Mary was saying, so she responded. "You ain't the only one that break their back around here," she yelled back at her. "I know I do!"

"But you can't complain to me like that. I done went out there and gotten them kids some noodles. I can see if I ain't trying, but you talking about they need some meat. It ain't like they gonna go to bed starving."

"They still need some meat, Mary!"

"I ain't got no meat!"

She was beyond frustrated at this point. "Chotcie ain't have no meat for me to get them! And, I ain't got no money!"

Zenani did not respond. Even she knew that Mary, who they often teased for being lazy, had done all that she could. Their frustration boiled over, and most of it had nothing to do with noodles or meat.

Iris kept crying. Her crying and what was left of the emotional outburst filled the temporary silence.

"Shut up, Iris!" Mary yelled.

Trayveon jumped in my lap and started play fighting with me as if he did not notice what was happening.

"I win."

"No, you didn't."

Then, when we paused for a minute, he asked, "Can I go to your house, please?"

"No, you can't go to my house. You got your own house," I responded softly.

His mother, who was just a couple of seats down, heard him.

"Sit your ass down," she said to him in a serious tone, "And stop all that damn playing."

When things quieted down a little bit, Zenani revealed why she was so upset with Mary. Whispering to Jamila and away from Painter, she explained that she thought she was pretty close to getting Painter to spend his money to go to KFC for some chicken and that Mary had foiled it by announcing that she got them some food. Being upset was, therefore, not just about her insistence that the children needed meat. It was also about missing out on potential resources. If Mary had not announced the noodles, they would have had fried chicken that night and noodles the following night. She was upset because she now had to keep looking for food.

From her seat in the living room, Jamila noticed that her flag was gone. She is a military veteran who has done several tours, most recently in Iraq. She speaks of her time in service ambivalently; she is both prideful and regretful. Her flag, which was displayed on top of the mantle in the dining area, was one source of pride.

"Where's my flag?" she asked.

No one responded. When she noticed that her American flag and the case in which she kept it were both on the floor, she got immediately upset.

"Who broke my flag?" she yelled. This time, she was screaming at the top of her lungs. The temporary peace was gone. Her yelling startled all of us, but the kids were especially shook-up. It brought the younger kids to tears. They all immediately denied it.

"It wasn't me," they whimpered.

"Oh, somebody is going to answer to this—I promise you!" Jamila ran out the door. She went to get a switch she would whoop the kids with. As soon as she walked out of the door, all the kids disappeared from the middle of the room. Mary's kids ran into the bedroom where they stayed. Zenani's kids ran to her and hid by her. They were fear-struck. Jamila came back with a perfectly cleaned switch.

"Who the fuck broke my case for my presidential flag? And where is my medal?" She lowered her tone to sincerely explain to them why she was so upset. "I told y'all not to mess with it. You can't go to the store to replace it. I been telling y'all. I give y'all everything. I let y'all do everything you want, but the one thing that means a lot to me y'all just had to go mess with it. Where they at?"

Zenani tried to explain the whole thing to Jamila. An hour or so prior, all the kids were playing, after which they were instructed to clean up. Tout, Zenani's daughter, used a broom that was taller than her, so as she swept near the mantle where the flag sat, the top of the broom caught an edge of the flag's case and pulled it off the shelf. The case fell and opened. She tried to close it and put it back, but she could not reach the mantle, so she just put it on the dining room table. The medal, which was by the case, also fell, but she did not notice it. Trayveon, Zenani's son, picked up the medal, put it around his neck, and ran around with it. After a while, the medal flung off the lanyard.

Jamila understood and accepted Zenani's explanation. She found the medal on the floor, put the flag back into its case, and took it to her bedroom. Mary was so upset at what happened, and perhaps still frustrated from her earlier fight with Zenani, she grabbed Jamila's switch and whooped her kids. She started with Caleb. He did not have on a shirt, so the sting of the switch directly hit his skin as his mother reached for him. Having received some whoopings in my day, I cringed as I watched the little boy squirm. Precious also got a whooping, and so did Iris, even though she was not even around when the incident happened.

After the whole incident, Billy, drunk and still drinking, commented to Zenani that she should have been paying attention to her kids as he had told her. "That don't do nothing to the situation, Dad. Just leave it alone. It's my kids, and I'll take care of them. I have been, by myself, all this time."

Jamila came back out of her bedroom. "Y'all come get something to eat and get ready for bed. It's damn near nine o'clock."

It was a school night too. She stepped back into her maternal role—she often cared for her nieces and nephews as if they were her own. She cleaned up the dining room table and instructed Precious to make the noodles. Tout made some noodles for herself, following her mother's instructions. Precious made noodles for Trayveon. And, he ate. Around the table, they all ate. And slowly, they drifted off to bed in the back rooms. Trayveon, still restless, could not sleep.

"Come here, baby. Let me rock you to sleep."

He climbed in his mother's arms. She held him tightly, kissed him on the back of his head, and swayed him back and forth. It calmed him. After a short while, he climbed down and went into the bedroom to sleep.

It was calm again, or so it seemed. Zenani still had to figure out what she was going to feed her children the next day. She borrowed my phone to make a couple of calls because Jamila was using hers. They were both still working to see if they could get some food, money, or both. As soon as Jamila hung up after an unsuccessful attempt, a call came in.

"Who's this?" Jamila asked.

We all listened in.

"You got my number from what pages? I don't think . . . Oh, you must be looking for my sister."

She handed Zenani the phone. After saying, "Hello," Zenani changed the tone of her voice. It seemed like she was trying to woo whoever was on the other line. She could not pass up the chance.

"$150 . . . Yea, for thirty minutes, but you know time doesn't really matter. . . . Yea, we keep going until, you know . . . Okay then."

She got up and went into her bedroom. A few minutes later, she was gone.

CHAPTER EIGHT

Ms. Bea

WE PULLED INTO A PARKING LOT and sat there, continuing a conversation we were having. I kept the car running for a while until I realized that we would be there for a while longer. It was my first week back to Jackson in 2016 in June. I had been gone since the fall of 2012. I was reacquainting myself to Zenani's life. She now had a third child, who was less than a year old. I had plenty of questions, and because I had built a good rapport with her during my last stay and had kept in touch while I was away, I asked my questions directly. And, she provided vulnerable, straightforward answers, which I took to be her most honest. She spoke in both details and abstractions about the strains of poverty, especially about how it affected her food decisions. In some ways, things had gotten better, but in other ways, they were worse.

"It might don't look like it, but I really have come a long way from the point that I was. So, I ain't gonna turn back, like . . . I've been triggered. . . . I gotta take everything little bit by little bit. Like, I can't plan nothing. I ain't had that type of lifestyle in a while."

She was tempted, but she no longer went out of town to dance with her friends for money. She admitted that she desperately missed the financial windfalls that those trips provided. She now had a job, but it did not pay enough to sustain herself and her family. So, she was stuck.

"When the money was coming in, I prolly took a hundred dollars to go buy groceries when we didn't have nothing and plan it out. But now, it ain't like that. . . . I gotta make my money stretch."

Her current job pays her $400 every two weeks. Thanks to a HUD certificate, she pays only $100 a month of her $800 rent—that is until they find out that she has a job. She got most of her housing covered because when she signed up she was pregnant and unemployed. After paying utilities and a few bills, she is left with about $200 to feed her family and cover all other living expenses, including diapers for the baby. She spoke to me like she was trying to convince me that she was doing all she could. I turned off the engine of the car. My body faced forward. She was sitting as far away from me as she could in the front seat of the car, but her body was facing me. She kept going back to how stressful it all was.

"Tell me about the stress."

"It's like when you got kids and responsibility, and you can't provide. Like, I literally didn't know how they was going to eat last night. I just happen to swipe my card and put it in the negative." The words rushed out of her mouth. "But, I just got this account, so that mean I'mma have to pay double back, that's the $39 for they fee, and that's the $20, you see what I'm saying." She admitted as well that she had no idea how they were going to eat that day. Another part of the stress came when she had to go to work, her mother was not able to watch the children, she had no money to pay the daily $175 for summer day care, and she had to choose between going to work and leaving them alone at home or staying at home and losing out on the money.

She paused and took a couple deep breaths. And then, almost as if she second-guessed herself about telling me, she blurted out, "Trayveon told me he wanted to be down there with his daddy." Trayveon's father had passed away a few years back, and he wished to be buried with him. "I'm like, 'Why?' And he's like, 'Momma, cuz you got so much stress on you.' That hurt me to my heart. That really took my soul. . . . It don't supposed to be like that. It don't."

I was sympathetic to how she expressed her hardships, not just because I had gotten to know her and her family and children so well but also because it made sense and matched up with how various scholars talk about life in poverty. The chaos and uncertainty of her life hung over all aspects of her life—it depleted both her mental and emotional energy.

8.1. Ms. Bea talking to her daughter in her kitchen

I found out that he was not interested in having me as a mentor or having a mentor at all. But, I kept going back to Ms. Bea's house because Ms. Bea kept inviting me back. I played with the other children, Deeunte and Da'kari (her grandkids) and Reuben (her nephew). And, I spent time with her in her kitchen watching her cook. As it was within her personality to do, she saw me as someone else to take care of. She fed me more times than I can count.

During my time with her, I saw Ms. Bea make different food choices than did Zenani. Simply put, she cooked more—a lot more. Ms. Bea's approach to her food choice was not as dominated by her present conditions as was Zenani's. Instead, it was led more by her past food traditions. To reach for one's past is not about mind-lessly following customs. It is not agent-less. Ms. Bea had to selectively recall the past and make the recollections fit within a present context. She had to also maneuver through different strategies to accomplish the recalled expectation.[1] Then, she drew on the appropriate resources including ingredients, cooking utensils, cooking skills—all of which are somewhat determined by the present context to reproduce what she remembered.

When Ms. Bea drew on her past, she recalled her 1960s Lexington, Mississippi household where her mother did all the cooking.

"Mother always had food on the stove when we got up," she recounted to me one morning around her kitchen counter. They had toast and bacon or sausage and grits for breakfast. "[It was] cold grits, but she always had breakfast ready." Her mother got up at 5 a.m. to fix it before going to work. She worked at a day care center and then at a hospital as a nurse's assistant at the OB/GYN unit. "She did it every morning and fixed my dad lunch every day. Every day!" she repeated slowly and emphatically. For dinner, her mother cooked when she returned from work around 3:30 in the afternoon. Her fondest memories of dinner were when they had cabbage, greens, cornbread, sweet potatoes, and fried chicken.

"Is that where you learned to cook?"

"In a way, yea. But, I wasn't the kitchen help. Liv, my youngest sister, was the kitchen help. Cuz, my daddy was funny about the food that he ate. He only ate food cooked from Liv and Dor." Dor was one of her older siblings.

She started cooking for herself when, after high school, she moved to Kansas City to live with one of her older sisters. Her sister, who worked two jobs and volunteered at church, was, in Ms. Bea's words, "a TV-dinner kind of girl." It was the mid-70s; Swanson had just launched its Hungry Man dinners and was advertising frozen dinners as a cheap alternative.[2] Ms. Bea resisted their appeal. She started cooking for herself by recollecting what dinners used to be like for her. She cooked some of the same meals as her mother—cornbread, collard greens, and black-eyed peas—but, she admitted, most of her ingredients came out of cans. Her comment made me presume that her mother cooked with fresher ingredients. In Kansas City, she did not have access to those ingredients, so she made her past recollections fit her context.

She was doing the same in 2012. Ms. Bea shopped at her local grocer on Fortification Street, about four miles from her house. When she received her food stamps (around $600) on the thirteenth of the month, she went to stock up. After several comments about how much food she kept at her house, she invited me to join her on

8.2. A young Ms. Bea

her grocery shopping trips. I took advantage of her wish to teach me how to shop as she did.

When we walked by the famous Pick-5 sales, which she often patronaged, she explained that she could get five items for $19.99. The most popular was the Pick-5 meat options, but there were also Pick-5 fruits and vegetables. The middle-class families with whom I visited the same stores often complained that the items included in the promotion were subpar throw-away quality, but Ms. Bea was not as picky. She bought three sets of meat, one set of fruits, and one set of vegetables. She bragged that her children love eating broccoli when I commented that they were not my favorite vegetables. Ms. Bea also often purchased several of the same items if they were on sale. When she saw that Kraft BBQ sauce was 88 cents, she bought five bottles. She also bought four bottles of mustard on sale. She grabbed a large packet of frozen ribs, three boxes of frozen sausage biscuit sandwiches for breakfast, and four cans of salmon to make croquettes. These were far from the ingredients her mother used to cook for her. In her kitchen one day, she shared her fond memories of picking fresh vegetables over the summer and canning and pickling them so they would last through the winter.

Washington 'Dition

The youngest child in Ms. Bea's household, Deeunte, was in the driveway when I arrived one Sunday morning. I went behind him and picked him up. I asked him if he was going to church. He mumbled a yes. He is a short and stocky boy. Even as an eight-year-old, he looked like a running back. I asked him if Ms. Bea was in the house. He nodded. He and his brother had awakened early to spend time with their mother, 'Mica. I was there on Ms. Bea's invitation to accompany them to church.

The smell of bacon met me at the door. Ms. Bea was already in her blue knee-length suit, ready to go. It was about 8:35 a.m. The other two boys, Reuben (her nephew) and Jeremiah (her adopted son) were just getting out of bed. Jeremiah pleasantly greeted me. I asked him about a paper that he and I had worked on. "I would have gotten an A if I turned it in on time," he responded. For breakfast, Ms. Bea fixed us bacon sandwiches—a few pieces of bacon in between slices of white bread.

After we all ate, we climbed into her big green van. The van was like her mobile office. In it, she had all kinds of pens, pads, water, and whatever other knickknacks she needed. She explained that the radio did not work—it had a broken circuit, so it came on and off on its own. "You just gotta hit the right bump for it to come on." We were driving to a church where her ex-husband's father pastors in Terry, Mississippi, about twenty miles or so south of Jackson. She had been going there on and off for nearly twenty years. She made the weekly drive because it reminded her of Lexington, Mississippi, where she grew up.

There were a dozen people, four men and eight women, in Ms. Bea's Sunday school class when we arrived. Six more people came in after us. The scripture that day was John 1:1–14. Each person stood up and read one verse. By the time we got to me, Ms. Bea had passed me a Bible to take my turn. Then the preacher, Rev. Ceaser (the founder of the church and Ms. Bea's ex-father-in-law, who was in his mid-seventies) preached. He wore a three-quarter length checked gray suit. His preaching entailed going through the read scriptures verse for verse and, along the way, making references to other verses. By the time the preaching was done, the children, who had been in their own Sunday school class, joined ours. They stood in front of the room, and one at a time, fielded questions about the Bible lesson to demonstrate what they had learned.

Then there were announcements, about ten minutes' worth. One announcement was about donated shredded wheat cereal that people could take. The person making the announcement joked that he did not like that type of cereal because it tasted like grass, but anyone who wanted them could take them. He leaned on the pastor's symbolic power to voice his dismissal.

"Y'all know that Pastor Ceaser and I don't like anything unless it's fried and has sugar in it, so this don't really taste good to me."

"But it's good for you. It's a good source of fiber," a man seated upfront playfully interjected.

"Oh yea, yea. It's definitely good for you. I'm just saying I don't like the taste." In his next announcement, he asked for prayers for a nineteen-year-old who was in the hospital because his "sugar" levels were high.

After Sunday school, we went to the real church service in the main sanctuary. Several chandeliers lit the space. Ms. Bea directed us to sit in the middle row of the left column. She asked me why I didn't introduce myself during Sunday school and made it clear that I would do so during the service. I resisted. She was not having it. So, after the introductory song and announcements—the nineteen-year-old with high sugar levels was mentioned again—they asked for newcomers to present themselves to the church, which I did. Then, a guest preacher preached an unprepared sermon. The church members moaned and groaned through it, both in praise and admonishment. When the service ended and we walked out, I saw the boxes of shredded wheat at the door. There was a dozen. About eight were still in there when we walked out and more than half of the congregation was gone.

Conversations about eating healthy, which the church announcements hinted at, were plentiful in Ms. Bea's life. Some of her sisters had diabetes, so she knew and saw the consequences of poor health. And, Ms. Bea was one of the few people who attended community outreach programs and parenting classes, including ones that covered health, that Jackson State University and other nonprofit entities organized. And, she was in constant contact with community activists and social workers, but even she could not make healthy food choices central to her diet. She did what some health advocates recommend: she cooked. But, the ingredients to which she had access and could afford undercut her efforts. Her life in poverty, even a relatively stable one, made it impossible for her to be more health-conscious. That, she had in common with Zenani. It got worse when her life became less stable.[3]

When we returned home from church, Ms. Bea fed us fried chicken, English peas, and white rice. She had prepared all but the chicken the day before.

Living with Ms. Bea

"I made some pork chops for you last night." She had fried them.

"Oh, I'm sorry I wasn't here to eat them. I'll eat them this morning," I responded. It was 2016. Ms. Bea was living near the southern tip of the city, closer to Byram than to Jackson proper. She had an empty bedroom in the house where she was staying, so she asked if I wanted to rent the room. I agreed to live with her. I paid my share of the household expenses. Living with her, I saw more closely how her present circumstances shaped her foodways.

After I got out of the bathroom, she had one egg over easy and one scrambled. She asked me which one I wanted. I picked the scrambled one. She was warming up my pork chop in the oven toaster. I made some toast with the Raisin Bran bread and she cooked some bacon. "You can have some of that too. I'll make enough for both of us." She put six slices in a pan. I complimented her on the aroma of the pork chops. In agreement, she commented, "You put some seasoning on here, that sucka taste righteous." She used Tony Chachere's Original Creole Spice. As we talked about the pork chops, she showed me what else she had in her freezer. She mentioned that she now bought a lot of her food from Dollar Tree. I did not know her to shop at Dollar Tree, but times were hard.

"'Mica put me on. This Baron pizza is a dollar. This steak is a dollar. These chicken biscuits are a dollar." She takes those to work.

If she does, she doesn't have to pay $2 for the same thing in the vending machine at work. She also mentioned that she did not cook as much as she used to cook.

"I make dinner and can eat it for three, four days. There're some days I don't even turn on the stove." She was no longer caring for children. 'Mica had the kids for the summer, Jeremiah was now living on his own, and Reuben was back with her mother.

Ms. Bea was renting from a woman who now lives in Chicago. The woman's children used to ride her bus to school. When the children told Ms. Bea they were moving, she called the woman. Ms. Bea was, at that time, in need of a place to stay. The bank had foreclosed on her house because she could not keep up with the payments—she had lost her jobs. As hard as she tried, she could not keep up with the competing demands of the two jobs she had in 2012. When the school district gave her more routes, the hours disrupted her work at the day care, so she was forced to stop working there. When the bus reduced her hours again, she could not go back to the day care. Eventually, she lost the job with the school district as well. Ms. Bea explained her situation to the woman who had moved to Chicago and the woman agreed to lease her house to Ms. Bea. Ms. Bea now worked at a temp agency. At that moment, her posting was coming to an end, so she would have to search for something else. She was hoping they would send her to Walmart. Her life was now closer to the economic precarity that Zenani faced.

When she brought over my plate, she jokingly, but sincerely, added, "Boy, you know I ain't finna serve you. Get your own plate next time."

"Yes, ma'am," I responded.

I ate the white rice with butter, the scrambled eggs, and the fried pork chop. It was all saltier than what I usually eat. She ate her sunny-side eggs and bacon. She had some rice on her plate, but she did not eat it. She told me more about the house as we ate. She wanted to buy it from the lady, but her financial situation at that moment put her far away from that wish. When she moved in, the ceiling and the plumbing needed some work. She paid for it and kept all her receipts, and hoped to deduct it from her rent.

Before heading to work, she took some of her groceries over to 'Mica's for the boys. Even though her grandchildren were not

8.3. Ms. Bea and her bus

with her, she still played an active role in their upbringing, including making sure they had enough to eat. 'Mica did not feed her
children the same way as did her mother. She cooked less, ordered
in more, and ate out more. I observed numerous instances when
Ms. Bea reprimanded her daughter for not cooking and "feeding
her children a bunch of junk."

Their dissimilarity draws out the differences between Ms. Bea's
approach to food choices. For her, even when sick, feeding oneself
meant cooking. Eating out was an occasional activity, not a quotidian
one. She ate home-cooked meals while growing up; she cooked for
herself while living with her sister in Kansas City, and she cooked for
her children and grandchildren. It was so inscribed in her that even
the stresses of her economically precarious life, which depleted her
bandwidth, did not prevent her from cooking. Eating by cooking was
how she was brought up. Research about how past habits, developed
throughout one's life, shape what we do proposes that "neither social
structures nor psychological traits in themselves determine habits
of action; rather, actors develop relatively stable patterns of interaction in active response to historical situations."[4] In other words,
habits developed throughout one's life come to be stable predictors
of behavior. The behavior is not really about the qualities of the person doing the action, nor is it just about the person responding to
their social context. Ms. Bea continued to cook the way she did, even
when her economic circumstances looked similar to Zenani's because
she was habituated to it. It was a "pre-reflective intentionality," her
taken-for-granted knowledge, her knee-jerk reaction to solving the
problem of feeding herself and her family. This was the case for neither Zenani nor 'Mica. Zenani was not socialized into feeding her
family like that; 'Mica might have been, but today's food system has
made it easier for her to feed her family without cooking.

I helped Ms. Bea load up her green van with groceries for 'Mica.
When we got there, 'Mica was sleeping. Ms. Bea had a key to her
place, so she let herself in and went straight to the kitchen.

"What should I leave out?" she called to her daughter.

"Who's cooking?" 'Mica responded.

"You! Get your ass up," Ms. Bea yelled back.

'Mica appeared from her bedroom still with sleep in her eyes.
She said hello. I responded and complimented her on her new car,

which I had, walked by in the driveway. Reuben's mother, Ms. Bea's sister, was also at 'Mica's house. She moved around in a wheelchair. One of her legs had poor blood circulation.

Ms. Bea went to work afterward.

One morning, Ms. Bea found me in the dining room. She had on a pink robe that went down just past her knees and, for the first time, I noticed two tattoos on her legs: a flower on one, and a tiger on the another. The concerned look on her face suggested that she may have been up before me, had a smoke or a cup of coffee, and sat with her thoughts for a while, perhaps still anxious about her impending unemployment.

She went straight to the kitchen. Her grandchildren were spending a couple of summer days with her, so the house was livelier than usual. They also woke up early to play video games. Before I made my way into the kitchen, Ms. Bea had already mixed up the pancake batter. A skillet was on the stove. Deeunte, her youngest grandchild, volunteered to help make breakfast. She had him figure out how many eggs they needed if every person wanted two eggs, and there were four of us. He took a moment to do the multiplication. He needed eight eggs, but unfortunately, there were only four in the fridge. When he reported that to Ms. Bea, she assured him that would be enough.

"We don't need no more than that. Everyone gets one."

She beat the eggs and added some butter. Then, she made the pancakes in the skillet and semi-fried them with oil that was being reused. While she finished that, Deeunte cut up the sausages.

As they cooked, Deeunte commented that his brother, Da'Kari, seldom helped with cooking. Ms. Bea agreed and added, perhaps trying to verbalize the importance of cooking, "He goin' starve. He gonna have to go out and buy food. He don't know how to cook; he just don't."

Da'Kari was sitting on the couch, playing on his cell phone. He heard their comments, but they did not faze him. The boys had gotten bigger since the last time I saw them. Deeunte now looked more like an out-of-shape linebacker than a running back. Da'Kari was taller, but had also gained weight, perhaps a towering lineman. He walked with a slight limp that suggested that his joints could not support all his weight. Ms. Bea was concerned about his weight, so whenever she caught a glimpse of the limp, she took it as an opportunity to comment on how 'Mica does not feed them well.

Ms. Bea had the boys get their food first, even though she worried they might eat it all. I had two pieces of pancakes, some scrambled eggs—an amount I took to be an equivalent of one egg—and two pieces of sausage. We ate together around a table in the kitchen. Deeunte first held the fork as one usually would and tried cutting with a knife. After a while, he dropped the knife and started using his hand. He held down the pancake with a fork and used his hand to tear a piece of it. We left some for Ms. Bea, but I did not see her eat.

After she cooked, she went into the back for a little while. When she came out, she had changed out of her robe and was ready to go out. She motioned for me to go with her and shouted instructions to the boys to put the rest of the food away and clean the kitchen. We were on a hunt for cigarettes. I never saw her smoke, but her bedroom smelled of it. We drove by a tobacco spot, which was closed, so we went to a gas station. On the way there, she told me about people messing with her at work—she worked on a factory line. When she mentioned to her supervisors that her hand was hurting, she was reassigned. Unfortunately, her coworkers complained to her managers that Ms. Bea simply did not want to work. A few days later, she was told not to come back to work, but she went in anyway. She desperately needed the job. Her manager allowed her back on the line, but gave her the evening hours, 2 to 10 p.m., which she hated. She received $250 every two weeks. From each check, she put $40 each toward her cable and light bills and $100 toward rent. Doing so, she had paid ahead for all of them. She spent the rest of it on other household needs, including groceries.

While we were driving around, she received an invitation from her siblings and her daughter to go to the casino. It was a welcomed distraction from her stress and a chance to win some money, so she accepted their invitation and extended it to me. I initially rejected the offer, but changed my mind.

'Mica and I found Ms. Bea on one machine. According to her daughter, it was one she plays often—it was one of her hot spots.

She was sitting and seriously and attentively staring at the screen. She had a drink in her hand. "It's 'Sex on the Beach,'" she responded with a girlish grin. Casinos are seductive places for people like Ms. Bea, people who are struggling to make ends meet. The music, the cheap drinks, and the games help them temporarily take their minds off the struggles of their lives. But the fact that they were playing with real money reminded them of their financial situations. Win or lose, they were forced to think back on how much money they did not have. [5] It was a dangerous mix of stimuli and depressants.

After Ms. Bea drank her drink, she lit a cigarette. I gave her the free $10 coupon I received at the entrance. She had me tap the buttons a few times. I noticed she was holding something, a small green genie. I laughingly asked if it was her good luck charm. Embarrassed, she ignored my question and went back to the game. She tapped the button with her left hand and rubbed the object with her right and whispered to herself, "I wish for big money, big money." With every turn, she commented on how much that round had brought her. She had won $5 one round and $6 another. When there was a bonus round and she won big—$10 or $20—she would be all smiles.

Ms. Bea's luck began to turn. She was not winning anything, and what she had won was disappearing. "They don't like us anymore," she repeated. She would try one more game, she decided—she hoped for a windfall. I thought of Zenani. Dancing for money was not the same as playing a game at a casino. But, the chance at a financial windfall, a chance to make a dent in their financial hardships, lured them both to engage in these different risky behaviors.

I did not want to watch her go through another losing streak, so I walked away as she continued the game. When I returned twenty or so minutes later, she was in the same position as I left her: performing the same routines, rubbing the genie, and tapping the buttons. I could not tell if it was going well or if it was going badly.

When I got close enough, she grabbed my arm and said, "I'm going to give you my ticket. Go over there and cash it for me."

I looked at her screen. She was up about $350. I commented that it was more than her two-week income.

"No shit," she responded.

I took her ticket, slid it into the machine, and brought back to her three $100 bills, one $50 bill, and four $1 bills. She received it with a big smile. In the interim, she had won $12 more.

She cashed that out immediately. "If I don't leave, they're just going to eat it back up." She walked abruptly away from the machine as if she had stolen that money. In just about thirty minutes, she had won what would take her two whole weeks, plus overtime, to earn. She told me she was going to add that to her account for rent. Not knowing if she was going to have a job past the end of July, she was saving up to be able to pay for as much of her rent in advance as possible—what she won would cover more than half of a month's rent.

As soon as we got home, she put some steaks in a slow cooker. We would have it for dinner with mashed potatoes and some rolls.

Part III

CHAPTER NINE

Davis Family—
Lumpkins BBQ

THEY WERE AT Lumpkins BBQ. Black mothers and grand-mothers, four dozen or so of them, gathered to learn about how they could confront the school district if their children were wrong-fully disciplined.

In front of them was a long-faced, tall, and lanky Californian white man, Jed, who spoke to them in his capacity as an advocate from the Southern Poverty Law Center. Most of the women knew him well and trusted him, an interracial trust that is hard to come by in their Mississippi. They had probably fed him at one point or another. Ms. Bea arrived late. I know for sure that she had fed Jed on several occasions. He was the one that introduced me to Ms. Bea.

Jed walked them through the process of successfully filing a claim, unveiling the bureaucratic process that was foreign to the women he spoke to. He had a white man's convictions, but he also acquiesced when members of his audience challenged and cor-rected him. That is how he earned and kept the respect of many of the social justice–minded people in the city, including the propri-etors of the restaurant where he held that event, Mrs. and Mr. Mel-vin and Monique Davis. On that Saturday, I had come to spend time with the Davis's and help out at the restaurant.[1]

When I got there, all six Davis children, Melvin Jr., James, Charles, Ava, Benjamin, and Daniel, ranging in age from eighteen to seven, were there. "Is the work over?" I shouted. It had become a running joke that I often showed when the work to be done was finished. They had more work that day. After Jed's program, we were to feed the attendees. Mr. Melvin, a usually casual and jovial man, was already in work-mode, giving orders. His work demeanor was a blending of his middle- and working-class sensibilities.

"Melvin," he addressed his eldest son, "cut up the cornbread."

He ordered me to put the plates out. Benjamin was to find gloves. James went to do something else. Daniel, the seven-year-old, was freely running around the kitchen. It was neither the time, the place, nor the mood to be doing so. He did not know any better, but he was going to learn that day.

"Do you want a whooping?"

Just the sound of his father's baritone voice almost brought him to tears. He nodded his head but said, "No." His fright confused him. We onlookers giggled at his indecision.

"Do you want a whooping?" Mr. Melvin repeated.

"No," Daniel said. This time he got it right. He said no and shook his head.

"Then go out there and play with the other kids."

Daniel hurriedly left the kitchen.

"Melvin, where are you?"

"I'm working on the cornbread."

"Finish that and then come over here. When you're done, you're gonna be working the window."

Melvin misheard. He thought he was told to bring the cornbread to the window.

"What are you doing with the cornbread? Is that what I told you?"

He attempted to answer, but he could not get a word in.

"That's not what I told you," his father blurted out. His voice and tone were reminiscent of Denzel Washington's as Coach Boone in *Remember the Titans*.

I had incorrectly arranged the plates on the table, so I had to rearrange them. I did not want to catch his gaze, so I kept my head down. Mr. Melvin had the same effect on me as he did on his children. Charles's job was to pass the plates to Mr. Melvin, who put corn on the cob on each plate, then smoked chicken and baked beans. Melvin handed the plates to the people who came through the window. When we got our assembly line properly arranged, we fed all the workshop attendees, about fifty people.

Ms. Bea had not yet received a plate because she was busy talking, so I took one to her when the line slowed. None of Ms. Bea's boys ate the food. They said they did not like that taste.

"It tastes like barf," one rudely said. Another laughed.

In response to my disapproving glance, the one who laughed gave another explanation. "It just tastes different than Ms. Bea's food. That's all."

Having eaten at their house on numerous occasions, I agreed. What he was tasting was not just the food; it was also the difference in class.[2] This difference in taste by class is what the three chapters in this section of the book explore.

After everyone was served, I got a plate for myself. I sat on one of the first tables in the dining area. The children joined me with their plates. As a respite for our hard work, we ate and laughed together. Mr. Melvin, who was back to his cheerful self, joined us and laughed with us. Ava got two ears of corn for her mother, who also joined in. The only one missing was Daniel, the seven-year-old—he was asleep in the office.

I was the butt of their jokes. They made fun of my Africanness—my slight accent marked me as different from an American Southern Black person, and it gave way for them to exaggerate the distinction. I would have found their jokes tortuous years ago as a new immigrant in middle school, but I laughed with them there. Their jokes were benign—I had heard much worse in rural Illinois and Upstate New York—but it revealed to me that the children had a profound understanding of the boundaries of blackness in the city where they now lived. They were new Black Southerners—none of them were born in the South—so they knew, not just from observation but also from experience, what it meant to be a different kind of Black. In my time with them, I heard them talk about being placed on the edge of the field of blackness because they were fair-skinned children of return migrants who also happened to be middle-class. How class intermingled with race in their lives is another subject of these chapters.

I returned to work at Lumpkins BBQ more frequently after that day—three days a week, four hours a day, for about eight weeks.

Two or so weeks after my first day, I met and started spending time with Ms. Monique and Mr. Melvin's children when they came to the restaurant to help, and then in their home. From about May to November 2012, and then again during the summer of 2016, I came and went from their house as I pleased. When Hurricane Isaac threatened to hit the Mississippi coast, I stayed at their home.

The Davis Family and Charles

On my first day as a volunteer worker at Lumpkins, an April morning in 2012, I walked into the restaurant around 10 a.m. I greeted Ms. Monique in her office, a small back room behind the buffet bar. Her computer was in the back-left corner of a rectangular room just past a beige couch. It was a messy office; papers lay every which way alongside things that might not belong in an office—a spatula near a screwdriver, an empty bottle of ketchup near a dead battery, and a comic book. In the messiness, I saw the history of their restaurant. There were fliers that advertised nights when they invited musicians to play. They charged $5 to enter, which would include a complimentary pulled pork sandwich. Stashed in another corner were newspaper clippings about the restaurant's opening. The office gave the impression that the life of their family had become the life of the restaurant and vice versa and that they were being subsumed by it all.

She seemed to be stressed and sleep-deprived by the look of the brownness under her eyes. Her somber mood suggested the same, especially for Ms. Monique, someone who was always upbeat, conversant, and quick to show a beautiful, inviting smile. My instincts were correct. After a warm embrace, I sat on the couch near her workstation as she, rather candidly, shared with me the difficulties they had been facing. In the preceding months, business had slowed from about three hundred customers a week to about one hundred. They ceased inviting musicians to play on weekend evenings because it was no longer profitable. She could no longer afford to pay for advertisements, so she often offered to feed the staff of local newspapers for a few ad spots. Catering was their most lucrative service. It helped them to pay more of their bills than did opening the restaurant.

When Ms. Monique ushered me out of the office, she explained to me all that had to be done for the restaurant to open. My first assigned task was to wipe down the tables in the eating area, arrange the tables and chairs, and sweep the floor. Ms. Camilla, who oversaw the cash register, had soul music blasting while she sang along. It made for a pleasant work environment. When I was finished with my tasks, I watched Ms. Camilla make sweet tea, which, to Ms. Monique's displeasure, was always too sweet and, therefore, unhealthy.

It was my first sight of how Ms. Monique thinks through what one ought to eat (and drink). From that moment on, I observed and recorded all that goes into what she considered good and healthy food. I saw these considerations in her decisions as a restaurateur, a friend, and a mother to growing children. I paid attention to how different factors influenced her food decisions as well as how the socioeconomic and cultural context of her life made it possible to entertain these influencing factors. I quickly learned that, for Ms. Monique, health considerations were an essential part of her food choices. When, a few weeks into my tenure, Ms. Monique saw me eating leftover mac and cheese straight from the cooking pan, she warned that I would gain weight from working with them. She advised, on her way out of the kitchen, that I should eat more vegetables. When I responded in jest that I would eat some fried green tomatoes, she responded with a stern motherly grin and, "Those don't count. Frying them takes all the ingredients out."

After finishing the prep work in the front of the house—restaurant parlance for the dining area—I went to the back, Robert and Kenny's domain. The stove sits in the middle of the kitchen if one entered from the corridor that connected the dining area and the kitchen. To its left was the smoker. According to Mr. Melvin, it was the biggest smoker in the state of Mississippi, which, if true, would be very impressive considering that smoked meat was an essential part of Mississippi foodways. They smoke the chicken for three hours and the brisket for at least ten hours. On the wall to the right were the washing sinks. And, near that corner was the boombox that blasted hip-hop music from 99 Jamz, the city's premier hip-hop station. Robert, round-faced, average height, and reserved, was the chief cook. Kenny, brown-skinned and slender, was the utility man. He washed dishes, swept the floors, and attended to whatever else was needed. He was at the lowest level of the restaurant's organizational chart, but his presence was severely missed when he was not around.

I apprenticed myself to Kenny and made sure not to usurp his job, given that my presence, as unpaid help, potentially challenged his paid position. He taught me how to set up the workstation, get the water to the right temperature, use the right soaps for each of the sinks, and properly scrub pots, pans, and racks on which the ribs were smoked. He gave me pointers on how to be efficient. For example, if you neglected to wear rubber gloves while washing the dishes, which I did a few times, your hands would get soft from being in warm water for so long and would be irritated by the dishwashing bristle used to scrub the pots and pans. Perhaps as a reward for being a good apprentice, Kenny, who was usually soft-spoken and quiet, disclosed to me the restaurant's inner workings and the relationships between the staff. Long before I observed their dynamics, I learned from Kenny that Robert was often frustrated by Mr. Melvin's forgetfulness—Mr. Melvin often returned from his trips to the grocery store without one or two key ingredients.

As we got closer to opening time on my first day, I helped Robert take the smoked chicken and side dishes appetizingly arranged in silver buffet pans from the kitchen to the serving line. He lit candles under them to keep them warm. When it was all set, we waited for our customers. The day was unceremonious. Customers came and went. It was not a slow day, but it was also not particularly busy. I stayed out of the way most of the time since I was still learning the ropes, but I contributed by taking on the simplest tasks—sweeping up dropped food, wiping down tables, and throwing out trash.

Ms. Camilla played and sang to her soul music in the front, and Robert nodded and mumbled to hip-hop music in the back. When the customers finally thinned out, around 2 p.m., Ms. Camilla, Ms. Monique, and I gathered in the dining area with two customers who were also good friends of the Davis's. Robert and Kenny either ate in the back, if they ate at all, or they stayed in the backyard, smoking and joking with one another. I never saw them eat in the dining room area. Their keeping away might be because Ms. Monique was their boss, and it was simply too awkward for them to dine with them at work. Or, perhaps it was that they viewed the front of the restaurant as outside of their terrain since they oversaw the back area. I read their distance as evidence of their class differences. Robert and Kenny were squarely working-class, while Ms. Monique and her friends were middle-class. Writers about the South frequently exclude these intra-racial class dynamics. The experiences of Black folks in Mississippi are often homogenized. It is easy to do this because the state is the poorest in the country and, in Mississippi, Black folks have the highest rates of poverty (30.5 percent). Still, this homogenization is not helpful. It blunts understandings of Black life in a place like Jackson. In Parts III and IV of this book, I write against this tendency.

Often, after the crowd left, Ms. Monique, Mr. Melvin, and her friends enjoyed long leisurely lunches when they debated politics, race matters, and what they had heard or read from NPR or the *New York Times*. On this occasion, Tracie (Ms. Monique's friend), Ms. Camilla, and Charles (a loyal customer and a dear friend of the Davis family) talked about colorism. I listened in. Tracie initiated this topic, following the trails of previous comments, recounting the differences in skin tone between her grandmother and her grandmother's sisters. Tracie also shared a story about being labeled as dark-skinned and, therefore, undesired by men she encountered. As the conversations unfolded, Charles and Ms. Camilla began their line of conversing with her narrating the skin tones of people in Ms. Camilla's family. Charles listened attentively as he carefully took the final bits of meat from her chicken bones. When I first met him, he was morbidly obese, standing at about five feet and six inches and weighing about 400 pounds. His patronage at the restaurant provided more opportunities to observe Ms. Monique's food consciousness. She often insisted that Charles eat more vegetables, shoving more green beans on his plate, even as she offered her juicy fat-ladened brisket.

When he came in to eat on subsequent occasions, I made time to sit and talk with Charles. He and I continued conversations about race matters, electoral politics, sports, film, and television. He is an intellectual with an encyclopedic mind filled with details of Mississippi's cultural history. In his commentaries about the day's news, he reached far and wide for references that were often way beyond my knowledge of the South—he taught me a lot. At the time, he worked as a professional photographer for the Mississippi Art Center. I followed him to his shoots on a few occasions. For some time, Charles stopped coming to Lumpkins to eat. When we reconnected and started spending time with one another again, I learned that he had to radically change his diet due to a health scare. He was now vegan. We began to meet and chat again over meals again, but this time, it was at various places around town that served vegan dishes. And, on a few occasions, I spent evenings with him at his apartment and watched him cook for his new diet. The third chapter in this part of the book, Chapter 11, focuses on my time with Charles.

I use the experiences of the Davis family and Charles's to characterize the lives of the middle class in this study. They are lower-middle-class Black Americans, which I will distinguish from the Black upper-middle class, on whom the fourth part of this book focuses.[3] I conceive of their middle-class experience as that of those who live on the wages of their employment. While some struggled financially, they had enough economic resources to squeeze out a decent living. Also, they were able to rely on their educational backgrounds and networks to survive on their own. Their class position is also relational, in the sense that it is embedded in their Mississippi social and economic context and that it is shaped by their networks, especially their relationships with others in and above their class position. These networks grant them access to additional resources unavailable to those in poverty. Put together, class in this study is thought of as a subjective location and a relational explanation of economic life chances.[4]

Black folks among the US middle class are different from their white counterparts. For one thing, their history of upward mobility has been more gradual because of paternalistic white supremacist policies that systematically blocked their economic progress.[5] For another, even as they have clawed their way into the middle class, Black folks do not benefit from their improved financial positions in the same ways as do white middle-class folks. To point to just one example, middle-class Black Americans live in more impoverished neighborhoods than do white folks with similar incomes.[6] Both of these distinctions factor in how they go about getting something to eat. The former matters in that the ancestors of today's Black middle-class families spent much more time in the depths of poverty and therefore experienced what it meant to live in deprivation and became socialized into and endeared to the survival foods of poor Black folks. The latter is important because, in a contemporary re-segregated America, the poorer neighborhoods they live in provide less access to healthy and diverse foodscapes.[7]

For those Black folks who get out of poverty, they are supposed to be welcomed into a new class stratum where they enjoy the fruits of their economic progress, including a different taste in, among many things, food. But, middle-class Black folks quickly find that there is an ambiguous place for them. In America, all the middle-class people are presumed to be white, all the Black folks are assumed to be poor, and Black middle-class folks are stuck in between their race and class. This in-betweenness is a third unique attribute of being Black and middle-class in America.[8] In addition to this, middle-class Black folks are susceptible to suffering another fate—the questioning of their racial identity by poor Black folks. Their aspiration for upward economic mobility is often misconstrued as an aspiration for upward racial mobility toward whiteness and, therefore, a rejection of their blackness. The Black middle class, then, are vulnerable to experiencing a double rejection, one of their class position from the larger (white) middle-class strata, and another of their race, from the larger (poor) Black American population.[9] I will show how all this affects how people like Charles and the Davises think about food.

Food Consciousness

How do members of the Black lower-middle class make decisions about what they eat? Their class privileges offer more relative stability, economic and otherwise, and so their food choices are shaped by a broader range of influences. Their navigations of socioeconomic structures do not deplete their time, energy, and resources as they do for those in poverty. Specifically, because they have stable housing and employment, they do not have to spend as much time navigating the housing market or applying for jobs. With more time and energy, they entertain different factors in their food choices.

To follow how I explained Zenani and Ms. Bea's food choices, how the past, present, and future elements of decision-making come to matter, I argue here that their food choices include more than just their past or present.[10] Their food choices include their projections of their future desires. So, how do they manage the various potential influences? The answer to that question lies in looking into people's food consciousness, an important but often ignored part of food discussions, especially food choices.

Sociologists who try to explain people's actions have wondered about the importance of consciousness, especially in how different actions become routines and habits. Here, I treat food choices as actions and place them in this same conversation. I am interested in understanding how various considerations (e.g., health and environmental) become part of someone's food decision-making, including how new considerations become included in decisions and eventually become taken for granted.[11] For one theorist, Anthony Giddens, consciousness exists on multiple levels: on the level of practical consciousness—where actors bring to their taken-for-granted actions and unnoticeable know-how—and discursive consciousness—where actors actively and reflexively bring and incorporate new knowledge into their acts.[12]

My exploration of food consciousness follows this line of thinking: it is as much at the level of practical consciousness as it is at the level of discursive consciousness. It is as much about day-to-day food decisions as it is about decisions to take part in diets, as much about the daily choices of Ms. Monique and her family as it is about deciding to follow the keto diet, for example. What is more, food consciousness does not live in one's head but in a social context, often racialized and classed. It is not just rationally weighing which foods are good for one's health or the environment. It is embroiled in the messiness of everyday life.

With these ideas in mind, I make the following case for how to understand how Black folks like Ms. Monique and Charles make decisions about what they eat. I show that, because they have more time and resources than those in poverty, their decisions are not just based on the present circumstances. Again, their present circumstance is significant, but not dominant. For instance, they have the resources to explore and develop different tastes because of their class background. These different tastes can be pleasurable lifestyle preferences, like developing new tastes in Japanese cuisine. In addition, their food choices might also be shaped by their desired future possibilities, such as the resources to become vegan. I examine these considerations by looking at their practical consciousness, their taken-for-granted habits and routines, as well as their attempts to incorporate new knowledge and habits. And, I show how these considerations fit within their peculiar race and class contexts. Lower-middle-class Black folks do not get to live in the same neighborhoods that give them the access to the amenities to live out their taste as do their white counterparts. Even more important, their acquired middle-class taste is deeply connected to their negotiated racial identity.

Rethinking Soul Food

"We have a big job today, Piko. We have to smoke 170 slabs of ribs. Then we have to do about seventy more." That is how Mr. Melvin greeted me when I walked into Lumpkins.

"So, I'm gonna learn how to smoke meat today?" I asked.

"Yes, you are."

Without further instructions, he darted out to run errands and handed me off to Robert. Because Kenny was not around, Robert pointed to a sink full of dishes that needed to be done. Usually, I hate the chore of washing dishes, but at Lumpkins, I enjoyed it. It provided a purpose for my presence and put me in the corner of the kitchen to observe the comings and goings without being in the way. I was useful, but not essential—the dishes would have been done with or without me. And, as a solitary activity, it freed me from social engagement and allowed me to pay close attention to micro details about the people about whom I was learning. It provided the mental space to more carefully observe the order and rhythm of their conversations, the moans and grunts between their words, the subtleties of their nonverbal cues—in short, the beauty of Black Southern expressions that Zora Neale Hurston was so good at hearing.[13]

When Ms. Monique came to the kitchen, she was surprised to see me.

"Pikooo. . . ." Her alto voice sang my name. By her accent, a non-Southerner would recognize her as a Southerner; a Southerner would recognize that she did not grow up in the South. "I didn't know you were here."

"Yup, I'm blowing in like the wind."

She seemed happy to see me, genuinely, and perhaps also because she was missing two employees on that day.

"Did your lady and her mother enjoy their visit?" She asked about my then partner's visit.

"Yes, they did. I managed to get them to say that they would move here in a heartbeat."

"That's how you do it, changing one mind at a time." Convincing non-Southern Americans about Mississippi has become part of her life mission. It was her way of challenging how the South exists in the imagination of the country.

"So, they liked it here, huh?" It was a question from Robert. He did not talk to me much, so his question surprised me. His conversations with me were usually in passing and during various tasks. For this question, he stopped what he was doing and waited for an answer. He wore a blank stare, but it was not one of disinterest.

"Yea, they did. Cuz, you know, a house cost cheaper, you know. Everything is just a little cheaper here, so if you make the same amount here as you'd make up North, your money can go further."

He took in my mumbled answer. "Uhhhhhh, huh." He responded with his usual casual exclamation. The first part of it is like a long-held note, followed by a staccato. "Yup, you right," he added.

Just as quickly, we both returned to our work. I asked him questions as I needed, to which he often responded with one-word answers. He was neither unfriendly nor was he dismissive of my presence, but try as I did, he never really opened up to me. I wanted to know more about him and his family and how he learned to cook, how he landed a job with the Davis family, and how he thinks about food, but I never was able to engage him. Perhaps it was a result of my ignoring sociologist Erving Goffman's advice that an ethnographer could not get in with a subordinate group if they had close relations with a superordinate group.[14] In my scenario, my inability to "get in" with Robert was perhaps the price I paid for being so close to his employers. Just as he did not eat in the dining room with Ms. Monique and her friends, he did not fully engage with me. That, too, was a marker of how class differences affect intra-racial interactions.

When I finished with duties in the back that day, I went into the dining area to help Ms. Monique. Earlier, I had asked and learned from Robert that Ms. Camilla was ill and hospitalized. She had heart problems.

According to Robert, it was less severe than it sounded. "Yea, she'll be fine. But you know what it is? Camilla need to stop drinking. The doctor done told her to stop drinking so damn much, but she don't listen."

Her absence meant more work to be done up front, and it fell mostly on Ms. Monique. Because the restaurant was not generating enough income, she had taken on a part-time job. On that day, she excused herself from her second job to ensure a smooth opening at Lumpkins. I put the tables in order as she mopped the floor.

Mr. Melvin had returned by that time, so he too helped. In between wiping tables, he answered a call from a customer that had placed the large order he told me about when I arrived. In addition to the 130 slabs of smoked ribs they had ordered, they wanted half a pan of baked beans, half a pan of potato salad, twenty pieces of smoked chicken, and a pan of peach cobbler. By the time they arrived to pick up their order, Mr. Melvin was tending to customers who had come to eat. Robert was busy cooking. So, it fell on me to handle the ribs.

Following Mr. Melvin's instructions, I put in 130 slabs and then took one hundred and readied the order for customers who had come from Rankin County, the affluent county north of Jackson. They were white. Surprised by my "Northern" accent, they engaged me in conversation about what I was doing in Jackson. To my response that I was a sociologist, one lady responded, "Yea, that's good. We definitely need some of that down here." I learned that they were part of a civic leadership training program and were purchasing ribs for a fundraising dinner to sponsor an educational program that gives awards to the best students in their school district. They shared that they loved Lumpkins because they loved the taste.

After the customers left, and after the rush of the day, Ms. Monique cleaned around the buffet area while Mr. Melvin rearranged what was left of the meat. In trying to explain to me, and perhaps to themselves, the decline in customers, they commented on why they offered the foods on the line. In their discussion, I began to hear the differences, real or imagined, between how they think about food and how some of their potential customers think about food. It was a window into their food consciousness. And, their comments illuminated how they imagined their classed racial selves in the community where they lived and worked.

"If you don't have greens and cornbread, people get mad," Ms. Monique started.

"Yea, but you do have greens and cornbread," I retorted.

"We have them, but we don't want to have them," Mr. Melvin and Ms. Monique responded in unison.

"Eventually, we don't want to have to have greens. We want to do sandwiches and french fries. That's what I want," Ms. Monique further explained. They had, earlier, hinted how much they disliked being thought of as a soul food restaurant. I wanted to clarify what they meant.

"If you say 'soul food,' and you have to have greens and corn-bread . . ." I began, but they both, separately, jumped in to finish my sentence.

"If you don't, they'd start laughing at you. They'll start talk-ing shit and walk out the door," Mr. Melvin mumbled under his voice, doing his best to allow Ms. Monique to give a fuller answer. Ms. Monique added more to my list.

"Mac and cheese and candied yams, like Sunday, like Big Momma, like . . ." She kept editing herself, but in her unfinished phrasing, I heard her trying to conjure up that old image of the Black matriarch, cooking a large meal for her large extended family. "Like what you think of traditional Southern cooking on a Sunday."

"If you don't have every single thing, Black people will walk out," Mr. Melvin jumped in again.

"Or dressing," Ms. Monique jumped in again. "If you don't have dressing and everything, they'll walk out."

"Yea, they'd walk out and be mad and call you a 'dirty son-of-a-bitch," Mr. Melvin added. Ms. Monique laughed at the latter, which, to me, meant that he was exaggerating a bit.

To the expectations that people have, Mr. Melvin added the following, "And you think I'm joking," the serious look on his face—wrinkled brow, pursed lips—said he was not. He paused from wiping the counter, "People come behind the line, and they mad at me cuz they think I'm too light-skinned to be cooking. . . ." He paused and stared at me to see if I believed what he was saying.

"Now, I always take what he says with a grain of salt," I mentioned as I looked at Ms. Monique to determine if I should believe him.

"That's true," she affirmed.

Mr. Melvin continued, "It's supposed to be a big old lady who jumped out the pancake box." He was referencing the image of Aunt Jemima.[15]

Ms. Monique continued, "Plus, everybody think they can cook soul food, so people are always comparing this to what their memory or genetic expectation is. So, the achievement level is very high." Her choice of word, "genetic," was perhaps metaphoric. I took it to mean that she was referring to some hard-to-reach level of imagined "authenticity."

"You can't get there because everybody's different," Mr. Melvin added. Instead of soul food, Ms. Monique and Mr. Melvin wanted it to be a BBQ place.

When I asked them how they dealt with the expectations that people bring to a BBQ restaurant, they provided two different answers. The first was that, technically speaking, people can't BBQ in their homes, at least not the kind they can make at their restaurant. Most people can grill their meat, but they do not have the equipment to cook meat over indirect heat the same way they are able to in their smoker.

Second, Ms. Monique explained, "People have a different expectation when it comes to BBQ. People are a little more forgiving. They are willing to try something new. Customers have a more definite idea of what they want soul food to be than they do of what they want BBQ to be." And their big smoker, she argues, allows them to make their BBQ the same way each time. Implicit in all their comments was their frustration that the (richer) white folks who lived across town were more interested in their food than the (poorer) Black folks who lived near their restaurant.

9.1. Mr. Melvin and Ms. Monique Davis on their front porch

Mr. Melvin added, "People who wanna have good food and just want to venture out of their palette, we don't have a problem with them. But, the people who aren't adventuresome who just wanna go to McDonald's, those are the ones we have problems with."

His wife agreed. "If you wanna meet interesting people and have a good conversation, and eat some good BBQ, then come. This is it. . . . When they come, we do pretty good. And we need them to come in larger numbers."

My mind lingered on the conversation I had with Ms. Monique and Mr. Melvin as I pulled out of the restaurant's parking lot at the end of the day. A red light stopped me at the intersection of Raymond Road and Terry Road. My mind kept trying to make sense of their attitude toward soul food. It could be read as a rejection of the South, as a snobbish Black return-migrant attitude buried under their seemingly amicable feelings toward being back in the region. Even if, à la Fred Opie, soul food was the "high cuisine of bourgeoisie African Americans," it had come to represent something in and about blackness in the impoverished South. Because I had spent time with Zenani's family, in their kitchens and around their dinner tables, I knew that contemporary poor Black Southerners were not regularly eating soul food. Still, soul food was celebrated food, a symbol of something—survival, maybe, for being Black, and poor, and Southern. Cars passed me by. My thinking made me drive significantly below the speed limit.

The Black people who walk out of Lumpkins in anger might have been disappointed that the restaurant did not have what they wanted to eat. They might have been upset also because they viewed Lumpkins and its Black proprietors to be, however implicitly, rejecting soul food and the symbolisms it evoked. Even though the restaurant was physically close to them, it felt socially far from them. Their lives in poverty precluded them from experiencing and acquiring the taste to enjoy what Mr. Melvin and Ms. Monique wanted to offer. They did not have the luxury of an expanded food consciousness, the luxury to try new things and broaden their tastes of good food, whatever that might be. Like Zenani and Ms. Bea, they were too busy directing all their time and resources to pressing, daily problems. When they came to Lumpkins, they wanted what they wanted. They wanted what they knew and liked. And, they walked out upset because they wished Mr. Melvin and Ms. Monique understood that.

Stretching my left arm out of the driver-side car window, the wind rushed through my fingers as I tried to grasp at something. My right hand swerved South Jackson potholes. Another red light—I was heading toward Jackson State University. I stared in my rearview mirror, looking back toward the restaurant's direction, and started thinking about the matter inside out. What to them, return-migrant lower-middle-class Black folks, could soul food mean? And, how do their meanings of soul food differ from that of Black folks in poverty? Answering this question, especially by comparing the foodways of Black people across class, is one of the advantages of my tiered research approach. I drove through the green light across Highway 80—Terry Road became University Boulevard.

Mr. Melvin and Ms. Monique may appreciate the symbolic significance of soul food to Southern blackness; after all, they had deep roots in the South and now call it home. But, to them, there was more to good food than soul food. Their aspiration for creating other kinds of good food was not necessarily a rejection of soul food, much in the same ways that aspiration for upward economic mobility was not a rejection of blackness and an aspiration for whiteness. For them, Lumpkins was a place that sought to add to the foods that were available for Black folks in Jackson. Perhaps unconsciously, they imagined their restaurant for people like themselves, those whose food choices are not defined only by availability, those who have the mental space for entertaining other influences, those who do not live in poverty. It included middle-class folks of all backgrounds, like the white folks from Rankin County who came for the ribs. But, they wanted it to be for Black people like themselves, Charles, and me. It was a way for them to live out their expanded class taste. They wanted it to be a symbol of the Southern Black middle class.

Unfortunately, it was not in the right location. To have been more profitable, it needed to have been in another part of town, in a place with more people who had the luxury of trying and learning new tastes. Unfortunately, the Davises did not have the wealth to afford a restaurant in another part of town.

CHAPTER TEN

Davis Family— Cooking with Ava

MS. MONIQUE AND DANIEL, the youngest Davis child, were in the front yard waiting for an update about Mr. Melvin. His car had broken down on the highway while he was taking Melvin Jr. to take his SATs. I was returning to their house after going to Mr. Melvin's aid. I ended up taking Melvin Jr. to his exam. After I recounted the events to Ms. Monique, she offered me coffee.

"The kids have drank up all the milk."

Milk was a staple at the house, so there was never enough of it. They drank it all the time mostly because, other than water, it was the only beverage at the house. Ms. Monique refused to buy juice, which she described as "nothing but sugar." When they ran out of milk, the children had to drink water until the next time their parents went to the grocery store. The day before, Daniel told me they had gone through two gallons of milk in a week. I drank the black coffee Ms. Monique offered with sugar while we sat in their living room. NPR played in the background on an old white Bose radio speaker. Both Ava and Benjamin, the fourth and fifth born, asked why I was drinking coffee since during one of my visits, somewhere as part of my answer to their barrage of questions, I had mentioned that I did not like coffee.

"Grown folks change their minds too sometimes," Ms. Monique defended me.

I grabbed an orange with my coffee.

"I don't know if the kids have told you, but I eat some of your oranges every time I come over." My admission was a subtle way of ensuring that my involvement in their lives, to the point of eating their fruits at home, was agreeable to her.

"That's what they are there for," she responded, implicitly consenting to my presence. "I try to keep fruits around. If it's in the house, it gets eaten."

"Why do you like oranges so much?" Daniel asked me. He stood in front of me as I peeled my orange.

"Because they taste good," I replied.

"Because they are good for you," Ms. Monique said almost at the same time that I gave my answer. It was a way for her to reinscribe in Daniel's thinking the importance of fruits. Relatedly, I mentioned that Pecan Park Elementary School, Daniel and Benjamin's school, offered apples, but oddly, the apples come wrapped in plastic. My random passing comment invited her to make a larger pronouncement about the availability and quality of fruits and vegetables in her neighborhood.

"Have you been to the McDade's around the way? The fruits over there are always in plastic. I don't understand. And, because I'm on the other side of town, the north side, [for work] most of the day, I notice that the fruits in the other McDade's isn't always in plastic. I think we get the reject produce over here. That's why our fruits are in plastic." She continued, "I understand that for something like hair products, it's important for us to have different things in the store, but I don't know why we get different kinds of produce. We used to have just one kind of lettuce, iceberg lettuce, but I've raised enough stink that now we have different kinds. Iceberg lettuce is nothing but water—there are no nutrients in them." She is not wrong. Research on quality, availability, and prices of fruits and vegetables across neighborhoods often finds that low-income areas of towns receive lower-quality produce.[1]

Ms. Monique herded us all outside when the day broke. She and I sat on the rocking chairs in the front porch and watched Benjamin and Daniel run around after each other on their front lawn. A refreshing summer morning breeze rustled the leaves on the trees. The sun shone brightly, but it had not yet warmed. We talked about a public forum that we attended the day before about the most recent rounds of public-school redistricting in Jackson. It had by then been routine for us to discuss Jackson politics. The Davis family lived in and around the poor neighborhoods that were so often the subject of these conversations. They stayed attuned because they had the time to, but also because it was another way their middle-class lives remained intimately connected with those who live in poverty. Ms. Monique was also attuned to international politics. It was June 2, 2012, the day that former Egyptian president Hosni Mubarak was sentenced to life in prison. So, like a panel on any twenty-four-hour cable news channel, informed or not, we gave our opinions on that and various other matters.

A few minutes into our conversation, Mr. Melvin arrived to enthusiastic cheering from his wife.

"Yay! Daddy's back! Daddy's back. Daddy, you're the man. Come here and give me some love." It was her way of comforting him for a stressful morning. He came over and kissed her.

"Ava, get your dad some coffee."

Ava returned shortly with a cup of coffee in a clear glass. "There wasn't a lot of milk left," she said apologetically.

"Is there sugar in here?" Mr. Melvin asked.

"Yes."

"Okay, thank you." He took a sip and exhaled. "Y'all go play. Grown folks talking now."

There was a big catering job that day, so as the morning turned into the afternoon, Ms. Monique organized the family to head to the restaurant. Because it was a Saturday, restaurant activity was also a family activity. The four younger children piled in my car, and James, the second eldest, rode with his parents to the restaurant. At the restaurant, the dishes in the sink looked like they had not been washed in several days, so as others went to their respective duties, I put on scrubbing gloves. Mr. Melvin and James went to the store to pick up a few items. Charles, the third oldest son, made lemonade, and Ava and Ms. Monique went to the office to do paperwork. Ava served as her mother's assistant.

"Piko," Mr. Melvin called to me when he returned. "Just sanitize the area so we can cut up this chicken. Right now, that's more important than doing those dishes. We need to put this chicken in the smoker as soon as possible. James, go over there and get the chicken ready."

I cleaned out the last two of four sinks and sanitized the counter. James got to work with the chicken. In the middle of that, Ms. Monique asked me to pick up Melvin Jr. from his exam. When I returned with Melvin Jr., I worked with James to season several dozen pieces of chicken thighs and drumsticks for the smoker.

It was now past noon, so some of the children cried hunger. Daniel, the youngest, wanted a pulled pork sandwich, and so did Melvin Jr. Ms. Monique could have easily satisfied her children's hunger by allowing them to eat the sandwiches. But, she did not. She may not have wanted her children to eat away at her profits. But, there seemed to be more to her thinking.

"Your father is coming back soon, and we'll all figure out what we're going to eat." Sure enough, Mr. Melvin arrived shortly from his second trip to Sam's Club and plopped himself on a couch in the office.

"Okay, Husband, we're gonna have to decide what we're feeding everyone. What do you want to eat?" Her question made her food decision active. If the homeless men who ate in shelters had virtually no options other than to reject what was offered to them and risk going hungry, Zenani often had minimal options. She ate and fed her children whatever was immediately available to her. Ms. Bea also ate and provided her grandchildren with meals she could prepare from whatever ingredients she had in her fridge, which often were whatever was on sale at the store.

But, for Ms. Monique, her food decisions for family required thinking through different options and making a conscious decision. For the most part, her decisions were at the level of her practical consciousness—they were day-to-day decisions that have embedded in them, taken for granted unnoticeable know-how. Her food decisions were not diets that were prescribed or dictated and regulated by some formula. They included preferences and tastes, which sometimes went against her health considerations. Even though Ms. Monique tended toward healthier foods, she did not bar her children from eating all unhealthy foods. In fact, they had "Junk Food Day," when the children could indulge in otherwise restrained urges.

"Husband, what are we going to feed the kids?" Ms. Monique repeated herself.

Mr. Melvin was only partially listening. An episode of *Law and Order* on the small television in front of him took his attention.

"Melvin, go to the kitchen and take a poll of what everyone wants to eat," he instructed his son.

"What do you want to eat, Ava?" Melvin Jr. began his assignment.

"I said go to the kitchen and do it!"

Melvin Jr. went out to the kitchen to conduct the poll. He came back a few minutes later with the following suggestions: pork chops, ravioli, and chocolate cereal.

"No to all of that," Ms. Monique shot back. "Mom overrules all those suggestions. We're going to have some cold cuts, some lunch meat." Her response was true to form. She controlled what the family ate.

"Yea, let's get some ham," Ava agreed with her mother.

"We can get some ham, but not the kind that's filled with nitrate. Let's get some turkey too. Okay, Husband, we need to go to the store and get some lunch meat, some tomatoes, and some lettuce."

When we all walked out of the office, Mr. Melvin announced that Sam's Club's manager had given him a couple of bags of cinnamon rolls. Because he frequented the store, he knew most of the workers. Mr. Melvin recounted how he got the rolls. "[The manager] said, 'I can't charge you for these, so you can have them if you want because I'm just gonna have to throw them away in a couple of days. And there's nothing wrong with them.' So, I took them."

They were Hostess cinnamon rolls. The children's eyes lit up, as did mine. Ms. Monique was not very happy. She had successfully skirted the children toward a relatively healthy lunch, but what Mr. Melvin brought from the store negated her efforts. We each grabbed a roll.

Ms. Monique's food choices fit in her immediate world and were entangled within all her life's social and cultural structuring. When Mr. Melvin and Ms. Monique went to the store to get cold cuts for us, I did not go with them. But, given the length of time they were away, I can assume that they went to a store close to their restaurant in South Jackson. Ms. Monique's (and her family's) food decisions are thus fashioned by what is available to her and what is around her. And, for lower-middle-class Black folks, what was close to them did not always allow them to be as health-conscious as they would like to be.

Moments after they returned from the store, Ms. Monique and Ava started fixing sandwiches on a large counter in their restaurant's kitchen. None of the boys helped. They were too busy playing, chatting, or attending to other things on the collective to-do list. The sandwiches, made on hamburger buns, had turkey lunch meat, lettuce, tomatoes, and mayonnaise.

"Everyone, grab a sandwich," Ms. Monique called out.

"Piko, I have your sandwich right here," Ava assured me. "Do you want water or root beer?"

"I don't know. What are you getting?"

"I'm getting root beer," she responded.

"Well, I want root beer too."

She pulled out one can of root beer for me from the dozen-pack Big K root beer box that her mother had purchased. She and her siblings enjoyed the rare occasion to drink soda.

"Okay, come get your food and go outside. Go have a picnic." Ms. Monique motioned for us all to go outside—it freed time for her to return to the office and get to what was on her to-do list. They headed out, each with a sandwich, a napkin, and a root beer. I followed Daniel, Ava, and James, who had grilled his meat and his bun. We walked toward a big tree and sat under its shade on overgrown grass.

After everyone ate, it was time to get back to work and finish preparing the catering order. Daniel had been warned earlier in the day to stay away when grown folks were trying to work. He did not listen, so he was taken to the back for a whooping. James pulled the chicken off the smoker. Mr. Melvin didn't buy covers for the aluminum containers, so they had to cover them with sheets of plastic foil. There were about eight trays: six with smoked chicken and two with cooked corn on the cob. After the truck was packed and after the trays were rewrapped several times to ensure they would not spill—Mr. Melvin made sure of it—James, Mr. Melvin, Ms. Monique, and I got in the truck to deliver the food. We were headed to a community center in North Jackson, around Hanging Moss Road and Northside Drive, for

10.1. Daniel enjoying his sandwich

a Black family reunion. They had become accustomed to taking their food from the poorer South Jackson to richer North Jackson. It made it more evident to them that if their restaurant was located farther north, they would have been more successful. When we got there and began to unload, Mr. Melvin, who was back to his usual jovial self, pointed out why he was so insistent on how the food was covered.

"Look at this, Piko," he pointed to one small pan that had not been properly wrapped. The strong wind had blown off the covering. "I know you thought I was being mean about it."

"No, I didn't say anything," I responded.

"I know you were thinking it, though," he added.

"Yea, you were thinking it," James echoed him, trying to get me in trouble.

On the drive back to their side of town, as we approached Farish Street—the once-vibrant commercial street that now was abandoned and impoverished—Mr. Melvin asked Ms. Monique if she wanted to go to Big John's Place for a sandwich. Big Apple Inn is still referred to as Big John's Place, after Juan "Big John" Mora, a Mexican immigrant who, in 1939, brought his street corner tamale operation into a storefront property on Farish Street. His proximity to the NAACP office, housed just above his spot, made his small restaurant a gathering place for organizing.[2] The Davises were good friends with Geno Lee, the fourth-generation restaurant owner who still sells their famous "smokes and ears"—hot smoked sausage sandwiches and pig-ear sandwiches. It was one of few businesses still operating on that street.

Ms. Monique did not want a sandwich.

"I want a sandwich and Piko wants a sandwich. Let's go," James added me to his appeal to his mother.

"No, we are not going to get a sandwich. You all have had enough processed meat."

They both dropped it because they knew that her say was final.

A short moment of driving in silence later, Ms. Monique made her own request. "Husband, let's get some beers before we get back to the restaurant."

James jumped on the opportunity to call out the contradiction of his mother's food decisions. "Wait, you don't want to get sausage sandwiches, but you want some beer? How's beer better for you?"

"Yea, you right about that. I don't know if beer is any better," I jokingly sided with James. Ms. Monique laughed along.

"Beer has saved generations," Mr. Melvin defended his wife.

"Smokes saved Farish Street," James responded. His parents let out a hearty laugh because they knew how right their son was.

The preceding section of this chapter has provided a sense of Ms. Monique's food consciousness in the practical sense. In the next section, we see more of this, but this time with a focus on how new considerations, her food consciousness in the discursive sense, eventually become taken for granted. Importantly, we also see how she passes on how she thinks about food to her children, her daughter especially. It shows how Ava learns to take up the responsibility of feeding the family. This exploration supports what we know about the gendered nature of cooking and eating in families and reveals the socialization that keeps this structure in place.

Cooking with Ava

When I arrived, the dog barked. Benjamin, the knee-baby, was surprised but happy to see me at the door. I think. We hugged each other. He had gotten taller. He announced my return to the rest of the house and ran back to whatever television show he was watching. When I walked in the house through the living room and the dining room, both of which were rarely used, Melvin Jr. was staring at his computer with his headphones on. He had not heard Benjamin's announcement. When our eyes caught each other, he hopped up with shock and surprise to greet me.

"You're still alive, Piko!" he exclaimed in jest. "I haven't seen you forever."

It had been four years. I had kept in touch, but it was my first time back since I left in November 2012. It was now June 2016. Since I left, Melvin Jr. had graduated from high school and enrolled in the University of Miami. It did not go so well for him in Miami, so he was back home. He knew I knew about Miami. When I asked him about it, his eyes dropped in embarrassment. Melvin Jr. is a brilliant young man. During my previous visit, I had seen letters from Ivy League schools that recruited him because of his high ACT score. He stumbled his words as he tried to explain why he had failed at the University of Miami. We walked through the kitchen to the back TV room. He said it was simply too difficult. He had since returned home and enrolled at Jackson State University.

Daniel, the youngest Davis child, was intently watching the movie, so he did not give me much attention. Ava was lying on the couch, half paying attention to the film. She had a summer job, but she was not working that day because she was getting over a cold. I followed her to their dining room table to catch up.

Ava, a middle child and the only girl among six siblings, is quiet when she's at home, but she is not a pushover. She knew how to defend herself against the boys when she had to. She described it as being a gang of one versus a gang of five. She was also a bit uncertain of herself, still unsure of how smart and beautiful she was. As she updated me about school, her social life, and her art, she mentioned that she had to get ready to cook and headed into the kitchen. It immediately reminded me that she was the one who

10.2. Three of the Davis boys fixing a tire

cooks at home most of the time. I asked why that was the case. She responded that she cooks because she does not like to do dishes. Her brothers did dishes. That was the deal she had made with her mother. That she was being socialized to take on the labor of feeding her family had perhaps not dawned on her. Maybe it never will—that is the cunning seduction of gendered socialization.

For as long as it has been studied, and most likely even before, women have been in charge of feeding the family, along with performing various other household labor.[3] According to researchers who measure this portion of household labor by hours, there is survey evidence that in the 1900s, women spent forty-four hours a week on meal preparation. In the 1920s, it dropped to thirty hours, then twenty hours (1950s), then ten hours (1975). These numbers always varied by class. Wealthier women often hired poorer women to take on these hours; in the South, Black women often fed wealthy white families before or after they fed their own families.

Several factors explain this steady decline in meal preparation time for women. Technological advancements—the inventions of stoves, fridges, and microwaves—made routine tasks more efficient. Then, importantly, there was the changing role of women in the labor force, especially after World War II. When many other American women became wage earners, as Black American women had been decades prior, there simply was less time to be spent on meal preparation. Trends in diets, especially toward simpler and leaner meals during mid-twentieth century wars, also changed cooking at home. Important still were transformations in American eating culture, the introduction of TV dinners, eating out, and fast-food restaurants. Even with all this, women were still in charge of feeding their families, but much of that labor became outsourced. By 1998, nearly half of family income spent on food was on foods prepared outside the home.[4]

More recently, interest in cooking at home has increased.[5] Medical professionals, celebrity chefs, and television shows have promoted a broader (classed) food culture that views a return to cooking as a solution for various social problems, most important of which is health problems.[6] Ms. Monique and her family are participants in this new cultural shift, a large part of which is the belief in the virtue of preparing food at home. More men are cooking today

10.3. Ava

than ever before. But, as in the Davis household—where Mr. Melvin and the boys are not entirely banned from the kitchen—women still do more of the cooking. According to a 2019 Pew Research Center report, women prepare 80 percent of the meals in families with children.[7] Most researchers examine this pattern's inner dynamics (including how women manage), but few investigate how the work, the expectation, and the stress of feeding the family becomes transferred onto women. Few scholars show how the duty of cooking for the family gets transferred from a mother (or guardian) to a daughter who becomes another mother (or guardian). Being around Ava, I got a look into this mechanism of social reproduction concerning cooking.

Ava explained to me how her family decides what they will have for dinner. "You know, there aren't a lot of things that are dinner food, if you really think about it," she said with a childish grin as if she had just opened my mind to something new. She was putting a leftover whole chicken in the oven. It was what she cooked the day before. They did not eat it all last night, so she was heating it for dinner that day. Beyond considerations for "dinner food," Ava and her mother also thought about, in her words, "some health stuff." They shopped for food twice a month, the first and the fifteenth, when their parents received a paycheck. She then started to describe how they choose what they eat by telling me about documentaries about food she watched on Netflix.

"You know," she began to open my mind up to more things. "The food industry . . ."

She went on an almost rehearsed diatribe about the ills of the food industry, the government's role, the ubiquity of sugar, the corporate farming and meat production industry, and the prominence and predominance of fast-food restaurants. She also mentioned television shows about healthy food lifestyles that featured celebrity chefs and food experts. She was an outgrowth of her mother's ways of thinking about food. Her brothers also watched the documentaries, but Ava was the one that practiced what they learned and made them routine. I saw how their ever-evolving food consciousness fit within the ambiguities of their class position. With Ava, I also got a glimpse of the intermingling of her race and class in her other interests.

When I returned three days later, it seemed like it had been a leisurely day. It was mid-afternoon, and neither of her parents had returned from work. They had closed Lumpkins BBQ because they never were able to make it profitable.[8] Ms. Monique now worked for a nonprofit Catholic agency and Mr. Melvin was a contractor for an insurance company. Ava's older siblings were also off to their various summer part-time jobs. She was home with the two youngest, Daniel and Benjamin, who were too young to work. When I walked in, Ava was finishing a documentary about dieting. She had, in and out of her sleep, learned about the addictive qualities of sugar and about how even fat-free foods included sugar. She gave me another mini-lecture, and then, out of boredom, took my phone, and using the stylus, drew. One was a self-portrait of sorts in which, in a cartoon-like aesthetic, she represented her curly hair, exaggerated lips, and pronounced pupils. On another page, she drew a vista of a sunflower garden with mature flowers. When she finished, she handed me the phone and walked away. She knew I was already a fan of her artwork, so she did not wait to see if I would be impressed.

As dinner was fast approaching, Ava drifted into the kitchen to pull meat from the freezer. According to their meal schedule, she was to prepare beef stroganoff. She noticed that there were avocados that were ripped, so she offered to make guacamole. While I conversed with Melvin Jr., who had returned from his day, Ava came back twenty minutes later with her creation along with cut-up tortillas that she had toasted in the oven. The look and texture of her guacamole were similar to what one might find at any small Tex-Mex restaurant. And, it tasted just as good. I mentioned that I would be willing to pay $8.50 for it. Despite my economical pricing, she took my comment as a compliment. We enjoyed the snack together.

Afterward, Ava reminded Melvin Jr. that it was his turn to do the dishes. He washed dishes while Ava prepared onions and garlic to be steamed with the beef. Daniel, the youngest child, and I watched on. The gentle humming of running water, the clanking of the dishes, and the rhythmic meeting of the knife blade and the chopping board played in the background. Ava also had us listening to a playlist of her favorite music—Chance the Rapper was at the beginning of his verse in Kanye's "Ultralight Beam."

"So, besides Ava, can anyone else cook in this house?" I asked.

"Charles can cook very, very well," Ava quickly responded, even though I intentionally directed the question to the boys.

Melvin Jr. started mumbling an answer, but Daniel raised his hand to speak.

"Can you cook very well?" I directed my attention to him

"No."

"Why not?"

"Because I don't wanna cook." As the youngest, he was the most unfiltered. He said whatever was on his mind, or whatever he had heard others say. He had on a mischievous smile, which meant either that he was about to say something he knew he is not supposed to say or that he knew he had a funny one-line response—he loved delivering good punch-lines. When I asked him why he did not want to cook, he responded, "I'm a working man, not a cooking man." I laughed out loud. His older brother, who had been trying to get the attention off Daniel, seemed embarrassed by his response.

"That's the exact wrong answer, but that's fine," Melvin Jr. blurted out.

"Who told you that was a good answer?" I chuckled my response, even as I took a mental note of the analytical weight of his jovial comment.

"James told him," Melvin Jr. answered.

After Daniel left the kitchen, there were a few moments of nervous silence. Kirk Franklin's interlude came on. It was out of place, but it aptly filled the space. I wondered if Ava was thinking about why what she did for the family was not considered work. If she were, she would be joining feminist scholars who have wondered the same for decades. Daniel, less than ten years old, was already convinced that work done out of the house was indeed more valuable than the work done in the house.[9]

"You heard what your brother said?" I asked Ava.

"Yea, I heard." Her response lingered.

She opened a can of mushrooms to pour into the cooking pot. "Does the can have MSG in it?" I joked with her. Earlier, while watching the documentary on dieting, she had heard about the health consequences of MSG, what Chef David Chang describes as the vilification of MSG.[10] She checked. It did.

"You know you feeding your family cocaine?" I jovially repeated the refrain we had heard in the documentary.

"They like it," she joked back.

Ava's nonchalant attitude toward MSG at that moment was not borne out of skepticism of what she had learned. Like her mother, her food consciousness, including her subscription to healthy food advice, is lived within the context of her life. Even if she adherently believed in what she heard about MSG, that can of mushrooms was what she had in her kitchen. It was likely all they had in the grocery stores near her home. There were no health food stores close by. Even if McDade's, the local chain food store—the one Ms. Monique complained about—carried cans of mushrooms without MSG, they would have them at the store in North Jackson. So, she used what she had. The recipe she was following, which she found online, called for half a can, but as she tried to pour it, the whole can of mushrooms went into the pot. Melvin, finishing his chore and providing master commentary on Ava's cooking, lovingly criticized her for not measuring or scooping the right amount. Ava seemed unperturbed by it.

After Melvin Jr. tended to his task, he left the kitchen, commenting sarcastically, "I've fulfilled my duties to society." He probably returned to what I had observed to be his post: the dining room's computer table. The kitchen was, for him, a place to perform his assigned tasks. He knew where everything in the kitchen was kept because he put his dishes away in the right places, but he was there only to perform his duty.

Ava's presence in the space was different. There was an ease and comfort to it like it was her own. Her legs, her arms, and her torso moved about the space with their own eyes. And, she felt at ease to stay and rest there, listen to music there, talk there, or just *be* there. This ease in the kitchen, I was sure, had been learned from all the time she had spent in there—she had become habituated to the space.[11] She was becoming a woman, and spending time in the kitchen was part of the becoming.[12]

She readied the pasta for the recipe, hesitating for a moment as if she had forgotten a step. She had not. The instructions were not in front of her; she knew it by heart, so my random questions seemed not to disturb her. For instance, when Tom Higgenson's voice on "Hey There, Delilah" caught my attention, I asked her about the band, which lead us to a conversation about concerts. She had never been to a concert and wanted to see Drake, Chance, or Bieber. She added chicken broth and then played me an old Bieber song. She was a bit shy to admit her fandom—she clarified that she liked the old Bieber. And then, while playing *Coloring Book*, she told me about *Acid Rap*, Taylor Swift, Adele, and The Weeknd.

"I like The Weeknd, but he is so vulgar, so I can't play him around the house," she commented.

"Do your friends listen to the same type of music?"

"No. They listen to basic stuff." "Basic" music to her was people like Rich Homie Quan and Drake. "Drake is good, and I like it, but it's basic." She named other friends who listen to more eclectic music, including FKA Twigs and Jaden Smith. We were waiting for the stroganoff to cook down before she made the noodles. She also needed to put sour cream in the beef.

When she asked me what I listened to, I mentioned that I enjoyed older East Coast hip-hop music, like Jay-Z, Nas, Lauryn, Jean Grae, and Biggie. She said she was a fan of Biggie. She laughed and said she thought Biggie was ugly. She also added Young Thug to her list of eclectic artists. I admitted that I did not like Young Thug because I could not understand what he was saying. To school me, she decided to play me a song. I was shy at listening to the explicit content with her, but she insisted. She turned off Adele's "Rolling in the Deep" and played Young Thug's "With That." After the first three bars, the confusion on my face affirmed that I did not understand any of the song's words. So, she rapped it for me, acapella. Even with her enunciating the words, I still had no idea of what the song was saying. After her acapella performance of the song, she played it and gleefully sang along. She was a young woman of her time and place and seemed to be as fluent in the Black vernacular of her day as any of her peers. She had all the Black cultural capital required to be a young Black teen in Jackson. As I would learn in this conversation, she also had a heap of other cultural capital: the competencies, skills, and know-how that illustrated her middle-class status. She had both Black cultural capital and (white) middle-class cultural capital, and she carried them with ease.[13]

"Do your friends have as wide a music taste as you do?"

She shook her head. She explained that she listened to different songs for various reasons. There are happy songs and sad songs. And then there are songs for different moments of the day. She listened to rap in the mornings to "get ready for life;" she listened to Drake at night before going to sleep; she listened to jazz while doing homework because it had no words, and she listened to everything when she was working on her art so that she could draw on various influences. As a cultural sociologist, one with a keen interest in music, I enjoyed listening to her articulate the basis of her preferences. At her mention of a documentary that she saw about hip-hop in London, we started talking about traveling. She'd never been out of the country, but was very curious, not just about where she would want to go but also about where I had been. Somewhere along our conversation, I asked about her taste in art.

"I like realism," she responded.

"What is realism? Explain it to me."

"It's like drawing exactly what you see and trying to get to be as realistic as possible. It's expressing it so that it looks the same, except you can use different colors. But it is still realistic. That's the reason I like it."

"Who's your favorite artist?"

"Mary Cassatt," she responded without hesitation. Never mind that Cassatt was more an impressionist than a realist, Ava explained that she was drawn to how she drew girls and flowers. Again, Cassatt's oeuvre was more expansive than what Ava saw, but somehow, she found herself drawn to a white woman born to wealthy parents in Pennsylvania and who lived much of her life in France. When I jokingly asked if she, too, was going to paint white people, she objected with a serious tone. "I'm going to paint people who look like me." And she was sure of it. To prove it to me, she showed me some of the sketches she had made.

Ava's omnivorous cultural capital, her appetite for both Young Thug and Mary Cassatt, show the in-betweenness of her being a lower-middle-class Southerner.[14] She lived within three miles of the city's most impoverished neighborhoods; she attended school across town, but her young siblings went to the neighborhood elementary school. Her family shopped at the same grocery stores as did Zenani, Ms. Bea, and other poor Black folks, but they bought and cooked different things because they thought about food differently.

By the time everyone made it home, Ava was done cooking. They all came for their servings dished out on white plates that Melvin Jr. had washed. They ate together with their plates on their laps as they watched TV. The channel was turned to MSNBC so that Ms. Monique could catch up on the day's news.

CHAPTER ELEVEN

Charles

"HE COMES HERE just about every day," the waiter commented about Charles as he handed us two menus.

It was the first time I had sat down with Charles in months. The last I could recall was at Lumpkins over ribs and a heated conversation with Ms. Monique and a few others about the Catholic church and abortion. This instance was a serendipitous encounter. As I stepped out of what used to be the *Jackson Free Press* office, where I had been an intern—a way to stay tuned to city-wide politics—I saw a big Black man waddle out of his truck. His movement looked like an exaggerated Denzel Washington walk. But, his walk was not a botched attempt at imitation; his knees and ankles needed to set themselves properly to carry his shifting 400-pound weight. Charles moved at his own pace, slowly, but he was quick with a "hello." His charm, warmth, and agreeable sense of humor was the first thing about him one would notice, not his short and wide figure. He took no shame in his morbid obesity and thus did not invite anyone's pity. Spend enough time with him and he would disarm any awkward stare with a joke and loud laughter. He knew just how to hypnotize others out of fat-shaming.[1]

But, even in the security of his persona, Charles's weight held him hostage. He waged a slow and constant war for his health. When I found him in that restaurant that afternoon, he was practicing one of his strategies to win some of the battles. Charles, this big Black man whom I had known through ribs and smoked meat at Lumpkins BBQ, was now a vegan. His decision stands in the face of the presumption that veganism is a white practice, as many scholars have documented and have reified in their documentation.[2] As a result, and in addition to the stigma that all vegans already endure, food scholars note that non-whites especially Black people, who practice veganism often experience a racialized form of stigma.[3] Notably, the stigma that Black vegans face comes from white vegans and from non-white (including Black) non-vegans. Specifically, Black vegans are charged with "acting white" or taking part in food practices presumed to be incompatible with their racial identity.[4]

Charles and I were at High Noon Cafe, an eatery attached to Rainbow Natural Foods & Co-op, which was then the only health food grocery store in Jackson—Whole Foods has since dethroned Rainbow. On their menu, I read the following disclaimer:

> All our lunch fare and deli foods are prepared without the use of trans-fats, hydrogenated oils, MSG, meat, or GMOs. We use only cold-pressed organic oils, and USDA certified organic dairy products. We strive to use certified organic ingredients in all of our High Noon creations, but due to our location in the United States, certified produce can be limited. In these cases, local organic and non-organic produce is substituted.

I presumed they were referring to how their location in the American South limits their access to these products. Even though the number of organic farms is growing more quickly in the South than in other parts of the country, Deep South states (Louisiana, Mississippi, Alabama, Georgia) still have the fewest number of certified organic farms.[5] In 2017, The Food Institute at UC Berkeley reported that the production of organic products in Mississippi was low because, at the state level, there were virtually no resources to aid those who may be interested. Just as the restaurant prominently displayed the difficulties they faced in achieving their mission, I wondered the same for Charles: How was he going to practice veganism in Jackson, Mississippi, of all places?

Over the months I spent with him, Charles proved that it was possible to be vegan in Jackson, but it required flexibility and trying inconveniences. That the food movement has a weaker hold on the foodways of Mississippians is, for one thing, a result of the fact that the region has a more strongly bounded food culture and thus was less influenced by the whims of food movement from elsewhere.[6] There is a Southern Foodways Alliance to guide, study, and celebrate it—Northern and Western Foodways Alliances do not exist, and, if they did, they would be nonsensical. For another thing, class matters a great deal in the adoption of ideologies that come with the practice of veganism. It is often perceived, however inaccurately, as an expensive food habit reserved only for more affluent folks.[7] Thus, in a state with a disproportionate amount of poverty, it would make sense for veganism to be disfavored.

The South does not provide fertile ground for veganism because, more than most other parts of the country, the diets of white, Black, rich, and poor Americans are more similar.[8] As such, veganism, a practice that seems to grow on segregated taste buds, might be at odds with the foodways of the South. With all this in mind, Charles's venturing into veganism, very much motivated by improving his health and less by animal politics, sits at the core of the concern of the chapters in this section of the book: How race (blackness), class (middle-classness), and region (Mississippi) influence one's food consciousness. With the case of the Davis family, I gave most of my attention to their practical food consciousness. Here, with Charles, I pay more attention to the development of his food consciousness on a discursive level—I show how he comes to incorporate a new food practice into his life.

I sat across the table from Charles at High Noon Cafe and several other establishments in the subsequent months, where he did his best to abide by the rules of his new diet. The places where we ate were not all vegan or even vegetarian restaurants, but he made do. He ordered what he presumed to be the most vegan-friendly options. Over dozens of meals, I was able to directly observe how he thought about what he eats and, by learning about his biography and the social context of his life, make sense of how he perceived himself in relation to what he was eating. At High Noon, in between his account of the drama at his work, we placed our orders: a black bean burrito with a wheat tortilla and vegan cheese and ginger tea for him, and for me, a steamed vegetable dish with carrots, cauliflower, broccoli, and edamame beans served with Thai peanut sauce, along with ginger lemonade.

We barely noticed the time passing as we waited for our food. Charles told me a bit about some of the high school football games he photographs for local newspapers. We talked about small liberal arts colleges, about which he had more than a casual knowledge, including their rankings. He then told me a few childhood stories, including ones about how his mother dealt with his allergy to heavy acid-based foods, like tomatoes. By the time our food arrived, we were onto talking about the NFL and then about James Meredith. Somewhere during all that conversation, I nudged for an explanation for why he chose to become vegan.

"I've seen you tear up some ribs. . . ." I joked.

"Yup, put a whooping on them. . . . But you know something, dude. I'd eat some ribs, and it'd be good for that minute, and then about two hours later, I'd be home, sick as a dog, laying in the bed sick."

"Like, when you would come to Lumpkins?"

"Well, Lumpkins wouldn't bother me that much. But, after eating them, my leg would swell up like a balloon."

"Really?

"Yeah. My left leg because I have cellulitis in that leg, and that leg has issues. Blood circulation doesn't go through it right, and then you put all that salt and stuff in my system, and then all of a sudden, *boom*."

Perhaps unfairly, I asked why he kept eating such foods if his body had such an adverse reaction to it. His simple answer, a subtle honesty, hints at the ill logic in assuming food decisions are rational decisions.

"You know, you want to eat," he said.

"Right, right, right," I responded, almost embarrassed at what I had asked. And then he gave me a bit more of his medical history. This time, the tone in his voice lowered, like he was delivering a serious monologue. It was a departure from his gregariousness. He played with his fork, a distraction to himself, as he told me about his bouts at the hospital.

"I got sick in August of 2009 and had to go to the hospital that whole month. August until the first of September. I was in Florida in the hospital. And then, when I got back, I stayed at home for about a week, and then I slowly went back to work. Then I was doing better for a while. I lost a bunch of weight—then, it just started happening again. And then I ended up in the hospital again last year, after about two years. Then I said to myself, 'You killing yourself, man. What's your problem? What's going on in your head that's got you doing all that?' "

After a beat, he continued.

"You know, when I look at people now, I see people do self-destructive things. I could understand based on my own experience, you know. People just do screwed-up stuff to themselves for whatever reason based on the historical stuff or what issues they have with themselves; you know what I mean? Or the gratification of being satisfied over here and not looking at the downside over there. But you live, you learn. Now, so one day, I woke up and I said, 'No more. No more.'"

"That's it," I offered in support.

"No! More!" This time, he repeated himself with an exaggerated Southern accent that jolted him out of his serious tone. He let out his signature laugh, one that comes from the pit of his stomach and attracts the attention of those nearby.

Two months and a dozen or so lunches later, Charles invited me to his home on a Sunday evening to watch football. I looked forward to it because I knew he would be cooking. He lived on Wingfield Circle, just three blocks from Prentiss and Robinson, where I first met Zenani, in a neighborhood that was once reserved for the middle class—the cul-du-sac mid-century architecture homes with their manicured lawns gave it away. It was where he grew up. The house he now lives in, which his aunt used to own, is next door to his childhood home. There was a sun porch at the entry of his house. The main entrance opens into a dining room and a charming sitting room where he had stacks of magazines spread every which way. And then, in a darker corner of the open space, he had two couches, perpendicularly arranged to face his forty-two-inch flat-screen TV.

I shook his hand.

"My hand is wet, man. I've been doing some dishes," he apologized.

"No worries, bro."

11.1. Charles

11.2. Charles

"Welcome to the crib," he added. "I made some food if you want some."

Of course, I did.

I lifted the lid off one pot. In it was a mixture of beans, tofu (which looked like chicken), some spinach, and a bunch of spices that I could not readily identify. In another pot were some wheat elbow noodles and a lot of quinoa, his new go-to food. Like many other health-conscious eaters, he had embraced the high nutrient grain.[9] In his household garb—a pair of gym shorts, an old t-shirt, and a pair of Crocs—he half-stood and half-leaned on his kitchen counter to finish washing his dishes. When I asked him about the cost of his change in diet, he asserted that it had been cheaper for him. "When you cut off the meat, you cut off about a quarter of the cost." He buys quinoa in bulk, for about $18, which he eats for about two weeks.[10]

When it was ready, Charles served his tofu stew on top of the quinoa and noodles. Bowl and fork in hand, we headed into the living room to watch football. It was the first time I had quinoa. It reminded me of couscous or gari, but more textured. It soaked up the juices from his stew. So did the tofu. If I had tasted tofu before that occasion, I do not remember it as distinctly as I remember eating it at Charles's places. As was usual, we talked as we ate, but we were also both glued to updates of scores from that Sunday's NFL games as we waited for the second half of the Giants game against the Steelers. He admitted that he was a Cowboys fan, not a Saints fan, like many Mississippians. When the third quarter began and after we were both done eating, I complimented and thanked him for the food. And then, quite pointedly, I asked him how he was doing with his new diet.

"Well, I had to do it, Piko, or die. And I hate to put it so gloomy, but that's what it was."

He responded with an earnest smile on his face. His food choices now were mostly dictated by his need (and desire) to create a healthier future self. This, having the mental space to think beyond his most pressing need, was part of the luxury that comes with his class position.

"So, have you slipped back in old ways at all?" I pushed.

He shook his head no, slowly. I believed his answer.

11.3. Charles at a health food store

"No, I knew there were certain kinds of foods that I liked. Mediterranean, Italian, and some Mexican food, so I stick with those and eat healthy from those." Here, again, we see a development of various kinds of taste, another attribute of class, which potentially allows him to live out his new eating habits.

"What about Southern soul food? I mean, you grew up on those?"

"Yea, but I had to cut that out completely."

He turned down the volume of the TV so we could hear each other better. Before I could ask a follow-up, he offered a further explanation.

"I've fallen prey to soul food, and I've fallen prey to falling off the wagon."

I gave him a confused look.

"I've read *Twelve Steps*, not the full thing, but I got the general idea, and I use that. Alcoholics, you can't have one beer, you can't have one drink, you can't have one turkey leg."

I busted out in laughter about his analogy. He, too, was amused, but he did not laugh like I did because he was, again, being serious. He did not say that he was addicted to soul food, but he treated it as such.[11] To treat something with AA's Twelve Step process is to recognize it as something perhaps more than a casual habit or a want. It acknowledges how permanent soul food is and has been in his life and the difficulty of dislodging it from his life.

Charles has deep roots in Mississippi. His father is from Water Valley, twenty-or-so miles from Oxford, and his mother is from the same town as Oprah, Kosciusko, some eighty miles south. As far as he knows, his mother's people were not sharecroppers.

"I take great pride [in that]. My mother's side of the family, they were never sharecroppers—they were landowners. My family has owned the same land since 1860. They originally owned like 300 acres." He did not mention how his family came to amass this large landmass.

Through the meekly organized and resourced Freedman's Bureau, the federal government sought to provide land for formerly enslaved people who had fought for their freedom, but it mostly failed even before their efforts began.[12] If his family was like other landowning Black folks, their strategy for acquiring land ranged from brute force, economic wit, and squatting on abandoned land, to working with and purchasing lands from former white plantation owners.[13] Like many other Black families, his family also lost much of their land.

Charles was telling me all of this over one of our lunch dates. We were eating at a Thai restaurant off North Frontage Road in North Jackson. It was one of the places that could support his new eating habit. As he describes it, "they're not purposefully vegan. They're just naturally that way." Even before the change in his eating habits, he had been going there, so when we entered, the owner, a middle-aged Asian man, welcomed him by name and invited us to sit wherever we wished. We ordered soup to start, to fend off the chill in the restaurant, and then tofu pad Thai for him and pad see ew with chicken for me. While we waited, we jumped into conversations about his photography and how much he enjoyed photographing football games, which somehow took us to talk about his family and upbringing.

Charles understood his family was not unique, that many other Black families had also lost their lands. "When the Great Depression hit, people's land started getting gobbled up because they couldn't keep going on their taxes, and then some people's land just got gobbled up just because you was a Black person with land and they wanted to get your ass out of it." By "they," he meant white Southerners. He was not too far off from the *Atlantic Monthly* journalist Vann R. Newkirk's reporting about the subject.

> Mass dispossession did not require a central organizing force or a grand conspiracy. Thousands of individual decisions by white people, enabled or motivated by greed, racism, existing laws, and market forces, all pushed in a single direction. But some white people undeniably would have organized it this way if they could have. The civil-rights leader Bayard Rustin reported in 1956 that documents taken from the office of Robert Patterson, one of the founding fathers of the White Citizens' Councils, proposed a "master plan" to force hundreds of thousands of Black people from Mississippi in order to reduce their potential voting power.[14]

Charles continued, "My great-grandfather, my grandmama's dad—he had seven children. His wife died young. He had raised all his kids, and he ended up going down to New Orleans, you know, to fight with whoever was over the land. So, they said, 'Well, this is what we'll do. You give up everything, and we'll let you keep sixty acres of it.' So, he made a trade-off to keep his sixty acres, and on that, but originally it was like three hundred acres."

Charles's grandmother was the eldest of the seven children that his great-grandfather raised on that land. His mother was raised on the portion of the land that his grandmother inherited. As a child, he saw a small bit of this dependence on the land, and as an adult, he intellectually understood that whatever wealth his family might have had was in the land they owned and how they worked the land. In his explanation, he referenced French Enlightenment economic theory.[15]

"You know, people were physiocrats. You are cash poor, land rich, so they always had somewhere to stay. They owned their own land. They had a cow, so she had a little meat. They could grow food, but they didn't have any money. She could feed the family, but she couldn't do anything else, and she'd sell a little bit off [what she grew on the land], and you know, and buy flour. . . . You're going to buy flour, sugar, and salt."

"That's the only thing they bought?"

"That's the only thing my grandmother bought—from a rolling store. It was a store. Literally, a man would drive around a big truck, and they called it a rolling store, and he'd just ride around the community, and you'd buy off his store, buy off that."[16]

Charles's grandmother, whom he describes as having a "forward-thinking mentality," did not want her children to rely only on the land to survive. Maybe she anticipated that Black farmers would continue to lose their land, or perhaps she foresaw that, for subsequent generations, the growing arms of capitalism would make their physiocracy unsustainable. Whatever the reason, and amid protests from her siblings who took their children away from school during harvest season, she insisted that her children would be educated, and it began with Charles's mother, who happened to be a stellar student. She graduated from high school at sixteen years old. She enrolled in Piney Woods School, a private industrial junior college that followed Booker T. Washington's ideals. Even though the school targeted students from poor rural communities, his mother still could not afford the tuition, so she paid for her education by working in the laundry room.

"My mom could iron the hell out of a shirt. She could take a shirt and have that shirt looking like it came out of the cleaners," he joked. His mother had wanted to continue her education, but the family could not afford it. So, she returned to Kosciusko for a while until, through the contacts of some relatives, she earned a scholarship to Mississippi Industrial College and, when she finished, got a job as a teacher.

I was done with my plate, so I was engrossed in the absorbing and dynamic telling of his family history. He had taken only a few bites.

Charles's father was also a teacher and had gone to Rusk College, but his father's route to college was different. His parents did not raise him. "[My grandmother] married my grandfather, [when] she was young. . . . He got her pregnant. She had the baby. She left the boy [in Mississippi and went to Chicago]. She sent for [her husband]. She never sent for my daddy." So, Charles's father was raised by his father's aunties while his paternal grandparents stayed in Chicago. "Yeah. Mom used to tell me that my dad used to be really in a lot of pain about how his mother abandoned him." He got to know his grandmother a little, but not his grandfather. "I don't think I ever remember meeting him. I'm still trying to find the history of who his. His name was Tommy Smith, but I never got the history on him, unless he died or something. I know he had more than one son—my grandfather—because he was kind of a cat daddy." His grandmother lived and worked in Chicago and did not have any other children, but occasionally come down to Mississippi. "She'd come and stay with us. And she used to make the best fried corn I've ever had. Dude, I still haven't come across anybody who can make fried corn like that."

Charles was born in 1962 in his father's hometown, Water Valley, but his parents moved with him to Chicago. Like many other Black folks of the time, they sought a better life out of the shadows of Jim Crow South. After his father died, when he was just three years old, his mother did not want to raise him alone up north away from close kin, so they moved back to Mississippi, to Jackson, to Jones Street.

On a different day, when we were driving around West Jackson, he drove me to the apartment where he first lived.

"We lived on Jones Street. Me and my momma and my two first cousins and their mother. Used to be Smith Groceries, they sold a little bit of everything. Wasn't much of a grocery store, but it was there."

He slowed as we turned on the street. Jones Street is maybe half-a-mile long, one of the side streets between Valley Street and Dalton Street. I was a little familiar with the area because Ms. Bea lived on nearby Valley Street, near Jim Hill High School. Past the empty lots, where, I imagine, old houses were torn down, past Greater St. James Missionary Baptist Church, and the row of shotgun

Part IV

CHAPTER TWELVE

Jonathan

"TELL ME ABOUT YOURSELF, beginning with the age of three."

Jonathan and I were sitting on a high table at the front end of a fine dining restaurant in Jackson on a February afternoon. I had been at a soup kitchen with Smack earlier when Jonathan called me to meet him at the restaurant, one on the other side of town. To travel from the impoverished Westside to the wealthy Northside, from the lowest to the highest social class, I changed from a t-shirt to a button-down shirt and from a baseball cap to a Kangol. He wore a dress shirt with the sleeves rolled up to his forearms and a pair of slacks. Jonathan is only in his mid-thirties, but he carries himself with a mature demeanor that makes him appear much older. When we sat down, he ordered crab cakes and vodka gimlets—with Grey Goose Vodka—for us. It was a sharp distinction from the leftover food that Smack and I were eating at the soup kitchen.

I told him about my background, beginning with being born and raised in Ghana, living in New York, attending graduate school in Wisconsin, and conducting research in Mississippi. I answered a few clarifying questions before turning the focus back to him. I knew bits and pieces about Jonathan before our meeting that day, particularly about his status as a well-respected businessman in the city. I was also acquainted with him because he co-organized and hosted a weekly community forum, of which I was a regular attendee. It was not our first conversation, but it was, by far, the most meaningful. Without prompting, he began by explaining how his family came into their wealth.

It all started with how his grandfather, while sharecropping in Mississippi, began to accrue land and set his family on a new path of economic ascendance. As was the case with Charles's family, upward economic mobility often involved accumulating and maintaining land.

"What Papa did, he realized that if you're leasing land from these people and you had to buy your supplies from the people you're working for, they'd put everything on your account, on your books, the seeds and all the stuff you needed to work the fields. The problem was, you never saw the books. So, whatever you'd take to their gin, they'd say, for example, you have $25 worth of cotton, but your bill is $30. You have no way of knowing how much your bill was, and of course, during those days, you didn't challenge it. So, even if you were keeping up with it, you never got out of their debt.

"I don't know how he did it, but [Papa] managed to get a small plot of land, [and] was smart enough to go to other farmers in the area. He'd say, 'Hey, I got a little cash, let me buy some seed from you and be done with it.' If they asked why he wouldn't go to the store, he'd say, 'I just need a little seed to get through this year, so let me pay you for it and be done with it.' He paid for all he needed for the year, kept his profit, avoided debt, and bought some more land. He'd pay some poor white guy to go down to the courthouse, as if it was him, and buy the property.

"It took a few years before the [white] farm owners realized that Papa was a landowner. And of course, they thought he had stolen the land, but he had the papers to prove it was his. He preyed on the ignorance of the poor whites and his Black neighbors. He was that kind of a guy, unfortunately, but that was how he amassed quite a bit of land. They accused him of stealing and was gonna kill him, so he took his family in the dead heat of the night and they moved to the Delta, and did the same thing over there."

Jonathan's father continued their family's upward class mobility after he returned from the war by working his way up the professional ladder and eventually starting his own business. Not all Black soldiers returning from World War II benefited from the GI Bill, but he did. He used his benefits to pay for his education after which he began a career with Ford Motor Company.[1] When he returned to Mississippi, he managed a Ford manufacturing plant in North Jackson for some time. He then transitioned to running his own plant in the early 1980s, amassing considerable wealth in the process. When NAFTA prompted large corporations to move their factories overseas, Jonathan's father left the manufacturing business. He founded his own company, Mississippi Products, Inc., a products and warehouse business that sells medical, janitorial, filtration, industrial, and administrative products to a wide range of companies. If his grandfather lifted his family from sharecropping poverty into the ranks of middle-income Americans, his father leaped into the upper class.

Jonathan's father's wealth accumulation and income were unusual, not just among his nine siblings, who were not as financially successful, but also among his cohort of Black Americans of his time. Among the top quintile of income earners in 1980, only 10 percent (among whom was Jonathan's family) were Black.[2] What these wealthier Black folks had made them stand out from the median African American family in 1983, who had only $13,000 as compared to $105,000 for the median wealth level of white families.[3] So, even as his family enjoyed upper-middle-class life, they were still connected to poorer Black Mississippians, including those in his family who were in poverty.[4]

As a result, most of Jonathan's sensibilities, dispositions, and taste—including in food—have been shaped by that of the average working-class Black person of his childhood. His sense of self was tied more to his racial group identification than it was to his class identification. But there always existed a tension. He and his family lived with one foot in a socioeconomically privileged world, in which there were few Black people, and another foot in a Southern Black American society, in which there were few rich people.

Jonathan unwillingly followed in his father's footsteps. When he graduated from high school, he enrolled at the University of North Carolina at Chapel Hill, but he did not last there. "I was there for two weeks. I had a roommate named Sal. He was from East Rutherford, New Jersey. And, by the end of the week, if I heard one more joke about Mississippi or the South, I was going to scream. And Sal was the worst proponent [of the name-calling.]"

In addition to living as a Black person at the margins of upper-class life and as a rich person at the margins of a poorer Black world, Jonathan learned that, as a Southerner, he lived at the margins of the nation's imagination. He called his father and asked to come back home to enroll at Mississippi State University after previously denouncing the school as a "waste of good ACT scores." He received both his bachelor's and master's degrees in business from Mississippi State University. He was set to enroll in a PhD program at the University of Alabama in higher education administration. To appease his father, who wished he would take over the family business, Jonathan postponed his start date. He planned to work with his family for a short time, but an unthinkable tragedy changed everything.

"I came home and just had enough time to understand what I was supposed to do with the project and start. My father went to the doctor for a checkup. I was around twenty-five or twenty-six. He came home told us he had cancer, and it was terminal. Eight months later, he died. He was fifty-six years old, not very old. He died of gastric cancer, which is very rare among African Americans. He was literally here and gone. He was a very dominant man. In my family, we had this term; he was the 'valedictorian' of the family. He made decisions for all his brothers and sisters. If you had any problems, you just go and give it to Junior Lee, and didn't have to think about it anymore. For me, [his death] was the first time I had to carry my own cross. The same faith you're supposed to have in God, I had in him.

"With [him gone], I knew that I was supposed to stay home. My mom was checked out. My sister was checked out. We had two offices, one on the coast and one here. We had several warehouses in Southern and Central Mississippi and were about to open another. And we had some real estate properties. I was left holding the bag in my mid-twenties. I was pissed because this was not my plan. Every waking minute of my first five years, I was afraid I was going to run the business into the ground. I just felt like I was going to fail."

When I met Jonathan in 2012, he had been successfully running his family business for a decade. Along with inheriting his father's business, he stepped into the community roles and board positions that his father vacated, including on the boards of one of the city's

major hospitals and a national bank. He was also one of the youngest members of his alma mater's board of trustees.

Having lived in his father's shadow for so long, Jonathan was
ready to take on a new challenge in 2012. I had heard rumors of
it, but during our conversation, he confirmed that he planned
to run in the city's mayoral election. He was motivated by noble
ambitions.

"The Chamber [of Commerce] did a study in October. They
polled people in the community and around Jackson. Seventy
percent believe that, if they are going to achieve the quality of life,
they and their children have to leave. That's why I'm running. I
often think about what attracts me to this place. Why didn't I leave
[for good]? Oh, it's the people, but I think it's the will of the people.
We may be on the bottom of everything, [but] everybody is trying to move the bar. We are so mired in our own social caste, us
against them, so much hurt that's unresolved that we've never ral-
lied around."

Jonathan viewed himself as the person to bring the city together,
to bridge the various castes, to use his language. He might have
been using caste in the way that Isabel Wilkerson uses it, with references to the caste system in India, or in the ways that other sociologists of the South do, comparing race and class structures between
white and Black Southerners.[5] But, given that Jackson, Mississippi,
is 81 percent Black, I cannot help but presume he might have also
been referring to intra-racial class divide.

When Jonathan announced his bid for mayor of Jackson, he
did so in Georgetown, a neighborhood in which, during the 1970s,
Black folks across class lines lived near one another. As a volunteer
for his campaign, I took photographs of him, his wife, and his pastor as they addressed the press corps who came to cover the event.
In their speeches, they touted his business acumen, his youth, and
his maturity. They also made sure to make it clear that, even though
he lived across town in a wealthy and racially integrated neighborhood, through his grandmother, he has always been connected to
the plight of Black Jacksonians in poverty. His campaign anticipated that his political opponents would frame his class status as
a sign that he was disconnected from the average working-class

12.1. Lee for Mayor

Black person, so they relied on a narrative about how Black women transmit cultural traditions across generations.[6]

Upper-middle-class African Americans like Jonathan occupy a peculiar position in America's racialized and classed stratification order. Research about this group, going as far back as Du Bois's *Philadelphia Negro*, has documented their lives as paradoxical. On the one hand, they enjoy the privileges of their class position. On the other hand, they continue to encounter racial subjugation intertwined with various other portions of their identities.[7] Like the Davis Family and Charles's experiences that were explored in the last chapters, their class privileges are shaped by their racial subordination. However, different from them, Jonathan and other upper-middle-class Black folks explored here live their day-to-day lives further away from those in poverty. The sociologist Karyn Lacy, who distinguishes elite middle-class Blacks from the core middle-class population, explains that elite middle-class Black people often align themselves with their white counterparts in segregating themselves from those who are less well-off.[8]

Even though they are physically distant from many Black folks in Jackson, elite middle-class folks strive to maintain and nurture their racial identities. They employ what Lacy calls "strategic assimilation," which allows them to simultaneously live out their racialized and classed selves. They live in wealthier white neighborhoods, but they maintain ties in Black communities by participating in, among many things, Black churches and historically Black and civic associations.[9] They know that they will never be completely accepted in their white neighborhoods or their white job settings because they know that, in America and in the South, racial boundaries are more binding than class boundaries.[10] Their class mobility does not make them immune from racism. They nurture their racial identity also because they know their successes were a result of the Civil Rights Movement, a cross-class Black social movement for social and economic progress.[11] Their success and well-being are intricately tied to "the struggle."

Thus, maintaining their blackness requires that they stay connected to "the movement," that they "stay woke," even as they move farther away from the day-to-day hardships that most other Black folks continue to face. Blackness is much more than "the struggle," but a distancing from the latter is a distancing from the former.[12] The chapters in this section detail how these elite middle-class Blacks in Jackson use food to nurture their racial identities.

The German phrase, *"Man ist, was man isst"*—"You are what you eat"—is often cited in conversations about food and identity, but it is seldom unpacked. How is it, really, that we are what we eat? Claude Fischler, a food anthropologist, approaches this question through the omnivore's paradox. Humans, as omnivores, can survive on a wide range of diets. Unlike specialized eaters like carnivores or herbivores, the human species can learn and adapt to various forms of nourishment.

There is freedom in this, but there is also anxiety and danger. "Every omnivore, and man in particular, is subject to . . . a double bind between the familiar and the unknown, monotony and change, security and variety."[13] The foods that we choose to negotiate this paradox contribute to a making of oneself on at least three levels. At the most basic and biological level, ingesting certain foods is to take in the biochemicals of that food, which provide the energy the body needs and, in part, shape and maintain the very substances of the body. What you become is, literally, often shaped by what you eat. On another level, you take up the symbolic significance of what you eat—here, one thinks of how eating red meat, for instance, is associated with masculinity. On yet another level, to eat certain foods is to join the group of people who, over time, have solved the omnivore's paradox by settling on those specific types of food to survive. It is a way of registering one's membership. So, indeed, "you are what you eat." If that is true, then the inverse may also be true. In Fischler's words, if "food makes the eater: it is therefore natural that the eater should try to make himself by eating."[14] This chapter explores how elite middle-class Black folks make themselves—nurture their racial selves—through eating.

Foodways in a Day

Jonathan invited me to follow him around one August day. It was not a typical day for him, he explained, but it sufficiently demonstrated how he spends his days as a politician trying to raise funds and ideas for his campaign. On this day, he had three main meetings that included food: one with members of the city's chamber of commerce, another with a political consultant, and a casual get-together with his mentor at The Penguin, a restaurant near Jackson State University.

Our first stop was the Greater Jackson Chamber of Commerce meeting. At the time, Jonathan was the president of the organization—one of the high-level community positions he inherited from his father. As soon as we arrived, he notified the meeting organizer that he would be leaving early because of another appointment.

"See," the lady said to me jokingly, "I don't even know why he would schedule a 12 o'clock when he's got my meeting." I smiled and nodded in agreement. She invited us to get some food before more people arrived. Politely declining, Jonathan explained that we would not eat because our next meeting was over lunch.

The meeting attendees warmly greeted each other. When we sat down, Jonathan whispered to me that their friendliness did not necessarily mean they were all friends. He considered one lawyer who had been chitchatting with us a "former friend." His political ambition had earned him some "former friends." When I wandered over to where the food was arranged, I saw that they were serving baked chicken, baked beans, potato salad, rolls, and sweet tea. The food was in aluminum pans. Styrofoam cups with ice were arranged on a table. The attendees served themselves on heavy-duty paper plates and ate with plastic forks. Neither what they ate nor the plates and utensils signaled their class position—the food and tools did not look different from anything one might find at a neighborhood picnic. But not everyone could be in that room; the setting and the people are what highlighted their class positions.

After getting their meals, they returned to the meeting room, a U-shaped room with leather chairs, and they ate as they conversed. When I returned to my seat, I caught the mayor preparing to take his first bite. Before he raised a fork of beans to his mouth, he paused for a moment to say a prayer. After his bite, he turned to someone next to him to respond to a question. The newly hired school superintendent was also in attendance, and so was a well-known developer charged with bringing Farish Street back to prominence—I recognized him because he was continuously scrutinized on the local TV station, WLBT 3 On Your Side. The man next to him, a powerful lawyer, struggled to cut the chicken with his fork. Most of them did, but none picked up the chicken with their hands. It seemed inappropriate in the setting.

Because they were gathered for another purpose, it was almost as if the food was not present. No one commented on it. The eating happened without any fanfare. Like the homeless men I followed, these businessmen and politicians probably did not know what was going to be served before they walked into the room. They had relatively little choice in what was offered. But unlike the homeless, they knew that the food would be appropriate to their tastes, not just to their taste buds but also to their social taste—the appropriate food choices were made for them. And if they did not find the food being served to their liking, or like Jonathan and me, if they had any other reason to not partake in the meal, it was of very little consequence to them.

When most of the people were finished with their meals, a moderator stepped to the podium in the corner of the room and called

She had ensured that the batter for the chicken did not include any eggs. She laughed and described both her husband and her daughter as "picky eaters." She joked as well that her daughter often prefers "cheap" animal crackers over the brand-name one she buys. And as she watched Jonathan eating the wings, she commented, "Jonathan just likes things that are simple and plain."[16]

"I don't want any eggs on my pizza," he responded to her comment. She had chosen that pizza because she thought Jonathan, who typically likes poached eggs, would like the white cheese pizza.

Jonathan did not always partake in the food offerings at fine dining or high-end restaurants, even if he might enjoy the company of the people. His job and his political aspirations necessitated that he dine in those places, but they were not his go-to places to eat. These finer eateries in town seemed to require certain sensibilities that he did not have and did not particularly care to develop.

Jonathan related to food differently at a place like The Penguin. The Penguin opened in December 2011, a month before I arrived in Jackson, as a tribute to a popular food stand on Jackson State University's campus. Around twenty years ago, The Penguin was a hot dog stand. The revived restaurant was an elegant setting that served Jackson State University faculty, administrators, and other city professionals. There were few white patrons on any given day because, for the most part, it served a Black middle- and upper-class clientele. It was a Black space.[17] The front doors of the restaurant opened to the main seating area with black tables and chairs. From the entrance, one can look past the white pillars to the black granite bar. There were two large wide-screen televisions affixed between all-black cabinets at the bar. Dozens of recessed lights, along with decorated low-hanging round crystal light shades by the windows and in the center of the seating area, illuminated the space. There was a stage along one side of the space for nightly music performances. Some patrons dressed casually, in jeans and a shirt, but others, who came as the establishment would prefer, wore a nice button-down shirt and a sports jacket (for the men) and a dress or a skirt and blouse (for the women). In many ways, The Penguin communicated to its patrons that it was a space for the aesthetic taste of middle-class Black people.

At the same time, the establishment strove to not present itself as too highbrow. Its tagline was "upscale but not uppity." Their decor was upscale, so how did they ensure they were not uppity? What did it even mean to be uppity? In decades past, whites in the Deep South insisted that Black folks would not be uppity, that Black folks would not mistake their class ascendance as protection from racism. It was a term "applied to affluent Black people, who sometimes paid a horrific price for owning nicer homes, cars, or more successful businesses than whites."[18]

As used by The Penguin in a contemporary context, they implied that they serve people for whom a working-class racial identity superseded their privileged upper-class economic position. They did so by ensuring their menu included humble non-uppity foods. The menu included fried catfish, fried chicken, and hot dogs along-side crab cakes, duck breasts, and steaks. On some Sundays, they served neck bones, chicken, and waffles, and on the first and third Sundays of the month, chitterlings. Interestingly, their menu did not reflect the foods of today's working-class Black people but those of yesteryear. The menu reflected how Billy and Ms. Bea grew up, not how Zenani and her children are growing up.

Jonathan is among a collection of investors who made The Penguin possible. When we met there at the end of the day of meeting with the chamber of commerce and the political consultant, we were joined by Dr. Bill Cooley, or "Doc," a man Jonathan considered a "surrogate father." He, too, was an investor in the restaurant. Doc is a retired businessman and arguably the wealthiest African American in the city, though one would not know it from being around him—he is very humble and modest. His upbringing from share-cropping Hollandale, Mississippi, also allows him to play down his class status. Both Jonathan and Doc are regulars at The Penguin; they eat and drink there as often as three or four times a week.

The sun behind us was going down when we arrived that day. Other professionals strolled in to catch happy hour. We ordered drinks and appetizers and caught up on the day. Jonathan told Doc about his meetings. Between the updates, they laughed, joked, and even gossiped a little. It was the most at ease I had seen Jonathan all-day. Watching them at the moment, I thought of the anthropologist John L. Jackson Jr.'s idea of racial sincerity when people perform their understandings of their racial identity, not for the sake of proving their blackness to onlookers. Watching Jonathan and Doc enjoy a classy space and food that was "not uppity" was not a performance of racial scripts and it was not a display of their racial authenticity. Their racial and classed sincerity was, to use Jackson's words, "the something-elseness" that can make racial identities feel "so obvious, natural, real, and even liberating. . . . [and serve] as invisible links to other people."[19] To the best of their ability, they were being how they conceived of themselves.

I observed something similar on another day when I went with Jonathan and Doc to CS's, a well-known soul food restaurant. Jonathan and I were chatting after one of the Friday morning community forums when Doc asked if we wanted to go to lunch. He suggested CS's. It is a place known for its burgers, most prominently the Inez Burger, an open-faced burger with chili and nacho cheese. According to Doc, who was already seated when we arrived, it was once a major hangout for nearby Millsap students. Now, it appeared to be a place for young professionals, both Black and white. Being there provided an opportunity to see how they use food to connect with a working-class racial identity, even with considerable wealth.

The restaurant's owner recognized Jonathan and came to say hello as soon as we walked in. He knew Jonathan was running for mayor, so he asked about the campaign; Jonathan had held an event at the place the week prior. After the owner left, Jonathan mentioned that his father's aunt works in the kitchen. When she got word that Jonathan was around, she came out to say hello. She was an eighty-something woman. Doc and I were not sure what we were going to have until she came out and assured us that the chicken and dumplings was pretty good because she makes it. We laughed at her admission, but we both adhered to her suggestion. Jonathan ordered their fried pork chop, which his great aunt prepares as well. We were all salivating when our food quickly arrived on teal-colored plates. The fried pork chops were exactly to Jonathan's liking. Doc noted how good it looked.

"Here, grab you a piece," Jonathan offered.

While Doc looked happy to hear the offer, he was a bit apprehensive. We all knew that it was not in his health's best interest to be eating fried pork. We also knew that his daughter would not have allowed him to take a bite. He tried the pork chops anyway.

"Oh, I'm gonna tell on you to Toni," I teased him as he chewed. He smiled, enjoying the pork. I also tried a piece: it was crispy and succulent.

"How's you guys' plate?" Jonathan asked.

Doc mumbled his satisfaction first.

"It's great," I added. It was more food than any of us could eat.

As we approached the end of the meal, the owner came and took Jonathan to meet a table of lawyers who might be supporters. When he returned, his great aunt came to check on us. She saw that the only finished plate was the fried pork, so she brought an extra piece for us to share. Unlike at high-end restaurants, or even at the gourmet pizza shop, Jonathan did not have to navigate gluten-free or artisan cheese options. It was the simple food that, according to his wife, he enjoyed.

eat. As self-proclaimed foodies, they were excited about my project and curious about my findings.

When the waiter came back around, they ordered another round of drinks and appetizers. They might have come to the restaurant because they were hungry, but they stayed for as long as they did to socialize. The food and drinks had a social function, one markedly different than for people like Smack. For the men in homelessness, food was an interruption to socialization. With this group, it propelled socialization.

"I got a question for you." Adrianne, who seemed the most intrigued by my study, asked in between bites. "How come there aren't a lot of Black folks when we go to fine dining restaurants?"

Her question was one I contemplated as I shucked oysters in the ice bar that overlooked the seating area. I counted the number of non-whites I would see at Parlor Market, and in the three months that I worked there, I counted about fifteen people. If fine dining restaurants were one way of living out one's class position, how come elite Black folks hesitated to partake? I did not have a clear answer to her question, and I did not want to dodge the subject, so I offered my best guess.

"I think a lot of Black folks, richer Black folks, don't really use what they eat as something to mark their social status. In fact, they do not want to eat fine dining out of fear of rejecting their blackness. They might use the car they drive or whatever other things to show they are well-to-do. You all, on the other hand, like to come here because it's one of the ways to show that you are of a certain status. Cuz, you know, it's not just about the food."

"Yea, well, no," she politely interrupted. "The food is important. It *is* about the food." She ignored all of what I said before the comment about the food. I do not know if it meant she agreed with it or not.

"Yea," I attempted to explain what I meant, "but you also like how the place looks, [and] how you are served. The whole eating experience is important."

"Yea, I think you're right," Adrianne hesitantly agreed. She was not completely satisfied with my response. Neither was I. "I can't wait to read your dissertation. Matter of fact, you should include us in your study." It was music to my ears.

Before the evening ended, Dorian invited me to be a part of their Friday Cocktail group. They meet after work at upscale restaurants around the city to drink and enjoy appetizers. The rules were, as she explained them, as follows: "I'll send out a text message around 3 p.m. You have to respond if you are going to make it or if you are not going to make it. If you don't respond three times, you get taken off the list. So, you should come on Friday. You are on probation status." Othor laughed; Adrianne rolled her eyes. I quickly learned that Dorian managed group activities—she was affectionately referred to as "the Queen Bee."

To make the invitation more welcoming, Adrianne added, "We really enjoyed your company, so you should come."

From that day in mid-September till the end of November in 2012, and then in the summer months of 2016, I attended as many of the Friday Cocktail gatherings as I could, about three-quarters of them. Upon their invitation, I spent time with them during the day at their workplaces to get to get a fuller sense of their lives and their foodways.

Eating at Work

When I arrived at Dorian's office on my first day, she was standing in the corner of a large open-space room where there was a refrigerator and a coffee maker. I was getting ready to apologize for being late when Dorian greeted me with, "You have perfect timing. I just got in." It was around 11:30 a.m. She introduced me to Vicky, a friendly full-faced white woman in her mid-thirties with blond hair and an inviting smile. Vicky sat in one corner of this open space room near the refrigerator. Dorian offered me something to drink and then ushered me into her office to talk about my tasks. We agreed on three projects I could work on, all dealing with issues of liability for the school district she represented. I was free to come and go as I pleased, but I assured her I would work three days a week from mid-morning until the office closed.

As we finished our initial meeting on my first day, Vicky knocked on the door to ask if either of us needed anything. "Do y'all want me to get you some lunch?"

We both answered, "No."

My assigned working area was their conference room. From there, I could hear Dorian on and off phone calls. For the most part, she worked quietly at her desk for several hours at a time, and so did Vicky. If Dorian stepped out, it was to refill her tea or talk and joke with Vicky. Their relationship was one of an employer and employee, but it was also kind and warm-hearted.

When I returned the next day, I knocked on her closed office door to greet her before getting back to my tasks in the long conference room, which overlooked the sidewalk on which, several months prior, I traveled with homeless men on our way to breakfast. Dorian worked through lunch. Vicky ate a Stouffer's meal—one of the half-dozen boxes I saw in the office freezer—at her desk, and I ate granola bars I brought with me. Occasionally, I stepped out of the conference room to ask a question, borrow a stapler, or print a document. I entered Dorian's office intermittently to use a reference book. On most occasions, I found her at her desk and working on the computer, diligently reading and typing away. I did not see her come out of her seat or out of her office that day. As I walked by her office in one instance, I saw an open family-sized bag of tortilla chips on her desk.

After working in the office three times a week for three weeks, I got the sense that my observations of the first few days well-represented life in the office. Dorian usually does not eat breakfast and works through lunch. She eats her biggest meal after leaving the office.

Adrianne has similar eating habits. "I'm not a breakfast person," she confessed. "I like to have one big meal a day, where I can eat and drink at home. I know it's bad, but that's just the way it happens for me." She begins her day at 9:00 a.m. and works until 6:00 p.m. When I spent time at her office, I observed her eating bits of food here and there, a practice known as "grazing," eating or drinking while engaging in some other primary activity.[2]

I did not observe Dorian eat lunch until nearly a month after I began working with her. Popping out of her office, she announced, "I remembered that I have food today." She explained that her memory was jogged during a phone call when someone asked about her lunch plans. She went into the fridge and took out some turkey lunch meat, which she neatly arranged on two pieces of sliced bread. I could not tell if she put anything else on it.

13.1. Dorian at work

"Y'all can have some [of the meat] if you want some."

Vicky and I both politely declined and chuckled at the sight of her eating during the day.

"Now, I need some chips," she said, as she walked back into her office, "Who eats a sandwich without chips?"

Observing it all made me wonder if not eating lunch was simply a matter of her not having food at the office. She did not lack food in the same way that Zenani did, but Dorian ate as infrequently as Zenani did. Since I ate only when those around me did, I remember feeling as much hunger around Zenani as I did around Dorian. In fact, I was least hungry around the homeless men. So, what explains their similarity in how infrequently they ate? It turns out they have something in common: scarcity.

Zenani ate infrequently due to her financial constraints, and the time she spent working to solve never-ending and pressing problems, like finding a safe place to live or securing a job, interfered with a regular meal schedule. In Dorian's case, her eating habits appeared to be shaped by the scarcity of time, but that scarcity was the result of a busy job schedule. For many upper-middle-class professionals, career demands require so much focus that it causes a sort of tunnel vision, limiting or distorting their "bandwidth," or their ability to address other needs, including their eating needs.[3] However, while Dorian and Adrianne experience time scarcity with similar results on their eating habits as those experienced by Zenani, their scarcity of time ends with the workday. When they leave work, their economic resources relieve them of the scarcity. That is to say, their scarcity is not permanent, as it is for those in poverty.

Eating Out

One evening after work, Dorian invited me to join her and a group of friends for dinner. We met at a high-end restaurant called Shapley's, a place she used to frequent because a former coworker was a partial owner. Our party—Dorian, Othor, and me, along with Dorian's yoga instructor (Amy) and John, a bartender/sommelier— was ushered to our white-linen-covered round table. The serving staff—clad in white shirts, bow ties, and black vests—made themselves available to our every whim. John stepped into his role and chose a bottle of wine for the table. The rest of us discussed appetizers. We agreed on crab cakes and scallops for appetizers. When they arrived, Dorian was the first to taste the crab cakes, performing a ritual I had, by then, begun to recognize.

After she put a bite in her mouth, she held up the hand holding her fork to her shoulder's level and stared off for a second while she mindfully chewed. It was as if she was collecting and analyzing the data that her taste buds provided before providing a report to the rest of us. "It's pretty good."

And, during this instance and other instances, she would provide some assessment of the ingredients, their quality or freshness, and an evaluation of how well the dishes combined, noting if, positively or not, one overpowered another. We all joined in after we tasted the crab cakes, commenting on the proportion of crabmeat versus the other ingredients, the freshness of the crabmeat, and the spices used. The wine we sipped paired nicely, as well. Those who knew better took turns describing various characteristics of the wine and justified why it worked with what we were eating. I just nodded along. To be honest, eating as they did was foreign to me. In my immigrant lower-middle-class household, it would have been considered excessive to spend the amount of money we were spending that night on a meal.

The dinner conversation flowed smoothly, covering a wide range of various topics. We laughed over the worst jobs we had ever had, each taking turns talking, listening, and adding to one another's stories. The food was a quiet part of the conversation. Most of the time, it just lay in the background, and we talked and laughed over it, politely passing it to one another. But, occasionally, a taste would catch and demand our attention, and we would give it, discussing the particular flavor for a few minutes before swaying to another topic.

The ease with which one does this dance, between ignoring and making precise comments about the food, while also gliding through various topics, is part of what it means to eat with class. We had been there for an hour, nibbling on bread and appetizers and sipping wine before our entrées arrived. No one seemed to be in a hurry. While the pressures of Dorian's workday kept her from eating most of the day, it is in these settings that she can put a pause on her worries and engage all her senses in the eating process. When the entrées arrived—ribeye steak, herb-crusted chicken breast, grilled salmon fillet, and rack of lamb, served with an assortment of sharable sides, potatoes au gratin, creamed spinach, mashed potatoes, and grilled asparagus—the dance continued. When we finished, the servers asked about dessert.

"I don't know the last time I had dessert. I'm trying to figure out if I can have dessert today to reward myself," Dorian shared.

"Do it," someone moaned. The rest of us cheered for ordering dessert, and someone put in an order for bread pudding. Another ordered the restaurant's well-known cake à la mode.

"Okay, you've twisted my arm." Dorian gave in.

The desserts arrived with spoons for all of us to share.

On another weekday evening, I joined Dorian, Adrianne, and Othor for dinner at Parlor Market, where I first met them. Parlor Market, a place they more often frequented, is different from Shapley's. Parlor

13.2. Parlor Market Kitchen

13.3. Parlor Market Kitchen

13.4. Parlor Market Kitchen

Market is much more creative and adventurous. Shapley's offers its customers staples prepared with high-end ingredients served in an elegant setting. And they make this clear on their menu. As a prelude to their seafood offerings, they mention: "We take in only the finest and freshest seafood we can find and prepare them in a simple fashion that allows you to enjoy them as nature intended." And, about their meats, they say the following: "All our beef is trimmed and aged in-house and served with our famous beef reduction sauce and served with our famous fries like the good ole days!" So, even though Shapley's foods are out of the price range of many, their food offerings are familiar.

Parlor Market refines Southern staples. They strip them down, embellish, and introduce new ingredients and create new pairings. For instance, they serve duck confit with duck crackling and they put fried eggplant on their burgers. On their list of appetizers, they offer spicy pork rinds as well as a charcuterie board with an assortment of cheeses. Despite their differences, both restaurants situate themselves in their region—they reflect their region's food history. Most other restaurants of their caliber do the same. To be in the South is to be preoccupied with it. In the South, perhaps unlike in other regions of the country, high-end restaurants remain grounded in Southern cuisine, which is itself rooted in what came out of the kitchens of Black cooks in the big house.

Because of this tendency, even places like Parlor Market, are not, taste-wise, culturally far for people like Dorian and Adrianne. If they are, the distance is surmountable. But, when Parlor Market thinks about their primary clients, Black folks of any class stripe are not at the forefront of their minds. Again, this has less to do with the sophistication of the food and more to do with the racialization of the space. Parlor Market is an example of "white spaces," in the sense that the sociologist Elijah Anderson describes them—"[their] most distinctive feature is their overwhelming presence of white people and their absence of black people."[4] White and Black folks alike know these spaces as such. These tacit understandings were some of the residuals of Jim Crow. There are no brazen "Whites Only" signs, but it is understood. In all the time I spent with Jonathan, I never saw him eat there—I never even heard him consider it. Most Black folks who could afford to dine at a place like Parlor Market knew that Parlor Market did not think of them, so they too rejected it. This was not the case for Dorian, Adrianne, and Othor. No. They leaned into what they were denied. They participated in what the restaurant offered, enjoying much of it, while simultaneously, resisting it.[5]

One example of this resistance was my observation of how Dorian reads a menu. For her, the menu explained the dishes, but it also gave her clues of the kinds of ingredients they had available in the kitchen. When she orders, she often combines portions of various dishes to create what she wants. Dorian enjoys and appreciates the chef's creativity and expertise, even mentioning that "I come to these types of restaurants because they make things that I can't make for myself at home." But ultimately, she and her sister did not completely place their tastes in the restaurant's hands—their (racial) sense of self did not let them. And part of this is because she knew the chef did not have her in mind when creating the dishes. It was a small act of resistance. From spending time with the chefs and cooks in the kitchen, I heard how irritating they found such customers. When one of the chefs saw that I was paying attention to his complaining, he came to me to explain his annoyance.

"I'm going to kill the people at this table." He showed a ticket with a whole bunch of red marks on the order ticket. "Look at this. For every single thing they ordered, they changed something. Who the hell comes to a restaurant like this and changes up the menu? I hate that shit." Later on, he came to me to add that he was going to start charging people for changing stuff on the menu. For the chefs and their mostly white staff, it is a subtle way of saying that those who alter the menus do not belong at the restaurant.[6]

I sat with Dorian, Adrianne, and Othor at their usual spot, the long booth near the front entrance. John, who had been with us at Shapley's, was taking care of our drinks. Adrianne was debating between the lamb burger sliders and the General Tso pork belly.

"I had a lot of bread today, so I don't think I'mma go with the sliders," she thought out loud to herself. "But I do want something that soaks up these drinks. Okay, let me get the pork belly." It was served with sesame, scallion grits, local green kimchi, and pimento cheese wontons. After she placed her order, Dorian provided her assessment of the pork belly—she had had it when she visited the place a few days prior.

"I liked the pork belly, but when I got to the bottom, there was, whatever the oil that they cooked it in, it was too much, and it had permeated the taste of the rice, and it had messed up the flavor. But I liked it, except for the bottom."

Dorian ordered their duck sausage served with Delta Grind grits, muscadine jus, kale, and duck crackling. Othor and I were not very hungry, so we munched on charcuterie and mini crab legs. When the dishes arrived, as was their custom, they each took turns tasting them. We took note of the oil at the bottom of the pork belly dish because we had been primed. For the most part, we agreed with Dorian's assessment. We also shared and tasted the duck sausage.

"That's really good. Maybe I should've taken a bigger piece," Othor began.

"I told you, I like the sausage. That is so good," Adrianne agreed.

"And what's that sweet aftertaste? Is it maple? And it tastes smoked almost. Was it smoked?" Othor asked.

"I don't know," Dorian responded. "I have no idea, but it's good. The grits is good too."

Adrianne began with suggestions on how to make it better, their attempt at how to include their taste into the restaurant. "I would just change this up a little bit. I would make it a sandwich."

"Yea, a po-boy," Dorian pitched in. We all responded enthusiastically. "That's what they need to do," she continued. "But they need real French bread—Gambino's French bread—and some mustard. What kind of mustard? It needs a special kind of mustard."

"Oh yea, that mustard we had the other day, or was it mustard? Yea, it was. What was that?" Othor contributed.

"That habanero mustard. That's what it needs."

As they brainstormed, Adrianne took another bite of the sausage and grits and tasted the duck crackling.

"It took me three tastes to get some of the crackling, but it is good too." She directed us all to have another bite of the sausage with the crackling and grits. Othor does not eat grits, so he avoided it, but made sure he got a nice piece of crackling. After a few chews, he commented, "I would want that crackling to be more dry. And then I'd sprinkle some hot sauce on it, that's how country I am." We all laughed at his admission.

"Man, dry crackling and some hot sauce, that's good eating, man. I know that's so country, but I'm telling you." He let out his signature loud and infectious baritone laugh.

Othor grew up differently from Dorian and Adrianne. He was born in nearby Canton, but moved to Jackson at a young age. His family lived in one unit of the eight-unit Christian Brotherhood Apartments in Northwest Jackson when they first arrived in the city. Even though he lived in an all-Black neighborhood, he went to an integrated school. His cohort was among the students to integrate the school district in Jackson, and he remembered the terror of that experience.

In an interview with him, he recalled the first time being called a nigger on the playground by a white kid. "What I also remember very vividly was the teacher washing my mouth with soap, and not his." He had retaliated and called the boy a honky or cracker. "She literally washed my mouth. Oooh, my momma came to that school and did some cussing." His neighborhood, by contrast, was nurturing. His mother worked different shifts to take care of him and his siblings. So, she was not always home when he returned home

13.5. Othor at work

from school, but Ms. Miles, a neighbor who lived in one of the other units, looked out for him and other children in their apartment complex. She always had cake and cookies for them. Othor's elder sister also fed him when his mother was not around. "At that point, the only thing she knew how to cook was grits. That's all my sister used to cook. And, that's all I would eat until my mother came home." It is why Othor now refuses to eat grits.

When I mentioned that I had never had crackling, Dorian responded with, "Piko, where the hell you been? You just had crackling? This is so good."

"I'd want just a little more sausage. And definitely more crackling."

Adrianne and Dorian sought similar control over their taste when they went to their neighborhood Mexican spot. They came there twice a week, once on a weekday and once on the weekend. Dining with them on one of my last Sundays in Jackson, I asked them to talk more about how they think about their dining experiences. Adrianne was waiting impatiently for the waiter to come for our order. Dorian was eating chips, and as she picked up each one, she would cover it in chili powder before eating it.

The restaurant was empty. There was only one other table with customers. As we looked at the menu, I asked them for recommendations. They mentioned a few dishes, but it seemed like they ordered the same meals every time.

"So, out of the fifteen or so meals that you have a week, what percentage of that is at home?" For Adrianne, it was 50 to 60 percent. For Dorian, it was about 25 percent.

"I eat at home when I can't find someone to go out to eat with, and even that, I'll go by Subway or something to get a salad. I don't cook. I cook only when I'm entertaining," Dorian explained. "And I don't cook [because] I don't know how."

I added that I, too, didn't know how to cook and that if I had unlimited income, I'd hire a personal chef. Adrianne agreed with me. Dorian disagreed. She spoke about how much she enjoys the social aspects of eating out.

"I like eating out. I wouldn't wanna eat out every night, but I like eating out. I just think the whole process of eating out is fun. To me, eating out comprises of every delight that I enjoy. Eating out is like music to me—I love music." Adrianne added that, for her, the actual flavor of the food mattered a great deal.

She told a story about dining in California and befriending the table next to them. They were going to order a meal that was paired with wine, but they learned from their new friends that the wine was not very good. They also learned that when their new friends complained about the taste of the wine, the restaurant manager responded that it was because they did not know how to appreciate the wine.

"So, I said to them, 'Wait, you paying all this kind of money, and he said to y'all . . .' Oh, I would have gone off on them. Now, I always feel obligated to try stuff. I'll try new stuff, but you know, I also worry about if all of it is healthy for you."

"No, I don't worry about none of that."

When our meals arrived, I watched them manage how their food tastes. After the waiter placed Dorian's taco in front of her, he didn't get far before Dorian got his attention.

"Excuse me, you have my cut-up lime for me, right?"

He smiled, knowing that he should have known better.

13.6. Dorian and Adrianne

And, after she ate, her refried beans had gotten cold, so she asked the waiter to warm it up for her. After she had had her initial meal, Adrianne got the attention of the waiter to place another order. She gets flustered when placing an order, out of a need to be precise with what she requests.

"Okay. What do I want? Let me see. I want one more taco. Do I want another drink? Yea, let me think. Yea, give me one more taco and a margarita on the rocks, premium shelf, and I'll be good."

Adrianne, Dorian, and Jonathan were friends. They grew up in the same circles of elite Black families in Jackson and, to different degrees, experienced and responded to similar tensions between their race and class. For many, this tension does not play itself out in overt ways. It does not usually take up central places in their thinking, but it gently tugs at their every move. Adrianne, Dorian, and

Jonathan may not, because of this tension, have "split personalities" or "pathologies," as sociologist E. Franklin Frazier once described, but they are "insiders" and "outsiders" in both their privileged, classed worlds and their subordinated racial worlds, as political scientist Martin Kilson once described.[7] As Kilson further suggests, with a jest reference to Frazier, "The current 'split-personality' pressures facing some members of today's Black bourgeoisie are a comparatively minor burden to bear."[8] It usually is, but when Jonathan ran for mayor, it became a much more substantial burden. The tension became more explicit. It brought to the fore a subtle aspect of what it means to be Black in the American South today.

CHAPTER FOURTEEN

Running for Jackson

WE GOT TO THE PENGUIN early to grab a drink as we waited for Pam, a woman whom Jonathan respects a great deal. He called her one of the smartest minds in the city. He wanted to pick her brain about his campaign, about identifying which of the city's myriad problems he would pitch as the most pressing and, equally important, about how to present himself. As a first-time politician with low-name recognition going against an incumbent, he needed to craft a compelling story about himself. This already arduous task was further complicated by the dynamics of racial politics in city-wide elections. In our conversation, as we waited, he distilled to me what he hoped would be his campaign strategy.

The table that Jonathan picked for us was in one corner of the restaurant—it shielded him from customers going in and out, but it also kept us from the servers' attention. So, for the first thirty minutes, we conversed uninterrupted. He explained Jackson city politics by establishing that political power lay in Black folks' hands, but economic power was still in the hands of white people.

"So, it is an 'us' versus 'them,' right?" I asked.

He disagreed and corrected me.

"It's not an 'us' and 'them.' It is an 'us,' the other 'us,' and then a 'them.'"

The first "us" were the masses of Black folks in the city who were predominantly poor and were the ones being governed. The "them" were the white folks, who were mostly middle and upper class and held the economic power. The "other us" were the elite Black folks who held the political power. The constant battle in the city's politics was whether the "other us" would conduct politics to benefit the Black folks or if they would favor white people. Race theorists have observed this dynamic in their study of elite Black folks. According to Martin Kilson, "On some issues, upper-stratum Black will converge with upper-stratum whites. On other issues, however, upper-stratum Black will converge with middle- and lower-stratum Black and the broader African American community."[1]

Even if motivated by noble ambitions, Black politicians had to determine if they could gain and maintain political power by presenting themselves as primarily representing poorer Black folks or if they had to campaign as the candidate for both white and Black electorates. There was a fine line to be walked even in these two approaches. If they presented themselves as strictly appeasing Black people's demands, they might be deemed too radical and lose the support of some Black voters and the votes and economic support of most white voters. If they presented themselves as more concerned with white folks' interests, they would be deemed a "sellout" and lose the attention of Black voters. Political scientists characterize these strategies as the difference between race-specific versus de-racialized political campaigns.[2] These strategies were evident in the history of Jackson's mayoral campaigns beginning in 1993.

According to Jackson State University professor of political science D'Andra Orey's analysis, when Harvey Johnson Jr., a Black man, sought to unseat incumbent white mayor Kane Ditto in 1993, he chose to run a de-racialized campaign. He declined an invitation to attend a convention at which local Black leaders decided the candidate they would endorse because he wanted to be a candidate that was "sensitive to the needs and interests of all the parts of this city."[3] His strategy proved ineffective—he lost.

So, four years later, in 1997, he ran a race-specific campaign. He won the endorsement of Black leadership and, in his public speeches, made it clear that he sought to be the first Black mayor of Jackson. That strategy worked—he won. He used the same tactics in his reelection campaign and won again. When he ran for a third term in 2005, he was defeated by another Black man, the charismatic and controversial Frank Melton. Using his television show on the local WLBT TV station, of which he was chairman and president, Melton bluntly eschewed racial politics to focus on the singular topic that concerned him, drugs and crime. His de-racialized campaign appealed to both Black and white residents. And he made the case that public safety equally affected all residents in the city. Unfortunately, Melton died at the end of his term in office after solidifying his legacy as a gun-toting crime-fighting mayor who caught both praise and criticism, including his share of legal troubles. In 2009, Johnson returned to the mayoral race with the same tactics to beat his opponent Marshand Crisler, a Black man who was less inclined to center his campaign on race.

Having studied these previous campaigns, Jonathan had to decide on the kind of campaign he would run, especially since he was going against Harvey Johnson. That afternoon, while we still waited in the corner of The Penguin for a waiter to get us something to drink, he provided an unrehearsed and, therefore, sincere response to how he would position himself.

"We're at risk of losing the base," he began. "I'm talking about survival. So, what I intend to do is to make a case for survival. [Like] it played out when the current mayor lost the last time."

He was referring to how Johnson lost to Melton and how Melton pitched his campaign to be about another survival issue—crime. "It was basic old public safety, whether you are Black or white. It's survival. So, my approach will be talking about basic needs. How I'm going to help you reach your basic needs."

He hoped to make the case that the city's infrastructure—roads, schools, and utilities—was broken. "So, the strategy is identifying things that are above the "us" versus "them" thing. That's the strategy. . . . When I say that I'm not running a racialized campaign, I'm saying that I'm going to stick to the issues."

Jonathan knew that Johnson would employ the same tactic he had used to win his last three elections and appeal to the electorate's racial senses. "He's not going to stick to the issues. His thesis will be, 'This guy is here to return the city to the white folks.' That's gonna be his plan."

In this scenario, Jonathan would be painted as the "the other us" who was more loyal to elite white folks than Black Jacksonians. He would be the "white folks" candidate. His blackness would be

14.1. Jonathan and his campaign manager listening to constituents

questioned. He would be described as someone whose class affiliations were stronger than his racial affiliations. Jonathan resented this characterization—it may even have been hurtful—but he knew it was coming. So, even though he did not want to run a racialized campaign, he would have to confront his racialization. To do that, he would reach into his family history and present himself as someone much closer to the plight of poorer Black Jacksonians.

"That's part of the whole dance. We're all one generation from poverty. I don't know a Black person in the South who ain't."

"I hear that, but some folks are still in poverty," I pushed back.

"Right, but my point is, I know where you live. My grandma may live next door to you, my great aunt . . ."

"I'm closer to you than you think," I offered in support.

"At the end of the day, that's part of my job. I gotta make that connection. I'm your Sunday school teacher's grandson. I'm your next-door neighbor's first cousin. I'm your preacher's oldest son."

He would reference that his father went to Lanier High School, one of the famous Black high schools that attracted socioeconomically diverse Black students. He would use that connection to gain some Black cultural capital. In doing so, he would also be continuously reminded that he, Jonathan, went to Northwest Rankin High School, a predominantly white and wealthy school in the suburbs. For that, he would lose Black cultural capital.

"I can see if we were generations away. But we're not." He paused for a couple beats, almost out of frustration. "That's why I was so floored to know that . . ." He did not finish his sentence. Frustration fell from the tip of his tongue. "I have been categorized as an elitist, whereas my father, who earned a living and provided for his family very well, was never categorized that way."

"Why do you think that it is?"

He started to answer that question using his father's life story, but he changed his mind and reached for another case. "Prime example: This lawyer in town, him and I been going back and forth. He grew up first-generation poverty, now he lives in [a wealthy suburb] and sends four kids to [a private school] at $14,000 a year, and he's calling me an elitist."

"Why?" I asked again.

"Because I didn't know the struggle. It all comes back to the struggle," he responded, this time without a beat.

We were no longer just talking about the campaign. We were now talking about this tension that he has lived with most of his life: the tension between his privileged class identity and subordinated racial identity.

On a casual Sunday, I dropped in on Jonathan at his home as he went about his weekend. His wife took the lead on caring for their young child, and he took pride in cutting his lawn as well as taking care of the laundry and cleaning the house. When I showed up that day, his wife and daughter were at a yoga class. We reflected on my visit, the previous week, at The Boulé, the elite fraternity of Black men of which he was a member. That conversation led to a discussion of his race and class. It was not that he denied he was much richer than most Black folks in the city. For him, it was that his economic well-being ought not challenge his racial loyalty. One ought to be able to be economically well-off and racially loyal. His evidence for this was the memory of a socioeconomically integrated Black life of past decades, like in Georgetown, where his father

other candidates. Harvey Johnson received 21 percent of the votes
and finished in third place. Jonathan had successfully beaten Johnson, but because he did not finish with at least 50 percent of the
votes, he had to compete in a runoff against the candidate who finished in second place, Chokwe Lumumba. In the runoff elections
against Lumumba, Jonathan lost. Eight months after Lumumba
took office, he tragically and suddenly died.

Lumumba was one of these larger-than-life figures who seemed
to have lived several lives.[5] He was born and raised in Detroit,
Michigan. In his early twenties and following a lifelong interest
and investment in Black political movements—most of which was
inspired by politically active parents—he was part of the Republic
of New Afrika's leadership. It was also when he changed his name
from Edwin Finley Taliaferro to Chokwe Lumumba. The goal of
the Black nationalist organization he served was to secure land in
southeastern states in the United States on which the new country would settle. That mission was what first brought Lumumba
to Mississippi and Hinds County. In his thirties, he finished law
school at the top of his class, joined the Detroit Public Defenders
Office, and founded his law firm, all while remaining active with
Black nationalist organizations. He represented political figures
like Fulani Sunni Ali, the rapper Tupac Shakur, and former Black
Panther Party members Geronimo Pratt and Assata Shakur. He
cofounded the National Coalition of Blacks for Reparations in
America and the Malcolm X Grassroots Movement. In the 1980s,
Lumumba returned to Mississippi, to Jackson, and continued prac-
ticing law and continued his political work.

In the third act of his life, Lumumba became part of the government, the entity against which his organizations had so often
fought. He was elected as a city council member in 2009. And, in
2013, he ran for mayor. In the first primary race, he outflanked
Harvey Johnson as the candidate for the Black populace, in a more
nationalistic sense than the general population was accustomed to.
So, in the runoff, Lumumba and Jonathan became caricatures of
the two proverbial Black candidates: "the radical" and "the sellout."
Their clash, especially the conversations around it, provided an
opportunity for deep reflections about the contemporary meaning
of being Black in Mississippi.

Not many people thought Lumumba could win, himself included. While attending the taping of a local news program where he was asked about his intention to run for mayor, I heard him express this uncertainty. He was viewed as a radical, and he knew that, so he was not sure if he could win a city-wide election. The small but economically powerful white block distrusted him, as did some Black folks. When I interviewed one local public figure, he explained it to me like this:

> There were a lot of people who didn't even think he would win his council seat just based upon his views and based upon the organizations he aligned himself with. A lot of folks who lived in the ward he ended up winning didn't necessarily align themselves with the same thought process. Ward 2 has the largest percentage of Black people in the city. That's where most of the Black folks doing good live. They figured that Chokwe's message wasn't going to relate. As in too radical. However, Chokwe's ground game was so strong. And he proved to be an excellent campaigner, and that comes from doing grassroots work.

The skepticism and embrace of Lumumba during the mayoral elections were partly due to the pragmatism rooted in Black American politics.[6] When he was doubted, it was because Black voters were concerned that he would pass up practical solutions to social problems in favor of ones that upheld his ideological leanings. But, against Jonathan, Lumumba presented himself as an answer to a fear that became associated with Jonathan's candidacy, a fear of the sellout, a fear of the city being returned to white folks. That same pragmatism drove them to vote for Lumumba.

"I don't think [Jonathan] ever gave enough credence to that."

Over breakfast, I listened to a local pastor reflect on the elections. Even as someone who supported Jonathan, he explained that there was indeed a legitimate fear of the sellout.

> This idea that we're a chocolate city with all of this political power did not happen accidentally. I think back in the eighties and nineties when my dad and some other attorneys went to the state to redraw the city government with this idea of a mayor-council model with seven wards. That wasn't always there. They sued the city, sued the state. The

fact that we got all these Black elected officials was the result of hard work of people who politically and legally forced that to happen. . . . And most people who are in the voting group, who actually do vote, grew up through desegregation. It wasn't until 1997 that we had a Black mayor. The majority of the Black voting body still had memories of a time when white folks ran the city, and Jonathan did not do enough to ensure them that he was not going to hand the keys to the store to white folks.

When I spoke to Lumumba's youngest son about the election, he offered that it was easy to paint Jonathan as "the sellout."

"Well, there were a number of things. One was his presentation, the way he spoke, the way he communicated."

I did not interrupt him to ask what he meant, but it is worth unpacking. As a first-time politician, Jonathan's stage presence was probably above average. But, in direct comparison to Lumumba—a seasoned orator, lawyer, and long-time activist—Jonathan appeared outmatched. Besides his communication, Jonathan's political affiliation came into question. He was accused of being a closeted Republican.

"Even little things, the smallest things. When you put 'Democrat' on your yard, [it says something]. Around here, everyone expects you to be. They presume that you're a Democrat. So, when they see that and hear language like 'unify Jackson,' people know. Black folks catch on to that." Also, the fact that he received donations from white folks made him an easy target.

These concerns came to a head in their final debate. I spoke to several people who pointed to the last debate as one of the campaign's turning points. Lumumba's son also mentioned it.

"So, in that debate, [the debate moderators] asked [Jonathan if he was a Republican], and my father said, 'I don't know if you're a Republican or not. You know what you are in your heart, young brotha. But what I am concerned with is why all your friends aren't our friends.' You can be a Democrat all you want, [but] it is a matter of who is supporting you." The questions around his political affiliation then became linked to his racial loyalty. "If you don't have a history of standing up for people's rights and standing up against these people who are donors for you, then not only do *we* not know what you are going to do, but *you* don't know if you have the power to stand up. It is an unknown for you."

Jonathan still helped with his family's business, but in 2016, he worked full-time for an international health technology company. He worked remotely, so he often used the offices of his family business located on Valley Street in West Jackson, not too far from where Ms. Bea once lived. I met him there the day we had our first serious conversation about the elections. As soon as I sat down, Jonathan motioned for us to get something to eat. We went to a Subway on Pearl Street. We sat at their high tables by their windows. He asked me about my new life as a faculty member, about the classes I was teaching, and about how I was adjusting to life in North Carolina. I asked about his new profession and his transition from working for a small company to a large corporation. My interest in his new line of work was sincere, so was his in mine, but we both patiently anticipated the conversation about his election. He ate quickly, as he often does, so when we got to having that conversation, he was free to talk. I listened.

He began with this: "I don't think anyone who is being honest and fair would tell you that I lost on issues or an honest belief that I couldn't do the job. I think it came down to, 'We think he's a sell-out.' That was the whole narrative." And then he very quickly added, "But it worked." It was his way of acknowledging that he may have been outwitted. It worked because it was a familiar strategy in the city's politics.

"Weeks after the campaign, some folks I'd known my whole life came up to me and said, 'Sorry we had to do that to you—it ain't nothing personal.'"

And to them, he said, "Yea, that's how you beat me. You made it personal."

He understood how it had happened. Over several conversations, he explained it all just as others did. After he won the first round of elections, he became a legitimate contender. That was when, according to Jonathan, the money from (white) Northeast Jackson that everyone talked about arrived. Per his account, that

14.2. Jonathan in 2016

money was not what decided the elections. It was not the rich white folks that decided the election. It was rich Black folks.

The ultra-Black elite, the 1 percent of Black Jacksonians, had to pick a candidate to support after Harvey Johnson was eliminated. When they approached Jonathan, he did not respond as they hoped. They sought his support for a contract that would prove financially beneficial if the incoming mayor signed. Jonathan refused to promise his support. Because of that refusal, the ultra-elite shifted their support to Lumumba. They may have been equally suspicious of Lumumba. But, with Lumumba, they could at least trust that because of his ideological leanings he would not turn to white business owners with business opportunities. Lumumba may or may not have capitulated to the demands of the ultra-elite Black folks, but his interests converged with theirs. He shared with them a common goal of winning an election.

For my purposes, how they went about it, the intra-racial and class dynamics it revealed, is most useful. Studying the food consumption of upper-middle-class Black folks pointed to something that studying this election more clearly unveiled. For upper-class Black folks, maintaining their racial identity requires a continuous connection with the struggles of blackness. Their class position does not make them immune to white supremacy, so they do experience their own class-based versions of racism. But, to publicly demonstrate their Black cultural capital more fully, they must highlight their connection to the struggles of poor Black folks. To do *that*, they often reach to struggles of Black folks from the past and not to the struggles of Black folks today. In a context like the mayoral elections of an all-Black Southern city, their connections to Black struggles become valuable and translatable into political and economic gains.

"This is a fact. Never in the history of [a mayoral election] had Black people spent this amount of money. And in a week, I was told, they had raised $200k." A week before the runoff, he was leading comfortably in the polls. "I had a fourteen-point lead the Friday before the election. Just like that, [it disappeared]. For the people that were funding it, it was about business, but they used this: 'He wasn't Black enough.' It was done in three days."

Most of the money raised was used to paint him as a sellout. "The prevalent thought, a large segment of the African American community, believed that I took a whole bunch of money from white people in exchange for affinity to them." Along with labeling him a Republican, his opponents also advertised and presented Jonathan's family in a way that fit the image of someone who was disloyal to Black folks. "It was about ideology. . . . They spent $20k on a smear and a pamphlet that accused my wife of being a white woman. I mean, that kind of stuff. I still can't get over that. They went door to door handing out [fliers]. . . . They had photoshopped me with Mitt Romney."

He understood the tactic—he had anticipated it—but he was surprised at the length to which his opponents went to characterize him as they did. "There was no evidence, so they flat out lied. There was not enough safeguard." By that, he meant there were not enough people who came to his defense to defend him. Some of the people who propagated the narrative were people he had known his whole life: he attended the same church with one, he was good friends with another, and another had thrown him a baby shower at their house.

"This argument is hard to refute. I don't know how to refute the argument that I'm not Black enough." It was an odd thing to hear him say. But, understanding the context as much as he did, even he knew that the charges against his blackness weirdly and absurdly added up.

Around 4:30 p.m., we left his office to go pick up his daughter. His post-election life continued to display signs of the struggles of Black life, the subtle, less pernicious ones that were still part of his life, and the ones borne out of poverty that he no longer faced. The race/class tension still existed, but it was now out of the public's eye. It had become quieter again like it was for Dorian and Adrianne and many other upper-middle-class Black folks. He needed not worry about fitting his every move into an image of blackness that would get him votes.

His daughter attends a $1,500-a-month private school summer camp for kindergarteners. To get her, we left his West Jackson offices and drove north on Interstate 55. When we got off at the right exit, the street, lined with perfectly manicured trees, sharply contrasted the trash-littered streets we had left. It was raining when we arrived, so one of the camp counselors held an umbrella for her from the entrance of the gym to the car. True to her character, she was all smiles when she hopped in the back of the car.

"How are you? Did you have fun?"

"Yea," she responded with a raspy voice.

Jonathan asked more about what they did at camp. When she got over the shyness that my presence introduced, she responded that they played volleyball and did hula-hoop, but the teacher was part of the hula-hoop competition, so she did not win. When I asked how old she was, she said she was five and three-quarters. My question prompted her to share with her father an idea for her upcoming birthday party.

"Daddy, for my birthday, I'm thinking a games party. Games for boys and games for girls."

"What are girl games?" Jonathan asked, trying to push her not to think so strictly in gendered categories. She could not respond, but added that both of her parents would have to play.

She told her father that she wanted to go to Wendy's. Jonathan chuckled. He was not going to feed her that.

"No, I'm going to make some pork chops at home," he attempted to redirect.

"I don't want pork chops; it's too spicy."

"Okay, I won't make 'em spicy."

"I want Wendy's." Her father refused again.

"No. No fast food today." I wondered if they had fast food other times.

She kept pressing. She was determined to win. Jonathan knew that it would be a losing battle, so he compromised and decided to take her to get something to eat from McDade's, a local grocery store chain.

"What's your favorite food?" I asked as we pulled into the parking lot.

"Salad. I like healthy food," she responded. I was surprised to hear that coming from a five-and-three-quarter-year old, and one who just asked for Wendy's.

Jonathan affirmed her response with a nod. "She loves her some salad."

She added that she likes lettuce and cucumbers in her salad and, sometimes, onions. At McDade's, we walked to their already-prepared food. She asked for steak. She and I shared a laugh when the store attendant thought she had asked for cake. For her sides, she chose mac and cheese and greens. While checking out, we ran into her best friend's father, a white man who, I learned later, was a doctor. Apparently, her friend had been absent from camp. The father explained that the best friend was visiting family in Alabama.

They were still moving into their new house, so it was not completely furnished. The house was built in the 1950s by a white judge who had the same last name as Jonathan. As we pulled into the garage, he explained that it was apparent that they had maids because of the layout of the house. And the maids were most likely Black women. The first room closest to the garage had been for the maid. The house also had two driveways, one for the homeowners and the other for the help.

The racialized architecture of their new home was not lost on him.[7] It was a reminder to Jonathan of the hundreds of Black women who worked in homes like the one in which he now lives. He was familiar with their stories. He knows that many of them lived in and around places like Georgetown and probably took segregated buses to work every day. He may even know some of their children personally, especially the successful ones who now live in neighborhoods like his. He is probably less familiar with the less successful ones, the ones who are still living in and around the neighborhoods in which they grew up, neighborhoods that have seen better days. Jonathan had turned the maid's room into his home office. His quick explanation, which he offered as soon as we entered his house, made it obvious that this symbol of past Black struggle stayed on his mind.

After he gave me a tour of the house, Jonathan changed from his dress pants, brown shoes, and dress shirt to a pair of gym shorts and a t-shirt. He got out the pork chops and soaked them in Worcestershire sauce. He then sprinkled garlic powder, salt, and pepper before taking it out to his gas grill. We watched PBS News as we grilled. A few minutes on the fire and the pork chops were done. We were both very excited about the meat, so we did not prepare any sides.

"You ain't a visitor no more, so you gonna have to serve yourself." We put two pieces of meat on our plates. Juice dripped from the center of the meat when I cut it, and the seasoning still sizzled on top of it.

His wife entered just as we were complimenting ourselves on how well-cooked and seasoned the pork chops were. She had given up meat at that time, so she was unimpressed. She was coming from her Junior League meeting—she was a member of the then all-white (and racist) organization conspicuously depicted in *The Help*. At their meeting, they held a session about food safety in preparation for volunteering at a local nonprofit. She shared some of what she had taken away from their session.

"The thing I learned from that session was that we are food snobs." The presenter, a health care professional, spoke to them about the many side effects of eating canned food. "I mean, who eats veggies from a can? I know some people do, but I'm definitely a food snob." I listened attentively.

She also mentioned how they had to do diversity training for the organization's members entering poor communities to take part in service projects. "And it wasn't just for the white people, but also for the Black people. Like, can you leave your $1,000 purse in the car as you go volunteer? Or, can you pay attention to the kids when you go be with them for thirty minutes instead of being on your phone? Or, can you mingle with the kids instead of clustering up in one corner?" She made more comments about her frustration with her peers in the group, especially the ones who are Black, who consciously lived so far from the experiences of poor people. She was indignant toward them, not in a holier-than-thou sort of way but in a "we should do better" sort of way. Her message seemed to be as much to her peers as it was to herself.

Their daughter watched the television that hung in the kitchen while she finished her meal. We stood around their island and continued our conversations, which oscillated through different topics. Eventually, it returned to the conversation that Jonathan and I began at Subway. Jonathan's wife does not like to talk about the campaign. She had never wanted him to run for office, but she lovingly played her role. For someone like her, a lawyer who is keen on protecting her privacy, the personal attacks were her nightmares coming true. At the same time, she was unsurprised by the argument that her husband was not Black enough. In fact, on some days, she expressed the same. She knew, as did Jonathan, that they were going to do that.

"You're so comfortable around Black people, [but] it doesn't seem like they're comfortable around you," she commented.

"I'm comfortable," he shot back.

"But they're not comfortable around you."

He did not have much of an answer. We switched topics again.

Several hours later, on my way out, past the elegant stairs that led up to their bedrooms, through their formal living room, down the stairs, and past the maid's room, Jonathan made one more comment about race and class.

"My dad didn't teach us to need no validation. We validate ourselves. [My wife] needs to be doing all that—The Junior League, Jack and Jill, all that—to feel validated. I don't need all that. I'm in The Boulé because of her and Dr. Cooley." I had heard him make some of these comments to his wife before.

I only halfway believed him. Maybe it was true that he did not need anyone to validate his blackness. It was also very true that his class invalidated his blackness. And that stung.

Conclusion

CHAPTER FIFTEEN

Studying Food, Race, and the South

I BECAME INTERESTED in this project three years before it began. After spending most of a late evening at the library, I plopped down on my couch to watch television before heading to bed. As had become my ritual during my first year of graduate school in the dairy state (Wisconsin), I was digging into a bowl of ice cream while channel surfing. I usually stopped on ESPN, but on this particular night, I turned to a documentary on BET called *Heart of the City: Dying to Eat in Jackson*.[1] It told stories about the eating habits of African Americans in Jackson, Mississippi, and about some of the pressing health concerns they faced. I found it fascinating because it attempted to understand a social problem by talking to researchers and health professionals and by showing the lives of ordinary people in their homes and communities. The people in the documentary explained that most of what they ate was what their mothers and grandmothers ate, and what their grandmothers ate was what *their* mothers and grandmothers ate. So, a significant part of their food culture came from family traditions going back several generations.

One gripping portion of the documentary covered a sixty-something-year-old diabetic woman who died and was buried next to several other family members who had also died from diabetes-related illnesses. In many ways, the story of her death served as the impetus for this project. It forced me to reflect on something I had never considered: how people make decisions about what they eat. Looking at my eating habits and how I seek out hard-to-find ingredients and call my mother in Ghana for instructions on cooking my favorite Ghanaian dishes, I could attest that family traditions mattered, but they are not all that mattered. The ice cream I held in my hand while watching the documentary was evidence. It had nothing to do with my upbringing, yet it became a staple in my diet. Unfortunately for those in Jackson, the documentary argued, the most meaningful foods to them are also foods that cause many health problems. Giving them up would be to give up a significant aspect of their cultural identity. So, as the title suggested, people are quite literally *dying to eat*.

The documentary and the puzzle it introduced remained with me for quite some time. This ethnography may not have answered my initial concern, but I think I have raised, and hopefully answered, questions that undergird the documentary's central thesis. I have asked about what Black Southerners are eating today. This concern has been couched in an exploration of the socioeconomic context of life in the South. I examined what has become of Southern food traditions. I reject the documentary's uncomplicated assertion that these food traditions have fully been passed down and reproduced. Finally, and more broadly, I have explored what all this says about Southern Black Americans in contemporary Mississippi.

One of my main goals has been to make more central to food studies an analysis of the socioeconomic context of life. I introduce a framework that I hope will serve other researchers. First, I propose that to explore food availability is to also look at how someone's life circumstances come to matter in how they feed themselves. I have illustrated that food availability, when objectively measured, misses how institutions that shape people's lives make certain foods available. As I observed, food availability is as much about the foods to which people make themselves available as it is about the availability determined by cultural structures and social (and economic) structures. Through conventions and norms, the cultural structures we are born into or in which we choose to participate also shape our food availability. Black Southern culture, in varying degrees, influenced food availability for the different class groups. But, among the Black middle and upper class, the intersections of race and class allowed for their participation in the modern food movement.

For Smack and other men who are homeless and living in extreme deprivations, the shelters and other service providers essentially determined their food availability. They ate what the service providers decided. Those who lived in poverty appeared to have more available to them, but they too were heavily constrained by their engagement with and navigation through the many institutions that are part of living with poverty. Because those in poverty, those in the middle class and those in the upper class encountered different social and economic structures and institutions, they had available to them different kinds of foods. Put simply, living in poverty and dealing with the social welfare benefits shaped the food availability of poor people in ways unfamiliar to the upper-middle-class.[2] As it turns out, food availability is about more than how far one lives from the grocery store. It is also about the policies of homeless shelters and other service providers and about inequalities in housing, employment opportunities, and social welfare.

Second, studying food choice within this framework requires analyzing how someone navigates the structures they encounter. Looking at people's food choices, I insist, displays the resources they have available to them and how they use their resources to solve the quotidian problem of getting something to eat. Even among those who are homeless, there remained a small semblance of control over what they put in their stomachs. Carl, Ray, Minister Montgomery, and the others at times rejected the foods they were offered. At other times, they refused to do what was required of them to receive the food. Among those living in poverty and especially for those in the middle class, understanding food choices came in better focus. With them, I saw how their varying life circumstances allowed them to make food decisions based on habits and traditions in their pasts, paradoxes, and problems they face in the present—as well as their efforts to resolve them and outlooks and projections of themselves in the future.

Food did not structure the day-to-day lives of people in poverty as it did for the homeless men, but it was a constant and significant source of stress. Because they spent a lot of energy attempting to mitigate other concerns, like finding a decent apartment and a job, they attended to their families' need for food at the eleventh hour, when they could no longer bear the hunger. Interestingly, this was much more the case for Zenani than it was for Ms. Bea. Food was more scarce for Zenani than it was for Ms. Bea. When the poverty that Ms. Bea lived with became more uncertain, it markedly changed how she cooked the traditional meals she was accustomed to eating. The drain of poverty restricted their food choices so immensely that I came away from my work convinced that any successful food policy also has to be an anti-poverty policy. If social programs that attempt to change the food choices of people who live in poverty have any chance of success, they have to be equally committed to easing poverty constraints.[3]

Finally, studying food consumption in the manner I have proposed provides an avenue for social-psychological analysis, especially the relationship between food and identity. I use my exploration in taste to look at the internal dynamics of blackness. Ms. Monique and Charles experienced in their food choices some of the same contradictions and tensions they lived with as members of the Black lower-middle class. They exhibited some of the taste preferences of their white middle-class counterparts, but they lived in parts of town that did not have amenities for them to sustain their tastes. At times, they had also to negotiate their taste and racial identities. This tension was one reason the Davises had to close Lumpkins— they were not able to offer their clients in West Jackson the kind of soul food they wanted.

When Dorian, Adrianne, and Othor went to high-end restaurants, they were often the only Black folks there. Their presence stuck out to them and to the servers and chefs and everyone else who looked on, knowing that they were in a "white space." Because they did not wish to forsake their racial identity for their class identity, most wealthier Black people voluntarily chose to align themselves with foods of working-class Black people. For instance, Jonathan mostly rejected "fancy" foods and, instead, preferred foods that are considered staples of a (Black and poor) Southern diet—chicken, greens, cornbread, and fruit pies.

About race and blackness, I, first, make a case for food scholars to view food not as a reflection of race and racialization but as a part of it. Food is one of the tools used to construct, refine, and reconstruct racial boundaries. This was as true during the slavery and Reconstruction Eras as it was during the Civil Rights and Obama Eras. The second goal in this work is to illustrate and encourage a return to studying Black life across class groups. As I have demonstrated, doing so shows the different ways Black folks across class groups encounter racialized social and cultural structures, how they navigate their encounters, and how their encounters and navigations reflect changing racial identities. These differences disrupt homogenizing the contemporary experiences of Black folks in the South. They highlight what it means to be Black in different class groups today.

Given that Black folks exist in the public imagination as the most marginalized racial group in America, the homeless men I got to know viewed their lives as manifestations of that sentiment. Even with their lives in disarray, they did not experience a disjuncture between their race and class identities, as did well-to-do Black folks. Instead, they viewed their lot in life as what was to be expected. They sharply and harshly contrasted their lives with those of white folks who were also in homelessness. For those who endured poverty, one of the few areas of tranquility in their lives was their racial identification. Their blackness was the default blackness. The perpetual equation of Black Mississippians with poverty made them the epitome of blackness. When politicians wanted to show their Black cultural capital, they touted their connections with poor Black folks. People in poverty found solace and strength in their racial identity—they lived the "Black struggle." For those in the lower-middle class, their food consciousness illustrated the tension between their race and class; their food choices, which were based on attributes generally ascribed to the (white) middle class, rubbed against their racial identity, which was often classed as poor. Members of the upper-middle class experienced this tension as well. It existed implicitly and quietly in their lives, especially in the segregated spaces in which they often "intruded"—their all-white workplaces, neighborhoods, and social clubs. It became more explicit for Jonathan when he ran for mayor and his class status became a challenge to his racial identity. He lost the race because his opponents made the class that he was a sellout to his race.

In terms of what we can learn about the South, my objectives have been humble. At its most basic, it is to showcase to more scholars, particularly sociologists, the importance of recasting our gaze below the Mason-Dixon Line, a region of the country that is often ignored. It is to bring us closer to the intimate details of life in the South and, in so doing, resist the simple caricatured story that most Americans believe about a place like Mississippi. At another level, my goal has been to add fire to the realignment of a sociology of the South and a sociology in the South. It has been to show that social problems in the US South resemble those elsewhere. Even if they might manifest differently, and even if solutions to these problems may require local strategies, many of today's pressing issues—police brutality, housing inequality, and food injustices—are rooted in similar large-scale nationwide concerns. Another part of my agenda has been to insist that historical explorations of the South ought to be coupled with investigating the contemporary South. All efforts to reconcile with the region's past that excludes an honest engagement with the present is, in my view, futile.

As of April 2021, Jonathan still lives in Jackson with his family. He watches on as the city continues to struggle with some of the same problems he hoped to fix as a mayor. When I last spoke to him about the elections, I could tell that it still dug at him. He still believed he could have served the city well. Chokwe Lumumba tragically passed away less than a year into his term. So, after an interim mayor, his son, Antar Chokwe Lumumba, ran and won. He is now in his second term. He is a dynamic leader, but in Jonathan's eyes, the younger Lumumba still has not been able to get a handle on the city's infrastructure problems. The last time I saw Jonathan, we were both in Paris, France. I was spending my leave there. He had come to visit with his family. We sat at the bar of the restaurant where he was staying and laughed as we had done at The Penguin.

Dorian, Adrianne, and Othor are all well. COVID-19 shut down the activities of the Friday Cocktail group. Othor has an online live-stream show where he discusses city politics. I have enjoyed revisiting the city through this show. In several conversations with

Charles, we have continued our discussions about national politics. I was delighted to learn that he has returned to graduate school to study public policy. He is going to get the PhD that he so richly deserves. I last saw all of them in 2018.

Among the Davis family, Melvin Jr. finished his engineering degree at Jackson State. He now lives and works in Texas. James graduated from Tuskegee University and is also an engineer. He's also experimenting with starting a consulting firm and sharpening his stage presence as a stand-up comic in Tennessee. Charles graduated from Rice University. He's taking a year off before applying to a PhD program in the natural sciences. Ava is a second-year student at Tulane University studying studio art and early childhood education. Ms. Monique and Mr. Melvin are almost empty nesters. Benjamin is a senior in high school and Daniel is a freshman. I have not seen any of them since my 2018 visit, but I have been in touch via phone, especially with James and Ava.

Zenani and her sisters still live in the same neighborhood in Jackson. Life has gotten a little kinder to her. She has a steady job at the VA hospital. When she got the job a few years back, she called me to share the good news. She believes the job was from an application we filled out together. Things are more stable, but poverty still weighs upon her life and that of her sisters. And the pandemic has made it heavier to bear.

The last time I saw Ms. Bea, she had moved again into an apartment in West Jackson, just down the street from The Opportunity Center. She was all smiles, but she also admitted that things were hard. When her daughter's employer in Mississippi transferred her to a new post in Iowa, she decided to go with her. She has been living there for three years. She goes back to Jackson every once in a while to visit.

I have lost touch with most of the men in homelessness. I have not seen or heard from Smack, Minister Montgomery, or Charles since I left Jackson in 2012. When I returned in 2016, I ran into Toni, Minister Montgomery's friend who got banned for the cookies. He was a home health aide for an older Black woman. I have also lost touch with Carl, Ray, Eric, and Willie. The Opportunity Center is now run by Christie Burnett, who has been transforming the place, according to Heather Ivery, the former director.

COVID-19 has made her job more difficult. One of the places that provides beds closed out of fear of the virus spreading. Others significantly reduced their intake to adhere to social distance regulations. At the height of the pandemic, there were only eleven beds available. The OC also closed at first, but reopened in November and has remained open, twenty-four hours a day. Staying open has been a response to the sharp rise in homicides that Jackson, and many other cities, are experiencing. Christie remains optimistic about the work that she and her staff are doing. They are using rapid rehousing tactics to get as many people as possible into their own housing and off the streets. Matthew, the man who had gotten banned for pushing a white man, is one of her success stories. He still comes to The Opportunity Center, but he comes to help serve the current clients.

CHAPTER SIXTEEN

Afterword and Acknowledgments

ETHNOGRAPHIC PROJECTS often leave an indelible mark on their authors. This left the same on me. It grew me. It turned my curiosity about the region into a love for it. It shook my understanding of my profession, for the good and the not-so-good. And, it shaped my taste.

Before this project, I did not know much about the South, but I was curious about it, owing to my days as an MLK scholar as an undergrad at Ithaca College, where we read about the region's importance in discussions of racial inequalities. While in graduate school, I followed my roommate to his home in Nashville on several occasions. He took me around his city and showed me Fisk, where I bowed to the statue of Du Bois, and Tennessee State University, where I experienced a proper homecoming. Those visits and a few others endeared the South to me. After living in Jackson for those thirteen months and after graduating, I welcomed the opportunity to make a home in North Carolina. For me, the South feels more like being in Ghana than being anywhere else in the United States for many good and not-so-good reasons. It is warm in temperament and temperature, but it is also intolerant. I enjoy the good parts, and the bad parts remind me of the work yet to be done. What I learned in Jackson, especially about the importance of local politics, has stayed with me.

My time in Jackson also transformed how I think about my profession. Those months put me closer to the sources and mechanisms of poverty than any reading I have ever done. Most importantly, I witnessed the lived human consequences of American poverty and homelessness. It was a critical education. It burned into my consciousness a sense of urgency for engaging in social reform through my scholarship and all other means. It also proved to me the human capability for abundant empathy and the deep fulfillment of communing with people who are consistently ignored.

At the same time, this project also revealed the brutal personal consequences of conducting research in this manner. Ethnography may expand our humanity and make us better and more sympathetic professionals, but it often also has the opposite effect on our personal lives. It takes us away from our homes and leaves to our partners the labor of caring for our households and our children. The time and obsession that this craft requires for any chance of success can be destructive. It was a significant part of the end of a marriage for me. This project is probably not to blame, but it certainly did not help. Then, there is the guilt it brews inside us; the guilt of trading dirty stories of pain for money and prestige, as another ethnographer put it.[1] The guilt can be a source of motivation to keep pushing on, but it can also be disheartening. No amount of work on my part can even the equation.

Finally, the project shaped my taste. Because, on any given day, I went from eating at a soup kitchen to eating at the most elegant restaurants that Jackson has to offer. This project quite literally calibrated my taste buds. I ate some nasty food and some fantastic food. I ate things that I never want to see again, some things that I would be happy to eat every day, and some things that were good at first try, but no longer interest me. And, it was not just with foods; it was also with cocktails. It is singularly responsible for my appreciation for the differences between an Old Fashioned, a Sazerac, and a Vieux Carré.

Acknowledgments

Mustafa Emirbayer, you were the first person with whom I shared the idea for this project. I know it was a decent one from how your face lit up. Thank you for your constant support. I hope you know how much influence you have had on my professional life. I'm also so grateful for your friendship.

Matt and Tessa Desmond, thank you for exhibiting to me how to balance family responsibilities with this type of work. I treasure our abiding friendship. Craig Werner, you believed in this project from the get-go, even though, at the time, I had never been to Mississippi. I'm so proud to be one of your students. Justin Schaup, Wes Markofsi, Regina Baker, Victor Ray, Anna Haskins, Sarah Bruch, Meagan Shoji, Celson Villegas, Elena Shih, Anima Adjepong, it gives me so much joy to cheer for all of you from afar. Thanks for your friendships. Ethan, bro, I'll never forget when we ran around the city and took one thousand photos. Thanks for adding your touch to this project.

I am mentored by three amazing Black (women) sociologists who probably think of me not as a mentee but as a friend. Christy Erving, Jean Beaman, and Tiffany Joseph, I'm talking about you three. Thank you.

Bobby Smith II, writing with you made this project better. Thanks for helping me get an article. B. Brian Foster, I can't tell you how many times I tried to steal so many of your words, but nobody can do it like you do it. I'm thrilled to have a front seat to watch your rise.

Zandria Robinson, remember when I came up to the University of Mississippi to visit you? You assured me that this project would be something. Thank you. I also met the good folks at the Southern Foodways Alliance during that trip. John T. Edge, Mary Beth Lassetter, and Amy Evans, I don't know what made you put a graduate student who barely knew anything about the South on the main stage. I am so grateful to you and the whole SFA staff for believing in this work.

Gayle Kaufman and Gerardo Marti, I am immensely grateful for your support and mentorship at Davidson College. When you hired me, I had not a single publication to my name. Thanks for believing in my potential. Amanda Martinez and Aarushi Bhandari, we have a lot to live up to. I am excited to work with you and continue to build our department together.

Hilton Kelly and Laurian Bowles, two-thirds of the Cape Town Trio, thanks for all the work you do to support and protect us from an institution that is trying to get itself out of its white supremacist roots. It is not lost on me that I am because you are—I hope you both know that. Fuji Lozada, thanks for always talking sense into me, even when I did not want to hear it. John Wortheimer and Julio Ramirez, thank you for your close mentorship. Thank you for encouraging me to follow some of my crazy ideas and for showing me how to sanely carry them out. Alice Wimers, Takiyah Haper-Shipman, Sundi Richardson, Daniel Lynds, Daniel Layman, Kuba Kabala, Mary Muchane, LuAnne Sledge, and Helen Cho, thank you for making Davidson a warm place to work.

Meagan Levinson, the praise you get from all your authors is so well-deserved. Let me add mine: You are the Phil Jackson and the C. Vivian Stringer of the editing game. You saved this work from so many random metaphors, puns, academic jargon, and clunky sentences. Thanks for always bringing me back to the important ideas. The book is better for it and I am a better writer because of it. I hope the stars align for us to work together again. And to Ellen Foos, Katie Stileman, Kate Hensley, and the rest of the staff at Princeton University Press, thank you for being so good at what you do, and for being so kind. Diedre Hammons, thanks for sharpening my voice.

Jason Thompson, thank you for the long conversations. You know, for most of this research, I slept under a roof that belonged to you. Thank you for that and for your friendship. Jed, thanks for reading everything and providing line-by-line comments. You might have a career as an editor, man. R. L. Naves, thanks for all the conversations on Taco Tuesday.

Camille Rogers, Dalayna Tillman, Shatina Williams, Lonna Dawson, Tashonda Frazier, Edward Cole, Kwadwo Owusu Ofori, Greg Okotie, C.J. Harmon, Courtney Peck, and Patrick Lee, y'all give me life and hold me down. Torsheika Maddox, Heather O'Connell, and Michelle Robinson, you always give me a place to come back to when I drift away. Thank you.

Mama, the pages in this book reflect just a small portion of how you taught me to relate to people. All I am as an ethnographer comes from you. Dad, I am eternally grateful that you passed on to both Ce and me the love of books and words. Bonzi Wells (aka Joe Bronko), we got another one! Dr. Vicky, Pastor Nana, Ms. Samuela,

Mr. Jaydon, Mr. Oliver, and her Royal Highness, The Queen Mother (Mama Benny), thank you all for the love and support.

Stevo, Uncle, chale, what's up!

To my extended family worldwide, especially The Youngsters, I am so glad that we are pulling closer together despite the recent family tragedies. Sometimes, I wish we lived closer to each other, but then again, isn't it so amazing that our family covers so many continents? Kukuwa Ashun and I are getting ready to tell our story.

Caroline, my love, us finding each other is, I believe, an act of God. You've read every page of this and offered thoughtful feedback. More importantly, you have provided a warm and loving home to grow as a person and a scholar.

Jaden, what a joy it has been to witness your growth? I'm so proud of who you are and who you are becoming. While working on this project, I learned an important lesson from you. When, or if, you get around to reading this note, which will probably be when you are a bit older, come and ask and I'll share with you what I learned. Josephine, you came into our lives right as I was finishing this project. I'm listening to you breathing and cooing. At just twelve days old you have made our lives so much fuller.

To the residents of Jackson, Mississippi, everyone who has been named in this book and hundreds more who have not, words can't express how much richer my life now is because of the time I spent in your city. Writing about you is, by far, the most difficult intellectual exercise I have ever taken on. The fear of misrepresenting all your complexities never left me. I hope some of you will look fondly at what I have done. I hope the rest of you will forgive my shortcomings.

Finally, I thank the Ford Foundation Dissertation Fellowship, the American Sociological Association Minority Fellowship Program, and Davidson College, especially the Malcolm O. Partin Endowed Chair for their support as I finished the manuscript.

Chapter 1. Getting Something to Eat

1. Founded in the early 1900s in Philadelphia, The Boulé's mission was to bring together accomplished and educated men who were, at the time, isolated from one another and from the masses of Black Americans who remained under racial subjugation. Membership to the fraternity is, as it has always been, by invitation only. And, today, the annual dues cost thousands of dollars.

2. Sabrina Pendergrass, "Routing Black Migration to the Urban US South: Social Class and Sources of Social Capital in the Destination Selection Process," *Journal of Ethnic and Migration Studies* 39, no. 9 (November 1, 2013): 1441–59.

3. Howard Winant, "The Dark Side of the Force: One Hundred Years of the Sociology of Race," in *Sociology in America: A History*, ed. Craig Calhoun (Chicago: University of Chicago Press, 2007), 535–71.

4. Sheldon Hackney, "The Contradictory South," *Southern Cultures* 7, no. 4 (November 1, 2001): 70.

5. Larry J. Griffin, "The Promise of a Sociology of the South," *Southern Cultures* 7, no. 1 (February 1, 2001): 352–53; Zandria F. Robinson, *This Ain't Chicago: Race, Class, and Regional Identity in the Post-Soul South* (Chapel Hill, NC: University of North Carolina Press, 2014).

6. Mary Lou Finley et al., eds., *The Chicago Freedom Movement: Martin Luther King Jr. and Civil Rights Activism in the North* (Lexington: University Press of Kentucky, 2016); Charles Earl Jones, ed., *The Black Panther Party (Reconsidered)* (Baltimore, MD: Black Classic Press, 1998).

7. Charles Johnson, *The Negro in Chicago: A Study of Race Relations and a Race Riot* (Chicago: University of Chicago Press, 1922).

8. Hackney, "The Contradictory South."

9. David Bateman, Ira Katznelson, and John S. Lapinski, *Southern Nation: Congress and White Supremacy after Reconstruction* (Princeton, NJ: Princeton University Press, 2018).

10. Howard W. Odum, "Notes on the Study of Regional and Folk Society," *Social Forces* 10, no. 2 (1931): 164–75.

11. Anna Julia Cooper, *A Voice from the South by A Black Woman of The South* (Aldine Printing House, 1892); Howard W. Odum, *Race and Rumors of Race* (Chapel Hill, NC: University of North Carolina Press, 1943).

12. Karida L. Brown, *Gone Home: Race and Roots through Appalachia* (Chapel Hill, NC: University of North Carolina Press, 2018); Sabrina Pendergrass, "Routing Black Migration to the Urban US South: Social Class and Sources of Social Capital in the Destination Selection Process," *Journal of Ethnic and Migration Studies* 39, no. 9

(November 1,): 1441–59; Vanesa Ribas, *On the Line: Slaughterhouse Lives and the Making of the New South* (Oakland: University of California Press, 2015); Robinson, *This Ain't Chicago* (2014); B. Brian Foster, *I Don't Like the Blues: Race, Place, and the Backbeat of Black Life* (Chapel Hill, NC: University of North Carolina Press, 2020).

13. Carol Anderson, *White Rage: The Unspoken Truth of Our Racial Divide* (New York: Bloomsbury USA, 2017).

14. Timothy Williams and Alan Blinder, "Lawmakers Vote to Effectively Ban Abortion in Alabama," *New York Times*, May 15, 2019, https://www.nytimes.com/2019/05/14/us/abortion-law-alabama.html.

15. Alan Blinder, "North Carolina Lawmakers Met with Protests Over Bias Law," *New York Times*, December 21, 2017, https://www.nytimes.com/2016/04/26/us/north-carolina-house-bill-2.html.

16. Edward E. Baptist, *The Half Has Never Been Told: Slavery and the Making of American Capitalism* (New York: Basic Books, 2016).

17. Richard Rothstein, *The Color of Law: A Forgotten History of How Our Government Segregated America* (New York: Liveright, 2017).

18. W.E.B. Du Bois, *The Philadelphia Negro: A Social Study* (Philadelphia: University of Pennsylvania Press, 1899).

19. W. Lloyd Warner, "A Methodological Note," in *Black Metropolis: A Study of Negro Life in a Northern City* (Chicago: University of Chicago Press, 1945), 776.

20. Eugene Robinson, *Disintegration: The Splintering of Black America* (New York: Anchor Books, 2011).

21. Some notable exceptions include Mary Patillo-McCoy's *Black Picket Fences* (Chicago: University of Chicago Press, 1999) and Annette Lareau's *Unequal Childhoods* (Berkeley: University of California Press), both of which compare the experiences of poor and middle-class Black Americans.

22. Robinson, *This Ain't Chicago*, 18, 29.

23. Jennifer Jensen Wallach, *How America Eats: A Social History of U.S. Food and Culture* (Lanham, MD: Rowman & Littlefield Publishers, 2012); Mario Luis Small, David J. Harding, and Michèle Lamont, "Reconsidering Culture and Poverty," *The ANNALS of the American Academy of Political and Social Science*, 629, no. 1: 6–27.

24. Margaret Lombe et al., "Examining Effects of Food Insecurity and Food Choices on Health Outcomes in Households in Poverty," *Social Work in Health Care* 55, no. 6 (July 2, 2016): 440–60; G. Turrell, "Socioeconomic Differences in Food Preference and Their Influence on Healthy Food Purchasing Choices," *Journal of Human Nutrition and Dietetics* 11, no. 2 (April 1, 1998): 135–49.

25. Alan Beardsworth and Teresa Keil, *Sociology on the Menu: An Invitation to the Study of Food and Society*, (New York: Routledge, 1997); Jack Goody, *Cooking, Cuisine and Class: A Study in Comparative Sociology* (Cambridge: Cambridge University Press, 1996); Marvin Harris, *Good to Eat: Riddles of Food and Culture* (Long Grove, IL: Waveland Press, 1998).

26. Jessica Greenebaum, "Vegans of Color: Managing Visible and Invisible Stigmas," *Food, Culture & Society* 21, no. 5 (October 20, 2018): 680–97; Eric Holt-Giménez and Yi Wang, "Reform or Transformation? The Pivotal Role of Food Justice

in the U.S. Food Movement," *Race/Ethnicity: Multidisciplinary Global Contexts* 5, no. 1 (2011): 83–102; Stephen Schneider, "Good, Clean, Fair: The Rhetoric of the Slow Food Movement," *College English* 70, no. 4 (2008):384–402.

27. William H. Sewell, "A Theory of Structure: Duality, Agency, and Transformation," *American Journal of Sociology* 98, no. 1 (1992): 1–29.

28. Mustafa Emirbayer and Ann Mische, "What Is Agency?," *The American Journal of Sociology* 103, no. 4 (January 1, 1998): 962–1023.

29. Itai Vardi, "Feeding Race," *Food, Culture & Society* 13, no. 3 (September 1, 2010): 371–96.

30. John Dollard, *Caste and Class in a Southern Town*, (Doubleday, 1957); St. Clair Drake and Horace R Cayton, *Black Metropolis: A Study of Negro Life in a Northern City* (Chicago: University of Chicago Press, 1945); Hortense Powdermaker, *After Freedom: A Cultural Study in The Deep South* (New York: Viking Press, 1939); Zandria F. Robinson, *This Ain't Chicago: Race, Class, and Regional Identity in the Post-Soul South* (Chapel Hill, NC: University of North Carolina Press Books, 2014); John L. Jackson Jr., *Harlemworld: Doing Race and Class in Contemporary Black America* (Chicago: University of Chicago Press, 2010).

31. Milton M. Gordon, "Social Class in American Sociology," *American Journal of Sociology* 55, no. 3 (1949): 262–68; Erik Olin Wright, "Social Class," in *Encyclopedia of Social Theory*, ed. George Ritzer (Thousand Oaks, CA: SAGE Publications, 2004) 718–24.

32. To understand their diverse experiences, I spent 80 percent of my time with persons in one class group and the remaining 20 percent of my time building and maintaining relationships with those representing the others. I spent 80 percent of my time during January, February, and March 2012 with people experiencing homelessness and 20 percent of my time building relationships with those who were working class, middle class, and upper-middle class.

Chapter 2. Soul Food and Jackson

1. Frederick Douglass Opie, *Hog and Hominy: Soul Food from Africa to America* (New York: Columbia University Press, 2010); Michael W. Twitty, *The Cooking Gene: A Journey Through African American Culinary History in the Old South* (New York, NY: Amistad, 2017), 163.

2. Opie, *Hog and Hominy*, 4.

3. William Dillon Piersen, *From Africa to America: African American History from the Colonial Era to the Early Republic,1526–1790* (Woodbridge, CT: Twayne Publishers, 1996), 11.

4. James A. Rawley and Stephen D. Behrendt, *The Transatlantic Slave Trade: A History* (Lincoln: University of Nebraska Press, 2005), 256.

5. William Dillon Piersen, *From Africa to America: African American History from the Colonial Era to the Early Republic, 1526–1790* (New York; London: Twayne Publishers; Prentice Hall International, 1996).

6. Rawley and Behrendt, *The Transatlantic Slave Trade: A History*.

7. Byron Hurt, *Soul Food Junkies*, DVD, Documentary, 2012.

8. Despite their efforts, revolt was the norm. For a thorough analysis of slave revolts, see Eric Robert Taylor, *If We Must Die: Shipboard Insurrections in the Era of the Atlantic Slave Trade* (Baton Rouge: Louisiana State University Press, 2009).

9. Sylviane A. Diouf, *Fighting the Slave Trade: West African Strategies* (Athens: Ohio University Press, 2003), 125.

10. In a forthcoming book, Bobby Smith II explores how, in the twentieth century, food continued to be both a source of and resistance to domination for Black Americans in the US South. Bobby Smith II, *Food Power Politics* (Chapel Hill, NC: University of North Carolina Press, Forthcoming).

11. John W. Blassingame, *The Slave Community: Plantation Life in the Antebellum South* (Oxford: Oxford University Press, 1979), 250.

12. Sam Bowers Hilliard, *Hog Meat and Hoecake: Food Supply in the Old South, 1840–1860* (Carbondale: Southern Illinois University Press, 1972), 56–69.

13. Sam Bowers Hilliard, *Hog Meat and Hoecake*, 251.

14. Opie, *Hog and Hominy: Soul Food from Africa to America*, 25.

15. Sam Bowers Hilliard, *Hog Meat and Hoecake*, 55.

16. Eugene D. Genovese, *Roll, Jordan, Roll: The World the Slaves Made* (New York: Random House Digital, 2011), xvii.

17. John T. Edge, *The Potlikker Papers: A Food History of the Modern South* (New York: Penguin Press, 2017).

18. Frederick Douglass and Harriet Jacobs, *Narrative of the Life of Frederick Douglass, an American Slave & Incidents in the Life of a Slave Girl* (New York: Random House, 2011), 140.

19. Frederick Douglass, *My Bondage and My Freedom* (Miller, Orton & Mulligan, 1855), 253.

20. John Blassingame confirms that most slaves who wrote about their experience "complained that they had at least one owner who did not give them enough food. Sometimes, even when slaves generally received enough food provisions ran low." John W. Blassingame, *The Slave Community: Plantation Life in the Antebellum South* (Oxford: Oxford University Press, 1979), 254.

21. Blassingame, *The Slave Community: Plantation Life in the Antebellum South*, 577.

22. Fredrika Bremer, Adolph Benson, and Carrie Catt, *America of the Fifties: Letters of Fredrika Bremer* (New York: Applewood Books, 2007), 122–23.

23. Harriet A. Jacobs, *Incidents in the Life of a Slave Girl*, ed. Jean Fagan Yellin (Cambridge, MA: Harvard University Press, 1987), 119.

24. In his recent book, *The Cooking Gene,* and in his presentations, Michael Twitty has archived and preserved some of these early cooking traditions. Twitty, *The Cooking Gene: A Journey Through African American Culinary History in the Old South* (New York: Amistad, 2017).

25. Marcie Cohen Ferris, *The Edible South: The Power of Food and the Making of an American Region* (Chapel Hill: University of North Carolina Press, 2016), 48–58.

26. Opie, *Hog and Hominy*, 50.

27. Henry Louis Gates, Mark Lund, and Winslow Andia, "Reconstruction: America after the Civil War," Documentary (PBS, February 2019), http://www.imdb.com /title/tt9701076/.

28. Rayford W. Logan, *The Negro in American Life and Thought: The Nadir, 1877–1901* (New York: Dial Press, 1954).

29. Stewart E. Tolnay, "The African American 'Great Migration' and Beyond," *Annual Review of Sociology* 29, no. 1 (2003): 209–32.

30. Frederick Douglass Opie, *Hog and Hominy*, 57.

31. Isabel Wilkerson, *The Warmth of Other Suns: The Epic Story of America's Great Migration* (New York: Vintage, 2011), 240.

32. St. Clair Drake and Horace R Cayton, *Black Metropolis: A Study of Negro Life in a Northern City* (Chicago: University of Chicago Press, 1945), 608.

33. "In years of low prices, a tenant's money and his store of pork, meal, and sweet potatoes are usually exhausted by Christmas, or even before. He then faces a period of from two and one-half to three months (before advances begin in late March or April), when he has neither money, credit, nor stored food. A second period of destitution follows the stopping of advances in July, when he is again without money, credit, nor stored food, and when the heat has withered the spring gardens," Allison Davis, Burleigh B. Gardner, and Mary R. Gardner, *Deep South: A Study of Social Class and Color Caste in a Southern City* (Chicago: University of Chicago Press, 1941), 378.

34. Opie, *Hog and Hominy*, 101.

35. Leda Cooks, "You Are What You (Don't) Eat? Food, Identity, and Resistance," *Text and Performance Quarterly* 29, no. 1 (January 1, 2009): 94–110; Opie, *Hog and Hominy*, 106.

36. Opie, *Hog and Hominy*, 125, 129, 132; William L. Van Deburg, *New Day in Babylon: The Black Power Movement and American Culture, 1965–1975*: (Chicago: University of Chicago Press, 1993).

37. Lawrence D. Bobo and Michael C. Dawson, "A Change Has Come: Race, Politics, and the Path to the Obama Presidency," *Du Bois Review: Social Science Research on Race 6*, no. 01 (2009): 1–14; Camille Zubrinsky Charles, "The Dynamics of Racial Residential Segregation," *Annual Review of Sociology* 29, no. 1 (2003): 167–207; Robert A. Hummer and Erin R. Hamilton, "Race and Ethnicity in Fragile Families," *The Future of Children* 20, no. 2 (2010): 113–31; Grace Kao and Jennifer S. Thompson, "Racial and Ethnic Stratification in Educational Achievement and Attainment," *Annual Review of Sociology* 29, no. 1 (2003): 417–42; Mary Pattillo, "Black Middle-Class Neighborhoods," *Annual Review of Sociology* 31, no. 1 (2005): 305–29; Sean F. Reardon and Kendra Bischoff, "Income Inequality and Income Segregation," *American Journal of Sociology* 116, no. 4 (January 2011): 1092–153; Sara Wakefield and Christopher Uggen, "Incarceration and Stratification," *Annual Review of Sociology* 36, no. 1 (2010): 387–406; David R. Williams and Pamela Braboy Jackson, "Social Sources Of Racial Disparities In Health," *Health Affairs* 24, no. 2 (March 1, 2005): 325–34.

38. H.W. Brands, *Andrew Jackson: His Life and Times*, (New York: Anchor, 2006); Robert V. Remini, *Martin Van Buren and the Making of the Democratic Party* (New York: Columbia University Press, 1968).

39. Sheldon Hackney, "The Contradictory South," *Southern Cultures* 7, no. 4 (November 1, 2001): 65–80; Charles Reagan Wilson, "Whose South?: Lessons Learned from Studying the South at the University of Mississippi," *Southern Cultures* 22, no. 4 (2016): 96–110.

40. Edward E. Baptist, *The Half Has Never Been Told: Slavery and the Making of American Capitalism* (Philadelphia: Basic Books, 2016).

41. Emory M. Thomas, *The Confederate Nation, 1861–1865* (New York: Harper & Row, 1979).

42. Carol Anderson, *White Rage: The Unspoken Truth of Our Racial Divide* (2017).

43. Richard Wright lived in and wrote about these times in *Black Boy*. Richard Wright, *Black Boy (American Hunger: A Record of Childhood and Youth)* (New York: Harper & Brothers, 1945).

44. John Dittmer, *Local People: The Struggle for Civil Rights in Mississippi* (Champaign, IL: University of Illinois Press, 1994), 88–89.

45. Raymond Arsenault, *Freedom Riders: 1961 and the Struggle for Racial Justice* (Oxford: Oxford University Press, 2007).

46. "State and County Quick Facts" (US Census Bureau, 2014).

47. Robinson, *This Ain't Chicago.*

48. Byron Orey, "Deracialization, Racialization, or Something in between?: The Making of a Black Mayor in Jackson, Mississippi," *Politics & Policy* 34, no. 4 (2006): 814–36.

49. These descriptions of Jackson are based on my experiencing of the city during the time of my fieldwork, January to November 2012 and summer 2016.

50. "State and County Quick Facts" (US Census Bureau, 2014).

51. "State and County Quick Facts" (US Census Bureau, 2014).

52. Charles E. Cobb, *On the Road to Freedom: A Guided Tour of the Civil Rights Trail* (Chapel Hill, NC: Algonquin Books, 2007).

53. Grace Britton Sweet and Benjamin Bradley, *Church Street: The Sugar Hill of Jackson, Mississippi* (Charleston, SC: The History Press, 2013).

54. "American Community Survey" (US Census Bureau, 2011).

Chapter 3. Smack—Late Afternoons

1. Single homeless adults are more likely to be men than women. The US Conference of Mayors reports that 67.5 percent of the single homeless population is male, and this single population makes up 76 percent of the homeless population surveyed (National Commission for the Homeless 2009). Additionaly, homeless men face harsher financial hardships than women because they seldom qualify for service programs that favor families (Barrett A. Lee, Kimberly A. Tyler, and James D. Wright,

"The New Homelessness Revisited, *Annual Review of Sociology* 36 (2010, 501–521). Several other studies explore the gendered nature of homelessness. (See, for example, Duneier 2001; Jasinki et al. 2010; Liebow 1993).

2. Martha R. Burt, *Over the Edge: The Growth of Homelessness in the 1980s* (New York: Russell Sage Foundation, 1993); Jana L. Jasinki et al., *Hard Lives, Mean Streets: Violence in the Lives of Homeless Women* (Lebanon, NH: Northeastern University Press, 2010); Continuum of Care Homeless Assistance Programs, "HUD's 2012 Continuum of Care Homeless Assistance Programs Homeless Populations and Subpopulations," 2012; Joel Blau, *The Visible Poor: Homelessness in the United States* (Oxford: Oxford University Press, 1993); Christopher Jencks, *The Homeless* (Cambridge, MA: Harvard University Press, 1995); Barrett A. Lee, Kimberly A. Tyler, and James D. Wright, "The New Homelessness Revisited," *Annual Review of Sociology* 36, no. 1 (2010): 501–21; Liebow, *Tell Them Who I Am* (1993); David A. Snow and Leon Anderson, *Down on Their Luck: A Study of Homeless Street People* (Berkeley: University of California Press, 1993).

3. Mitchell Duneier, *Sidewalk* (New York: Macmillan, 2001).

4. Elijah Anderson, *Streetwise: Race, Class, and Change in an Urban Community* (Chicago: University of Chicago Press, 1990).

5. Snow and Anderson, *Down on Their Luck.*

6. These observations hold for more recent works. See Teresa Gowan, *Hobos, Hustlers, and Backsliders: Homeless in San Francisco* (Minneapolis: University Of Minnesota Press, 2010); Forrest Stuart, *Down, Out, and Under Arrest: Policing and Everyday Life in Skid Row* (Chicago: University of Chicago Press, 2016); Brandon Andrew Robinson, *Coming Out to the Streets: LGBTQ Youth Experiencing Homelessness* (Oakland, CA: University of California Press, 2020).

7. Barrett A. Lee and Meredith J. Greif, "Homelessness and Hunger," *Journal of Health and Social Behavior* 49, no. 1 (March 1, 2008): 11.

8. Lee and Greif, "Homelessness and Hunger," 11.

9. Lee and Greif, "Homelessness and Hunger," 3–19.

10. Homelessness exposure types are defined in different ways by different scholars, but in general differ according to two factors: the number of episodes of homelessness experienced by an individual and the duration of each episode. Lee and Greif (2008) consider the *chronically* homeless to be those whose current homelessness experience has lasted at least two years and who have experienced two or more spells of homelessness during their lifetime. They consider the *transitionally* homeless to be those currently experiencing their first spell of homelessness and who have been homeless less than one year. Dennis P. Culhane et al., "Testing a Typology of Family Homelessness Based on Patterns of Public Shelter Utilization in Four US Jurisdictions: Implications for Policy and Program Planning," *Housing Policy Debate* 18, no. 1 (2007): 1–28, https://doi.org/10.1080/10511482.2007.9521591; Jeffrey Grunberg and Paula F. Eagle, "Shelterization: How the Homeless Adapt to Shelter Living," *Psychiatric Services* 41, no. 5 (May 1, 1990): 521–25.

11. Lee and Greif, "Homelessness and Hunger," 3–19.

12. Lee and Greif, "Homelessness and Hunger," 3–19.

13. This argument is not unlike Grunberg and Eagle's "shelterization thesis," wherein they argue that the longer a person stays on the streets, the less they aspire to get out of homelessness, partially because they learn how to acculturate themselves to the homeless life (Grunberg and Eagle, "Shelterization" 521–25). Snow and Anderson support this idea when they point out, in their typology of homeless life, that there are some who "drift further into street life, with both their cognitive orientation and their daily routine riveted on surviving on the streets rather than making it off." Snow and Anderson, *Down on Their Luck* (1993). My research departs from Grunberg and Eagle in one crucial way. I do not find that the homeless stay in homelessness simply because they acculturate themselves to homelessness. I find that, if people who have long spells of homelessness tend to remain homeless, it is because surviving homelessness leaves little room to work toward escaping it. Grunberg and Eagle blame the homeless for not finding a way out of homelessness. I am suggesting that surviving homelessness is a full-time existence that leaves little room for anything else. And, service provides have oriented much of their services for making homelessness bearable, but not for escaping homelessness.

14. For a discussion of homelessness and skidrow, see Stuart 2016.

15. Jacob Fuller and R. L. Nave, "Developing Jackson: A Decade of Progress," *Jackson Free Press*, September 19, 2012, http://www.jacksonfreepress.com/news/2012/sep/19/developing-jackson-decade-progress/; Robyne S. Turner, "The Politics of Design and Development in the Postmodern Downtown," *Journal of Urban Affairs* 24, no. 5 (December 1, 2002): 533–48.

16. Roberta Ann Johnson, "African Americans and Homelessness: Moving Through History," *Journal of Black Studies* 40, no. 4 (March 1, 2010): 583–605.

17. John Hope Franklin and Alfred A. Moss Jr., *From Slavery to Freedom: A History of African Americans*, (New York: McGraw-Hill, 1994).

18. Linda W. Slaughter, *The Freedmen of the South* (Cincinnati, OH: Elm Street Printing, 1869), http://archive.org/details/freedmenofSouthoslau.

19. W.E.B. Du Bois, *The Philadelphia Negro: A Social Study* (Philadelphia: University of Pennsylvania Press, 1899), 58.

20. Kim Hopper and Norweeta Milburn, "Homelessness Among African-Americans: A Historical and Contemporary Perspective," in *Homelessness in America*, ed. Jim Baumohl (Phoenix, AZ: Oryx, 1996), 123–31.

21. "Many Black tenant farmers were literally homeless; a roof over their heads meant just a sheet of tin or metal or even just a large tree that provided shade. Some relief officials rationalized Black homelessness as acceptable. Blacks, they thought, should feel comfortable living outdoors. One anonymous official of the Federal Emergency Relief Administration was quoted as saying that "local relief agents were more inclined to favor whites because the Negro is better adjusted to the open country environment and is accustomed to getting along on less" (M. Franklin, 1985 "Organizing for survival and change," unpublished ms., Amherst, MA). (Johnson 2010:594)

22. Johnson, "African Americans and Homelessness" 583–605; Gregory D. Squires, *Capital and Communities in Black and White: The Intersections of Race, Class, and Uneven Development* (Albany: State University of New York Press, 1994);

Jennifer R. Wolch and Michael J. Dear, *Malign Neglect: Homelessness in an American City* (San Francisco: Jossey-Bass, 1993).

23. US Department of Housing and Urban Development, "HUD 2018 Continuum of Care Homeless Assistance Programs Homeless Populations and Subpopulations" (Washington, DC, 2018).

24. Margot Sanger-Katz, "Hate Paperwork? Medicaid Recipients Will Be Drowning in It," *New York Times*, January 18, 2018, sec. The Upshot, https://www.nytimes.com/2018/01/18/upshot/medicaid-enrollment-obstacles-kentucky-work-requirement.html; Pamela Herd and Donald P. Moynihan, *Administrative Burden: Policymaking by Other Means*, (New York: Russell Sage Foundation, 2019).

Chapter 4. Minister Montgomery and Charles—Mornings

1. "Annual Statistical Report on the Social Security Disability Insurance Program" (Washington, DC: Social Security Administration, November 2013).

2. Kurt D. Johnson, Les B. Whitbeck, and Dan R. Hoyt, "Predictors of Social Network Composition among Homeless and Runaway Adolescents," *Journal of Adolescence* 28, no. 2 (April 2005): 231–48.

3. Siobhan M. Toohey, Marybeth Shinn, and Beth C. Weitzman, "Social Networks and Homelessness Among Women Heads of Household," *American Journal of Community Psychology* 33, no. 1–2 (2004): 7–20.

4. Erving Goffman, *Stigma: Notes on the Management of Spoiled Identity* (New York: Simon and Schuster, 2009).

5. Mario Luis Small, *Someone To Talk To* (New York: Oxford University Press, 2017).

6. Elliot Liebow, *Tell Them Who I Am* (New York: Simon and Schuster, 1993), 139.

7. Minister Montgomery's case is an example of how structural forces can produce homelessness. Scholars often attribute the causes of homelessness to large-scale factors such as macroeconomic conditions, housing squeezes (when affordable housing demand exceeds supply), demographic trends (immigration and changes in family structure), public policy shifts (welfare, mental health, housing), and drug epidemics (crack). See, Blau, *The Visible Poor: Homelessness in the United States* (Oxford: Oxford University Press, 1993); Martha R. Burt, *Over the Edge: The Growth of Homelessness in the 1980s* (New York: Russell Sage Foundation, 1993); Christopher Jencks, *The Homeless* (Cambridge, MA: Harvard University Press, 1995); *Helping America's Homeless: Emergency Shelter Or Affordable Housing?* (Washington, DC: The Urban Institute, 2001). Researchers have also learned that on an individual level, physical and sexual abuse, neglect, family conflict, poverty, housing instability, and alcohol and drug use increase the likelihood of homelessness. See Barrett A. Lee, Kimberly A. Tyler, and James D. Wright, "The New Homelessness Revisited," *Annual Review of Sociology* 36, no. 1 (2010): 501–21; Kimberly A. Tyler, "A Qualitative Study of Early Family Histories and Transitions of Homeless Youth," *Journal of Interpersonal Violence* 21, no. 10 (October 1, 2006): 1385–93; Kevin A. Yoder, Les B. Whitbeck, and

Dan R. Hoyt, "Event History Analysis of Antecedents to Running Away from Home and Being on the Street," *American Behavioral Scientist* 45, no. 1 (September 1, 2001): 51–65.

8. The debate over which set of factors matter the most has tapered in recent years and given way to an understanding that homelessness is the coming together of unfortunate circumstances. One argument might go like this: Structural difficulties (joblessness or housing squeeze) trigger individual vulnerabilities (divorce or drug use), which in turn create a situational crisis and lead to a short spell of homelessness. Another argument might go like this: Past sexual abuse increases the likelihood of drug use, which leads to being institutionalized (mental health hospital) and, upon discharge, a spell of homelessness (Maureen Crane et al., "The Causes of Homelessness in Later Life: Findings From a Three-Nation Study," *Journals of Gerontology Series B: Psychological Sciences and Social Sciences* 60, no. 3 (May 1, 2005): S152–59; Lee, Tyler, and Wright, "The New Homelessness Revisited," 501–21. Several studies have documented that about a tenth of homelessness occurs as a result of release from institutions such as foster care, treatment facilities, and prisons/jails. Dennis P. Culhane et al., "Testing a Typology of Family Homelessness Based on Patterns of Public Shelter Utilization in Four U.S. Jurisdictions: Implications for Policy and Program Planning," *Housing Policy Debate* 18, no. 1 (2007): 1–28; Peter J. Pecora et al., "Educational and Employment Outcomes of Adults Formerly Placed in Foster Care: Results from the Northwest Foster Care Alumni Study," *Children and Youth Services Review* 28, no. 12 (December 2006): 1459–81.

9. Edna Bonacich, "Advanced Capitalism and Black/White Race Relations in the United States: A Split Labor Market Interpretation," *American Sociological Review* 41, no. 1 (February 1, 1976): 34–51.

10. "American Community Survey" (US Census Bureau, 2011).

11. David A. Snow and Leon Anderson, "Identity Work Among the Homeless: The Verbal Construction and Avowal of Personal Identities," *American Journal of Sociology* 92, no. 6 (May 1, 1987): 1336–71.

12. Lee, Tyler, and Wright, "The New Homelessness Revisited," 501–21.

13. Daniel Kerr and Christopher Dole, "Cracking the Temp Trap: Day Laborers' Grievances and Strategies for Change in Cleveland, Ohio," *Labor Studies Journal* 29, no. 4 (January 1, 2005): 87–108.

14. Following Snow and Anderson (1987), personal identities refer to "meanings attributed to the self by the actor," different from social identities, which are "identities attributed or imputed to others in an attempt to place or situate them as social objects." Self-concept is "one's overarching view or image of her- or himself, Snow and Anderson, "Identity Work Among the Homeless," 1347–48.

15. Snow and Anderson identify the following elements of identity work: (a) procurement or arrangement of physical settings and props; (b) cosmetic face work or the arrangement of personal appearance; (c) selective association with other individuals and groups; and (d) verbal construction and assertion of personal identities.

16. Lee, Tyler, and Wright, "The New Homelessness Revisited," 501–21; Snow and Anderson, *Down on Their Luck* (Berkeley, University of California Press, 1993); Snow

and Anderson, "Identity Work Among the Homeless"; Mitchell Duneier, *Sidewalk* (2001).

17. Elijah Anderson, *The Cosmopolitan Canopy: Race and Civility in Everyday Life* (New York: W.W. Norton & Company, 2012).

18. James Baldwin, "On Being 'White' . . . and Other Lies," *Essence*, April 1984.

Chapter 5. Carl and Ray—Afternoons and Evenings

1. The public libraries were another place of refuge for people who are homeless. In fact, public libraries in some states (California, Minnesota, Illinois) are beginning to add services catering specifically to the homeless population that frequent their branches. Evelyn Nieves, "Public Libraries: The New Homeless Shelters," *Salon*, March 7, 2013.

2. Barrett A. Lee and Chad R. Farrell, "Buddy, Can You Spare A Dime? Homelessness, Panhandling, and the Public," *Urban Affairs Review* 38, no. 3 (January 1, 2003): 299–324.

3. US Census Bureau, "Decennial Census Datasets," 2010, https://www.census.gov /programs-surveys/decennial-census/data/datasets.html.

4. Robert Wuthnow, *Saving America?: Faith-Based Services and the Future of Civil Society* (Princeton, NJ: Princeton University Press, 2009); Manuel Mejido Costoya and Margaret Breen, "Faith-Based Responses to Homelessness in Greater Seattle: A Grounded Theory Approach," *Social Compass*, November 26, 2020, 7, https:// doi.org/10.1177/0037768620971211.

5. David A. Snow and Leon Anderson, *Down on Their Luck: A Study of Homeless Street People* (Berkeley: University of California Press, 1993), 79.

6. Rebecca Sager, "Faith-Based Social Services: Saving the Body or the Soul? A Research Note," *Journal for the Scientific Study of Religion* 50, no. 1 (2011): 201–10, https://doi.org/10.1111/j.1468-5906.2010.01560.x.

7. Rebecca Sager, "Faith-Based Social Services," 201–10.

8. Herbert J. Gans, "The Positive Functions of Poverty," *American Journal of Sociology* 78, no. 2: 275–89.

9. Snow and Anderson, *Down on Their Luck* (1993).

Chapter 6. Zenani—Younger Days

1. Colin Jerolmack and Shamus Khan, "Talk Is Cheap Ethnography and the Attitudinal Fallacy," *Sociological Methods & Research*, March 9, 2014, https://doi.org/10 .1177/0049124114523396.

2. Over time, I found that asking potential participants to teach you something, instead of asking to "study" them, was, in many cases, a more productive way to "get in."

3. Nancy Plankey-Videla, "Informed Consent as Process: Problematizing Informed Consent in Organizational Ethnographies," *Qualitative Sociology* 35, no. 1 (March 1, 2012): 1–21; Barrie Thorne, "'You Still Takin' Notes?' Fieldwork and Problems of Informed Consent," *Social Problems* 27, no. 3 (1980): 284–97.

4. Tanis Furst et al., "Food Choice: A Conceptual Model of the Process," *Appetite* 26, no. 3 (June 1996): 250–51.

5. Christine Blake and Carole A. Bisogni, "Personal and Family Food Choice Schemas of Rural Women in Upstate New York," *Journal of Nutrition Education and Behavior* 35, no. 6 (December 2003): 282–93; Cassandra M. Johnson et al., "It's Who I Am and What We Eat. Mothers' Food-Related Identities in Family Food Choice," *Appetite* 57, no. 1 (August 2011): 220–28, https://doi.org/10.1016/j.appet.2011.04.025; Mary C. Kirk and Ardyth H. Gillespie, "Factors Affecting Food Choices of Working Mothers with Young Families," *Journal of Nutrition Education* 22, no. 4 (July 1990): 161–68, https://doi.org/10.1016/S0022-3182(12)80917-4; Britta Renner et al., "Why We Eat What We Eat. The Eating Motivation Survey (TEMS)," *Appetite* 59, no. 1 (August 2012): 117–28, https://doi.org/10.1016/j.appet.2012.04.004.

6. Julie Beaulac, "A Systematic Review of Food Deserts, 1966–2007," *Preventing Chronic Disease* 6, no. 3 (2009): 1.

7. Beaulac, "A Systematic Review of Food Deserts, 1966–2007," 1.

8. Karen Glanz et al., "Nutrition Environment Measures Survey in Stores (NEMS-S): Development and Evaluation," *American Journal of Preventive Medicine* 32, no. 4 (April 2007): 282–89; Latetia V. Moore and Ana V. Diez Roux, "Associations of Neighborhood Characteristics with the Location and Type of Food Stores," *American Journal of Public Health* 96, no. 2 (February 2006): 325–31; Shannon N. Zenk et al., "Fruit and Vegetable Access Differs by Community Racial Composition and Socioeconomic Position in Detroit, Michigan," *Ethnicity & Disease* 16, no. 1 (2006): 275–80.

9. Alan Beardsworth and Teresa Keil, *Sociology on the Menu: An Invitation to the Study of Food and Society*, (New York: Routledge, 1997): 74; Mary Douglas, "Deciphering a Meal," *Daedalus* 101, no. 1 (1972): 61–81.

10. David Sutton, "Cooking Skills, the Senses, and Memory: The Fate of Practical Knowledge," in *Food and Culture: A Reader*, ed. Carole Counihan and Penny Van Esterik (New York: Routledge, 2012), 299–317; Pierre Bourdieu, *Distinction: A Social Critique of the Judgement of Taste* (Cambridge, MA: Harvard University Press, 1987).

11. Anne Bower, *African American Foodways: Explorations of History and Culture* (Champaign, IL: University of Illinois Press, 2007); Sheila Ferguson, *Soul Food: Classic Cuisine from the Deep South* (New York: Grove Press, 1993).

12. Byron Hurt, *Soul Food Junkies*, DVD, Documentary, 2012.

13. John McWhorter, "The Root: The Myth of the Food Desert," National Public Radio, *NPR*, December 15, 2010, http://www.npr.org/2010/12/15/132076786/the-root-the-myth-of-the-food-desert; John McWhorter, "The Food Desert Myth," *The Daily News*, April 22, 2012, https://www.nydailynews.com/opinion/food-desert-myth-article-1.1065165.

14. I am referring to Mustafa Emirbayer and Ann Mische's conceptualization of agentic orientation, which sidesteps many pitfalls and tensions in sociological theories of action. To begin with, Emirbayer and Mische view ends and means as being constructed together. In fact, as they mention, people come to value ends they have the means to accomplish. In addition, they view choices as intermittently determined by material conditions, values, tastes, and dispositions. Also, they dispense with

simply identifying the list of factors that matter for certain choices. Instead, they seek to understand how various factors converge within a context. Emirbayer and Mische, "What Is Agency?," *The American Journal of Sociology* 103, no. 4 (January 1, 1998): 962–1023.

15. Larry Tye, *Bobby Kennedy: The Making of a Liberal Icon* (New York: Random House, 2016). 348

16. John T. Edge, *The Potlikker Papers: A Food History of the Modern South* (New York: Penguin Press, 2017), 58; Monica M. White, "'A Pig and a Garden': Fannie Lou Hamer and the Freedom Farms Cooperative," *Food and Foodways* 25, no. 1 (January 2, 2017): 20–39.

17. Here, Bill is referring to the Commodity Credit Corporation. For more on this agency, see Reed L. Frischknecht, "The Commodity Credit Corporation: A Case Study of a Government Corporation," *The Western Political Quarterly* 6, no. 3 (September 1, 1953): 559–69.

18. Monica M. White, *Freedom Farmers: Agricultural Resistance and the Black Freedom Movement* (Chapel Hill: University of North Carolina Press, 2019).

19. Ralph Ellison, "Richard Wright's Blues," *The Antioch Review* 5, no. 2 (1945): 199.

20. Lisa Krissoff Boehm, *Making a Way Out of No Way: African American Women and the Second Great Migration* (Jackson: University Press of Mississippi, 2009).

21. This demonstrates research findings about the importance of food in how Black women define themselves, care for themselves, their families, and communities, and respond to inequalities. Psyche A. Williams-Forson, *Building Houses out of Chicken Legs: Black Women, Food, and Power* (Chapel Hill, NC: University of North Carolina Press, 2006).

22. Toni Tipton-Martin, *The Jemima Code: Two Centuries of African American Cookbooks* (Austin: University of Texas Press, 2015). Michael W. Twitty, *The Cooking Gene: A Journey Through African American Culinary History in the Old South* (New York, NY: Amistad, 2017).

23. Owen J. Furuseth and Heather A. Smith, in *Latinos in the New South: Transformations of Place*, ed. Owen J. Furuseth and Heather A. Smith (New York: Routledge, 2016), 1–19.

24. C. Vann Woodward, *Origins of the New South, 1877–1913: A History of the South* (Baton Rouge, LA: Louisiana State University Press, 1981). Charles Reagan Wilson, "From Bozart to Booming: Considering the Past and Future South," *Southern Cultures* 25, no. 1 (2019): 11, https://doi.org/10.1353/scu.2019.0001.

25. Sarah Bowen, Joslyn Brenton, and Sinikka Elliott, *Pressure Cooker: Why Home Cooking Won't Solve Our Problems and What We Can Do About It* (Oxford: Oxford University Press, 2019); Marjorie L. DeVault, *Feeding the Family: The Social Organization of Caring as Gendered Work* (Chicago: University of Chicago Press, 1994).

26. Megan Comfort, *Doing Time Together: Love and Family in the Shadow of the Prison* (Chicago: University of Chicago Press, 2008).

27. Frederick Douglass Opie, *Hog and Hominy: Soul Food from Africa to America* (New York: Columbia University Press, 2010), 129, 125, 132.

Chapter 7. Zenani—Today

1. Scott J. South and Glenn D. Deane, "Race and Residential Mobility: Individual Determinants and Structural Constraints," *Social Forces* 72, no. 1 (1993): 147–67; Matthew Desmond, "Eviction and the Reproduction of Urban Poverty," *American Journal of Sociology* 118, no. 1 (July 2012): 88–133.

2. Robert J. Sampson and Patrick Sharkey, "Neighborhood Selection and the Social Reproduction of Concentrated Racial Inequality," *Demography* 45, no. 1 (February 2008): 1–29; Robert Sampson, Jeffrey Morenoff, and Felton Earls, "Beyond Social Capital: Spatial Dynamics of Collective Efficacy for Children," *American Sociological Review* 64 (1999): 633–60; Shana Pribesh and Douglas B. Downey, "Why Are Residential and School Moves Associated with Poor School Performance?," *Demography* 36, no. 4 (November 1, 1999): 521–34.

3. Maxia Dong et al., "Childhood Residential Mobility and Multiple Health Risks during Adolescence and Adulthood: The Hidden Role of Adverse Childhood Experiences," *Archives of Pediatrics & Adolescent Medicine* 159, no. 12 (December 2005): 1104–10.

4. Shaila Dewan, "In Many Cities, Rent Is Rising Out of Reach of Middle Class," *New York Times*, April 14, 2014, http://www.nytimes.com/2014/04/15/business/more-renters-find-30-affordability-ratio-unattainable.html; Desmond, Matthew, "Housing Crisis in the Inner City," *Chicago Tribune*, April 18, 2010, http://articles.chicagotribune.com/2010-04-18/opinion/ct-oped-0419-evictions-20100416_1_housing-crisis-foreclosure-crisis-low-income.

5. Shaila Dewan, "Evictions Soar in Hot Market; Renters Suffer," *New York Times*, August 28, 2014, http://www.nytimes.com/2014/08/29/us/evictions-soar-in-hot-market-renters-suffer.html; Matthew Desmond, "Disposable Ties and the Urban Poor," *American Journal of Sociology* 117, no. 5 (March 1, 2012): 1295–1335.

6. "Extremely low-income households—a definition used by the US Department of Housing and Urban Development (HUD)—earn 30 percent of area median income or less" (MacDonald and Poethig 2014, 1).

7. Graham MacDonald and Poethig, "We've Mapped America's Rental Housing Crisis | MetroTrends Blog" (Urban Institute, March 3, 2014), http://blog.metrotrends.org/2014/03/america-rental-housing-crisis/.

8. Matthew Desmond et al., "Evicting Children," *Social Forces* 92, no. 1 (2013): 303–27; Gulf Coast Fair Housing Center, "An Audit Report on Race and Family Status Discrimination in the Mississippi Gulf Coast Rental Housing Market" (Gulfport, MS: Gulf Coast Fair Housing Center, 2004).

9. Peter Rosenblatt and Stefanie DeLuca, "'We Don't Live Outside, We Live in Here': Neighborhood and Residential Mobility Decisions Among Low-Income Families," *City & Community* 11, no. 3 (2012): 254–84.

10. Carol B. Stack, *All Our Kin: Strategies for Survival in a Black Community* (New York: Harper & Row, 1973), 43.

11. Disposable ties are "relations between new acquaintances characterized by accelerated and simulated intimacy, a high amount of . . . time spent together,

reciprocal or semi-reciprocal resource exchange, and (usually) a relatively short life span. Desmond, "Disposable Ties and the Urban Poor," 1311.

12. Neither the length of the relationship (short-term versus long-term) nor the depth of the (kin or disposable ties) seem to matter. From my observations, what mattered was that they were all living with so much instability that there was only so much they could do for one another.

13. "Temporary Assistance for Needy Families" (Washington, D.C.: Center On Budget and Policy Priorities, February 6, 2020), 1, https://www.cbpp.org/research /family-income-support/temporary-assistance-for-needy-families.

14. Greg J. Duncan and Jeanne Brooks-Gunn, "Family Poverty, Welfare Reform, and Child Development," *Child Development* 71, no. 1 (January 1, 2000): 188–96.

15. Fifty-five percent of Black children live in states with benefits 20 percent below the level of the poverty line, compared to 40 percent of white children. "Temporary Assistance for Needy Families" (Washington, D.C.: Center On Budget and Policy Priorities, February 6, 2020), 3, https://www.cbpp.org/research/family-income-support /temporary-assistance-for-needy-families.

16. Gene Falk, "Temporary Assistance for Needy Families (TANF): Eligibility and Benefit Amounts in State TANF Cash Assistance Programs" (Washington, D.C.: Congressional Research Service, July 22, 2014).

17. Drew Desilver, "Minimum Wage Hasn't Been Enough to Lift Most Out of Poverty for Decades" (Washington, D.C.: Pew Research Center, February 18, 2014), https://www.pewresearch.org/fact-tank/2014/02/18/minimum-wage-hasnt-been -enough-to-lift-most-out-of-poverty-for-decades/.

18. Rebecca Thiess, "The Future of Work: Trends and Challenges for Low-Wage Workers" (Washington, D.C.: Economic Policy Institute, April 27, 2012), 2, http:// www.epi.org/publication/bp341-future-of-work/.

19. Austin Nichols, "Unemployment and Poverty," Text (Washington, D.C.: Urban Institute, September 13, 2011), http://www.urban.org/publications/412400.html.

20. Amy S. Wharton, "The Sociology of Emotional Labor," *Annual Review of Sociology* 35, no. 1 (2009): 147–65.

21. Kelly Brownell and Katherine Battle Horgen, *Food Fight: The Inside Story of The Food Industry, America's Obesity Crisis, and What We Can Do About It* (New York: McGraw-Hill, 2004).

22. Derek Thompson, "How America Spends Money: 100 Years in the Life of the Family Budget," *Atlantic*, April 5, 2012, http://www.theatlantic.com/business/archive /2012/04/how-america-spends-money-100-years-in-the-life-of-the-family-budget /255475/; Derek Thompson, "Food Is Cheap," *Atlantic*, April 5, 2012, http://www .theatlantic.com/business/archive/2012/04/food-is-cheap/255516/.

23. Mustafa Emirbayer and Ann Mische, "What Is Agency?," *The American Journal of Sociology* 103, no. 4 (January 1, 1998): 994.

24. Emirbayer and Mische, "What Is Agency?," 994.

25. Sendhil Mullainathan and Eldar Shafir, *Scarcity: Why Having Too Little Means So Much* (New York: Macmillan, 2013); Cass R. Sunstein, "It Captures Your

Mind," *The New York Review of Books*, September 26, 2013, 3, http://www.nybooks
.com/articles/archives/2013/sep/26/it-captures-your-mind/.

26. Sendhil Mullainathan and Eldar Shafir, *Scarcity* (Macmillan, 2013); Jesse Singal, "Book Review: 'Scarcity: Why Having Too Little Means So Much' by Eldar Shafir and Sendhil Mullainathan" BostonGlobe.com, October 9, 2013, https://www.bostonglobe.com/arts/books/2013/10/09/book-review-scarcity -why-having-too-little-means-much-eldar-shafir-and-sendhil-mullainathan /iiIdalMtPBS01AKW339iII/story.html.

27. Sendhil Mullainathan and Eldar Shafir, *Scarcity*, 2013; Derek Thompson, "Your Brain on Poverty: Why Poor People Seem to Make Bad Decisions," *Atlantic*, November 22, 2013, http://www.theatlantic.com/business/archive/2013/11/your -brain-on-poverty-why-poor-people-seem-to-make-bad-decisions/281780/.

28. Kelley Fong, "Getting Eyes in the Home: Child Protective Services Investigations and State Surveillance of Family Life," *American Sociological Review* 85, no. 4 (August 1, 2020): 610–38, https://doi.org/10.1177/0003122420938460.

Chapter 8. Ms. Bea

1. Mustafa Emirbayer and Mische, "What Is Agency?," *The American Journal of Sociology* 103, no. 4 (January 1, 1998): 962–1023.

2. Lauren Gust, "Defrosting Dinner: The Evolution of Frozen Meals in America," *Intersect: The Stanford Journal of Science, Technology, and Society* 4 (October 13, 2011): 48–56; LeeAnn Smith, "Frozen Meals," *Journal of Renal Nutrition* 19, no. 3 (May 1, 2009): 11–13.

3. Leslie Hossfeld, E. Brooke Kelly, and Julia Waity, *Food and Poverty: Food Insecurity and Food Sovereignty among America's Poor* (Nashville, TN: Vanderbilt University Press, 2018).

4. Emirbayer and Mische, "What Is Agency?," 962.

5. Tara Hahmann et al., "Problem Gambling within the Context of Poverty: A Scoping Review," *International Gambling Studies* (September 21, 2020): 1–37, https://doi.org/10.1080/14459795.2020.1819365.

Chapter 9. Davis Family—Lumpkins BBQ

1. My research participants lived and/or worked around the same sections of the city, but their worlds rarely collided. This was one of the few rare occasions. Their lives in the city exhibited the old idea of city dwellers being physically close to one another, but socially distant. Louis Wirth, "Urbanism as a Way of Life," *American Journal of Sociology* 44, no. 1 (1938): 1–24.

2. Carlijn B.M. Kamphuis et al., "Bourdieu's Cultural Capital in Relation to Food Choices: A Systematic Review of Cultural Capital Indicators and an Empirical Proof of Concept," *PLoS ONE* 10, no. 8 (August 5, 2015); Wendy Wills et al., "The Framing of

Social Class Distinctions through Family Food and Eating Practices," *The Sociological Review* 59, no. 4 (November 2011): 725–40.

3. The middle-class folks in this section of the book are like those in Mary Pattillo-McCoy, *Black Picket Fences: Privilege and Peril Among the Black Middle Class* (Chicago: University of Chicago Press, 2000). The middle-class folks in Part IV are like those in Karyn R. Lacy, *Blue-Chip Black: Race, Class, and Status in the New Black Middle Class* (Berkeley: University of California Press, 2007).

4. Milton M. Gordon, "Social Class in American Sociology," *American Journal of Sociology* 55, no. 3 (1949): 262–68; Erik Olin Wright, "Social Class," in *Encyclopedia of Social Theory*, ed. George Ritzer (Thousand Oaks, CA: SAGE Publications, 2004).

5. William Julius Wilson, *The Truly Disadvantaged: The Inner City, the Underclass, and Public Policy* (Chicago: University of Chicago Press, 1987); Patricia Hill Collins, *Black Feminist Thought: Knowledge, Consciousness, and the Politics of Empowerment* (New York: Routledge, 1983); Courtney S. Thomas, "A New Look at the Black Middle Class: Research Trends and Challenges," *Sociological Focus* 48, no. 3 (September 2015): 191–207, http://dx.doi.org.ezproxy.lib.davidson.edu/10.1080/00380237.2015.1039439.

6. Mary Pattillo-McCoy, *Black Picket Fences*, (2000).

7. Ashanté M. Reese, *Black Food Geographies: Race, Self-Reliance, and Food Access in Washington,* (Chapel Hill: University of North Carolina Press, 2019); Monica M. White, *Freedom Farmers: Agricultural Resistance and the Black Freedom Movement* (Chapel Hill: University of North Carolina Press, 2019).

8. They live what one theorist calls "a subaltern life." The middle-class ideology, which on the one hand eschews aristocratic ordering of society in favor of the possibility of upward mobility of all citizens, also, on the other hand, includes exclusions based on race, class, gender, and other social markers. The subaltern middle class, like the Black middle class, are those who achieve middle-class status on the promise of an open society and upward mobility, but are denied of it based on discriminatory exclusion. For more on this, see Gyanendra Pandey, "Can There Be a Subaltern Middle Class? Notes on African American and Dalit History," *Public Culture* 21, no. 2 (May 1, 2009): 321–42; Gyanendra Pandey, ed., *Subaltern Citizens and Their Histories* (London: Routledge, 2009).

9. Elizabeth Ruth Cole and Safiya R. Omari, "Race, Class and the Dilemmas of Upward Mobility for African Americans," *Journal of Social Issues* 59, no. 4 (December 2003), https://doi.org/10.1046/j.0022-4537.2003.00090.x; Matthew O. Hunt and Rashawn Ray, "Social Class Identification Among Black Americans: Trends and Determinants, 1974–2010," *American Behavioral Scientist* 56, no. 11 (November 1, 2012): 1462–80, https://doi.org/10.1177/0002764212458275.

10. Mustafa Emirbayer and Ann Mische, "What Is Agency?," *The American Journal of Sociology* 103, no. 4 (January 1, 1998): 962–1023.

11. For a philosophical exploration of this, see John Dewey, *Human Nature and Conduct: An Introduction to Social Psychology* (New York: Modern Library, 1922), 15–42.

12. Anthony Giddens, *Central Problems in Social Theory: Action, Structure, and Contradiction in Social Analysis* (Berkeley: University of California Press, 1979).

13. Zora Neale Hurston, "Characteristics of Negro Expression.," *Negro Anthology*, 1934, 39–61.

14. Erving Goffman, "On Fieldwork," *Journal of Contemporary Ethnography* 18, no. 2 (July 1989): 123–32.

15. Toni Tipton-Martin, *The Jemima Code: Two Centuries of African American Cookbooks* (Austin: University of Texas Press, 2015).

Chapter 10. Davis Family—Cooking with Ava

1. Tatiana Andreyeva et al., "Availability And Prices Of Foods Across Stores And Neighborhoods: The Case Of New Haven, Connecticut," *Health Affairs* 27, no. 5 (September 1, 2008): 1381–88; Christina Black et al., "Variety and Quality of Healthy Foods Differ According to Neighbourhood Deprivation," *Health & Place* 18, no. 6 (November 1, 2012): 1292–99; Wendi Gosliner et al., "Availability, Quality and Price of Produce in Low-Income Neighbourhood Food Stores in California Raise Equity Issues," *Public Health Nutrition* 21, no. 9 (June 2018): 1639–48.

2. Geno Lee, Oral History Project: Jackson's Iconic Restaurant, interview by Amy Evans, March 24, 2011.

3. Suzanne M. Bianchi et al., "Is Anyone Doing the Housework? Trends in the Gender Division of Household Labor," *Social Forces* 79, no. 1 (2000): 191–228.

4. Douglas Bowers, "Cooking Trends Echo Changing Roles of Women," *Food Review/National Food Review* 23, no. 1 (2000).

5. Lindsey Smith Taillie, "Who's Cooking? Trends in US Home Food Preparation by Gender, Education, and Race/Ethnicity from 2003 to 2016," *Nutrition Journal* 17, no. 1 (April 2, 2018): 41.

6. Taillie, "Who's Cooking?," 41; Michael Pollan, *Cooked: A Natural History of Transformation* (New York: Penguin, 2014); Susanna Mills et al., "Health and Social Determinants and Outcomes of Home Cooking: A Systematic Review of Observational Studies," *Appetite* 111 (April 1, 2017): 116–34.

7. Katherin Schaeffer, "Among US Couples, Women Do More Cooking and Grocery Shopping than Men" (Washington, D.C.: Pew Research Center, September 2019), https://www.pewresearch.org/fact-tank/2019/09/24/among-u-s-couples-women-do-more-cooking-and-grocery-shopping-than-men/.

8. H.G. Parsa et al., "Why Restaurants Fail? Part II—The Impact of Affiliation, Location, and Size on Restaurant Failures: Results from a Survival Analysis," *Journal of Foodservice Business Research* 14, no. 4 (October 1, 2011): 360–79.

9. Martha MacDonald, Shelley Phipps, and Lynn Lethbridge, "Taking Its Toll: The Influence of Paid and Unpaid Work on Women's Well-Being," *Feminist Economics* 11, no. 1 (March 1, 2005): 63–94; Carmen Sirianni and Cynthia Negrey, "Working Time as Gendered Time," *Feminist Economics* 6, no. 1 (January 1, 2000): 59–76.

10. Despite substantial evidence to suggest otherwise, MSG's ubiquity in many foods, including in unhealthy foods like Doritos, has led it to be flagged as unnatural and therefore unhealthy. Paula Forbes, "David Chang's MAD Talk on the Stigma of MSG," *Eater*, (September 25, 2012), https://www.eater.com/2012/9/25/6542147/watch -david-changs-mad-talk-on-the-stigma-of-msg.

11. Jessamyn Neuhaus, "The Way to a Man's Heart: Gender Roles, Domestic Ideology, and Cookbooks in the 1950s," *Journal of Social History* 32, no. 3 (1999): 529–55; Lotte Holm et al., "Who Is Cooking Dinner?," *Food, Culture & Society* 18, no. 4 (October 2, 2015): 589–610; Nicklas Neuman and Christina Fjellström, "Gendered and Gendering Practices of Food and Cooking: An Inquiry into Authorisation, Legitimisation and Androcentric Dividends in Three Social Fields," *NORMA* 9, no. 4 (October 2, 2014): 269–85; Ashley Fetters, "The Man's Man's Kitchen," *Curbed*, (January 31, 2018), https://www.curbed.com/2018/1/31/16952460/kitchen-appliances-design-gender -men; Anna Bronnes, "Gender Roles and Food: Are We Sexist?," *Foodie Underground* (blog), (January 27, 2015), https://foodieunderground.com/gender-roles-and-food-are -we-sexist/; Rachel L. Swarns, "When Their Workday Ends, More Fathers Are Heading Into the Kitchen," *New York Times*, November 23, 2014, sec. New York, https:// www.nytimes.com/2014/11/24/nyregion/when-the-workday-ends-more-fathers-are -heading-to-the-kitchen.html.

12. Simone de Beauvoir theorized just as much in the following passage: "Suddenly in the kitchen, where her mother is washing dishes, the little girl realizes that over the years, every afternoon at the same time, these hands have plunged into greasy water and wiped the china with a rough dish towel. And until death they will be subjected to these rites. Eat, sleep, clean . . . the years no longer reach toward the sky, they spread out identical and gray as a horizontal tablecloth; every day looks like the previous one; the present is eternal, useless, and hopeless." Simone de Beauvoir, *The Second Sex*, trans. Constance Borde and Sheila Malovany-Chevallier (New York: Vintage, 1949), 540.

13. Mia Tuan, "Neither Real Americans nor Real Asians? Multigeneration Asian Ethnics Navigating the Terrain of Authenticity," *Qualitative Sociology* 22: 105–25; Carter, "Black Cultural Capital, Status Positioning, and Schooling Conflicts for Low-Income African American Youth," *Social Problems* 50 (February 2003): 136–55.

14. Josée Johnston, Shynon Bauman, and Merin Oleschuk, "Omnivorousness, Distinction, or Both," in *The Oxford Handbook of Consumption*, ed. Frederick F. Wherry and Ian Woodward (New York: Oxford University Press, 2019), 361–80.

Chapter 11. Charles

1. G. M. Eller, "On Fat Oppression," *Kennedy Institute of Ethics Journal* 24, no. 3 (November 12, 2014): 219–45.

2. Jessica Greenebaum, "Vegans of Color: Managing Visible and Invisible Stigmas," *Food, Culture & Society* 21, no. 5 (October 20, 2018): 680–97. For more on this, see Breeze A. Harper, "Going Beyond the Normative White 'Post-Racial' Vegan

Epistemology," in *Taking Food Public: Redefining Foodways in a Changing World*, ed. Psyche Williams Forson and Carole Counihan (New York: Routledge, 2013).

3. Khushbu Shah, "The Secret Vegan War You Didn't Know Existed," Thrillist, January 26, 2018, https://www.thrillist.com/eat/nation/vegan-race-wars-white -veganism; Kelly L. Markowski and Susan Roxburgh, "'If I Became a Vegan, My Family and Friends Would Hate Me:' Anticipating Vegan Stigma as a Barrier to Plant-Based Diets," *Appetite* 135 (April 1, 2019): 1–9; Jessica Greenebaum, "Veganism, Identity and the Quest for Authenticity," *Food, Culture & Society* 15, no. 1 (March 1, 2012): 129–44; Jessica Greenebaum and Brandon Dexter, "Vegan Men and Hybrid Masculinity," *Journal of Gender Studies* 27, no. 6 (August 18, 2018): 637–48.

4. Greenebaum, "Vegans of Color," 680–97; Jennifer Polish, "Decolonizing Veganism: On Resisting Vegan Whiteness and Racism," in *Critical Perspectives on Veganism*, ed. Jodey Castricano and Rasmus R. Simonsen, The Palgrave Macmillan Animal Ethics Series (Cham: Springer International Publishing, 2016), 373–91.

5. Kristi Walker and Kristen Bialik, "Organic Farming Is on the Rise in the U.S." (Washington, D.C.: Pew Research Center, January 10, 2019), https://www.pewresearch .org/fact-tank/2019/01/10/organic-farming-is-on-the-rise-in-the-u-s/; Laura Driscoll and Nina F. Ichikawa, "Growing Organic, State by State" (Berkeley, CA: Berkeley Food Institute, September 2017), https://food.berkeley.edu/organicstatebystate/.

6. Pierre Bourdieu, *Outline of a Theory of Practice*, trans. Richard Nice (Cambridge: Cambridge University Press, 1977), 164, 167, 169; Joseph C. Ewoodzie, *Break Beats in the Bronx: Rediscovering Hip-Hop's Early Years* (Chapel Hill, NC: University of North Carolina Press, 2017), 83; Julia Moskin, "Is It Southern Food, or Soul Food?," *New York Times*, August 7, 2018, https://www.nytimes.com/2018/08/07/dining/is-it -Southern-food-or-soul-food.html.

7. Jessica Beth Greenebaum, "Questioning the Concept of Vegan Privilege: A Commentary," *Humanity & Society* 41, no. 3 (August 1, 2017): 355–72.

8. Moskin, "Is It Southern Food, or Soul Food?"

9. Mariane Lutz and Luisa Bascuñán-Godoy, "The Revival of Quinoa: A Crop of Health," in *Superfood and Functional Food: An Overview of Their Processing and Utilization*, ed. Waisundara Viduranga and Naofumi Shiomi (Rijeka, Croatia: InTech, 2017), 37–54.

10. Scholars and advocates of veganism agree with his assessment. See Greenebaum, "Questioning the Concept of Vegan Privilege," 4. Also, there are various websites that argue that being vegan might actually be cheaper if one pays close attention to what they purchase. See "Eating Vegan on a Budget," https://animaloutlook .org/eating-vegan-on-a-budget/ and "The Actual Cost of Being Vegan," https://www .iamgoingvegan.com/cost-of-being-vegan/.

11. This reading of his comment does not deny the vast literature on the relationship between food addiction and obesity. It is only to suggest that Charles did not diagnose himself as being addicted but likened his relationship to soul food to addiction. For more on food addiction, see: Claire Curtis and Caroline Davis, "A Qualitative Study of Binge Eating and Obesity From an Addiction Perspective," *Eating Disorders* 22, no. 1 (January 1, 2014): 19–32; Jeffrey L. Fortuna, "The Obesity Epidemic and

Food Addiction: Clinical Similarities to Drug Dependence," *Journal of Psychoactive Drugs* 44, no. 1 (January 1, 2012): 56–63; Carrie R. Ferrario, "Food Addiction and Obesity," *Neuropsychopharmacology* 42, no. 1 (January 1, 2017): 361.

12. W.E.B. Du Bois, "The Freedmen's Bureau," *Atlantic*, March 1, 1901, https://www.theatlantic.com/magazine/archive/1901/03/the-freedmens-bureau/308772/.

13. "It was never much, and it was never close to just, but by the early 20th century, black people had something to hold on to. In 1900, according to the historian James C. Cobb, black landowners in Tunica County outnumbered white ones three to one. According to the U.S. Department of Agriculture, there were 25,000 black farm operators in 1910, an increase of almost 20 percent from 1900. Black farmland in Mississippi totaled 2.2 million acres in 1910—some 14 percent of all black-owned agricultural land in the country, and the most of any state." Vann R. Newkirk II, "The Great Land Robbery," *Atlantic*, September 2019, https://www.theatlantic.com/magazine/archive/2019/09/this-land-was-our-land/594742/; John C. Willis, *Forgotten Time: The Yazoo-Mississippi Delta after the Civil War*, 2000, https://www.upress.virginia.edu/title/1660; James C. Cobb, *The Most Southern Place on Earth: The Mississippi Delta and the Roots of Regional Identity* (New York: Oxford University Press, 1994), 91.

14. Newkirk, "The Great Land Robbery"; Lizzie Presser, "Kicked Off the Land," *The New Yorker*, July 15, 2019, https://features.propublica.org/black-land-loss/heirs-property-rights-why-black-families-lose-land-South/; Manning Marable, "The Politics of Black Land Tenure: 1877–1915," *Agricultural History* 53, no. 1 (1979): 142–52; Andrew W. Kahrl, "Black People's Land Was Stolen," *New York Times*, June 20, 2019, https://www.nytimes.com/2019/06/20/opinion/sunday/reparations-hearing.html; Pete Daniel, *Dispossession: Discrimination Against African American Farmers in the Age of Civil Rights* (Chapel Hill, NC: University of North Carolina Press Books, 2013).

15. Phillippe Steiner, "Physiocracy and French Pre-Classical Political Economy," in *A Companion to the History of Economic Thought*, ed. Jeff E. Biddle, Jon B. Davis, and Warren J. Samuels (Oxford: Blackwell Publishers, 2003), 61–77.

16. Emelyn Rude, "Like a Rolling Store: These Mobile Shops Changed Rural American Life," *Time*, May 24, 2016, https://time.com/4344621/history-rolling-store/.

Chapter 12. Jonathan

1. Sarah Turner and John Bound, "Closing the Gap or Widening the Divide: The Effects of the GI Bill and World War II on the Educational Outcomes of Black Americans," *The Journal of Economic History* 63, no. 01 (March 2003): 145–77.

2. Richard Reeves and Nathan Joo, "White, Still: The American Upper Middle Class," *Brookings*, October 4, 2017, https://www.brookings.edu/blog/social-mobility-memos/2017/10/04/white-still-the-american-upper-middle-class/.

3. Sara Lei, "Nine Charts about Wealth Inequality in America (Updated)" (Washington, D.C.: The Urban Institute, October 5, 2017), http://urbn.is/wealthcharts.

4. Richard Rothstein, *The Color of Law: A Forgotten History of How Our Government Segregated America* (New York: Liveright, 2017).

5. Allison Davis, Burleigh B. Gardner, and Mary R. Gardner, *Deep South: A Study of Social Class and Color Caste in a Southern City* (Chicago: University of Chicago Press, 1941); John Dollard, *Caste and Class in a Southern Town*. (Garden City, NY: Doubleday, 1957); Oliver Cromwell Cox, *Caste, Class, and Race: A Study in Social Dynamics* (New York: Monthly Review Press, 1948); Isabel Wilkerson, *Caste: The Origins of Our Discontents* (New York: Random House, 2020).

6. Josephine A. Beoku-Betts, "We Got Our Way of Cooking Things: Women, Food, and Preservation of Cultural Identity among the Gullah," *Gender & Society* 9, no. 5 (October 1, 1995): 535–55; Bernice Johnson Reagon, "African Diaspora Women: The Making of Cultural Workers," *Feminist Studies* 12, no. 1 (1986): 77–90; Angela Davis, "Reflections on the Black Woman's Role in the Community of Slaves," *The Massachusetts Review* 13, no. 1/2 (1972): 81–100.

7. W.E.B. Du Bois, *The Philadelphia Negro: A Social Study* (Philadelphia: University of Pennsylvania Press, 1899); Franklin Frazier, *Black Bourgeoisie* (New York: Simon and Schuster, 1957); St. Clair Drake and Horace R Cayton, *Black Metropolis: A Study of Negro Life in a Northern City* (Chicago: University of Chicago Press, 1945); Patricia Hill Collins, *Black Feminist Thought: Knowledge, Consciousness, and the Politics of Empowerment* (New York: Psychology Press, 2000).

8. Karyn R. Lacy, *Blue-Chip Black: Race, Class, and Status in the New Black Middle Class* (Berkeley: University of California Press, 2007).

9. Lacy, *Blue-Chip Black* (2007). Also see Lori Latrice Martin, "Strategic Assimilation or Creation of Symbolic Blackness: Middle-Class Blacks in Suburban Contexts," *Journal of African American Studies* 14, no. 2 (June 1, 2010): 234–46; Kesha S. Moore, "What's Class Got to Do With It? Community Development and Racial Identity," *Journal of Urban Affairs* 27, no. 4 (September 1, 2005): 437–51; Karyn R. Lacy, "Black Spaces, Black Places: Strategic Assimilation and Identity Construction in Middle-Class Suburbia," *Ethnic and Racial Studies* 27, no. 6 (November 1, 2004): 908–30.

10. Elijah Anderson, "The White Space," *Sociology of Race and Ethnicity* 1, no. 1 (January 1, 2015): 10–21, https://doi.org/10.1177/2332649214561306.

11. Mary C. King, "'Race Riots' and Black Economic Progress," *The Review of Black Political Economy* 30, no. 4 (March 1, 2003): 51–66.

12. John L. Jackson Jr., *Real Black: Adventures in Racial Sincerity* (Chicago: University of Chicago Press, 2005); John L. Jackson Jr., *Harlemworld: Doing Race and Class in Contemporary Black America* (Chicago: University of Chicago Press, 2010).

13. Claude Fischler, "Food, Self and Identity," *Social Science Information* 27, no. 2 (June 1988): 278.

14. Fischler, "Food, Self and Identity," 84.

15. A recent *New York Times* debate featuring a marketing professor, a dietician, two medical doctors, a food critic, and a cookbook editor discussed whether the gluten-free diet was a fad or if it had health benefits. "Life After Gluten," *New York Times*, http://www.nytimes.com/roomfordebate/2014/02/20/is-avoiding-gluten-a -risky-fad-or-a-healthy-diet/if-a-gluten-free-diet-helps-people-then-leave-them-be.

16. Jonathan's wife is not mentioned by name or included more substantially in this work because, even though she was supportive of my work, she requested to be excluded.

17. Anderson, "The White Space," 11–13.

18. Brent Staples, "Barack Obama, John McCain and the Language of Race," *The New York Times*, September 21, 2008, sec. Opinion, http://www.nytimes.com/2008 /09/22/opinion/22observer.html.

19. Jackson, *Real Black*, 15.

Chapter 13. Dorian, Adrianne, and Othor

1. Gary Alan Fine, *Kitchens: The Culture of Restaurant Work*, (Berkeley: University of California Press, 2008).

2. A 2006–2007 survey found that about half of American adults eat by grazing on a regular basis. Moreover, people with higher wages are more likely to graze than those with lower wages. Daniel S. Hamermesh, "Incentives, Time Use and BMI: The Roles of Eating, Grazing and Goods," *Economics & Human Biology* 8, no. 1 (March 2010): 2–15. Like binge eating, researchers have found that grazing is associated with higher risk for obesity. Ronna Saunders, "'Grazing': A High-Risk Behavior," *Obesity Surgery* 14, no. 1 (January 1, 2004): 98–102.

3. Oliver Burkeman, "Scarcity: Why Having Too Little Means So Much by Sendhil Mullainathan and Eldar Shafir—Review," *Guardian*, August 23, 2013, http://www.theguardian.com/books/2013/aug/23/scarcity-sendhil-mullainathan -eldar-shafir; Jesse Singal, "Book Review: 'Scarcity: Why Having Too Little Means So Much' by Eldar Shafir and Sendhil Mullainathan, *Boston Globe*," October 9, 2013, https://www.bostonglobe.com/arts/books/2013/10/09/book-review-scarcity -why-having-too-little-means-much-eldar-shafir-and-sendhil-mullainathan /iiIdalMtPBS01AKW339iII/story.html.

4. Elijah Anderson, "The White Space," *Sociology of Race and Ethnicity* 1, no. 1 (January 1, 2015): 13, https://doi.org/10.1177/2332649214561306.

5. For more on how middle-class Black people navigate white spaces, see Anderson, "The White Space," 13–15.

6. This is a subtle example of how, according to Elijah Anderson, white folks respond to Black folks in "white spaces." For more, see Anderson, "The White Space," 13.

7. Franklin Frazier, *Black Bourgeoisie* (New York: Simon and Schuster, 1957); Martin Kilson, "E. Franklin Frazier's *Black Bourgeoisie Reconsidered*: Frazier's Analytical Perspective," in *E. Franklin Frazier and Black Bourgeoisie*, ed. James E. Teele (Columbia: University of Missouri Press, 2002), 131. Kilson further describes the new Black bourgeoisie as follows: "Furthermore, the insider/outsider condition facing today's black bourgeoisie is influenced by the newness of today's full-fledged bourgeois sector among African Americans. The vast majority of the newly fledged black bourgeoisie (a bourgeoisie that is without or rather has fewer of the "pathologies" identified by Frazier) come from blue-collar or upper-working-class and lower-middle-class

African American families, with only a small section of today's black bourgeoisie having second-generation bourgeois origin (perhaps 10 to 20 percent). Thus, most of the new black bourgeoisie continue to have overlapping class and cultural ties deep in the everyday realities of black ethnicity." Martin Kilson, "E. Franklin Frazier's *Black Bourgeoisie* Reconsidered: Frazier's Analytical Perspective," in *E. Franklin Frazier and Black Bourgeoisie*, ed. James E. Teele (Columbia: University of Missouri Press, 2002), 131.

8. Kilson, "E. Franklin Frazier's *Black Bourgeoisie* Reconsidered," 132.

Chapter 14. Running for Jackson

1. Martin Kilson, "E. Franklin Frazier's *Black Bourgeoisie* Reconsidered: Frazier's Analytical Perspective," in *E. Franklin Frazier and Black Bourgeoisie*, ed. James E. Teele (Columbia: University of Missouri Press, 2002), 131.

2. Byron Orey, "Deracialization, Racialization, or Something in between?: The Making of a Black Mayor in Jackson, Mississippi," *Politics & Policy* 34, no. 4 (2006): 814–36.

3. Sarah Campbell, "Johnson Enters Mayoral Race Promising a Better Jackson," *The Clarion Ledger*, October 30, 1992, sec. A1; Orey, "Deracialization, Racialization, or Something in between?: The Making of a Black Mayor in Jackson, Mississippi," *Politics & Policy* 34, no. 4 (2006): 814–36.

4. Jonathan's wife is not mentioned by name or included more substantially in this work because, even though she was supportive of my work, she requested to be excluded.

5. Bhaskar Sunkara, "Chokwe Lumumba: A Revolutionary to the End," February 26, 2014, https://www.thenation.com/article/archive/chokwe-lumumba -revolutionary-end/; Herbert Buchsbaum, "Jackson Mourns Mayor With Militant Past Who Won Over Skeptics," *New York Times*, March 9, 2014, sec. U.S., https://www .nytimes.com/2014/03/10/us/jackson-mourns-mayor-with-militant-past-who-won -over-skeptics.html.

6. Eddie S. Glaude Jr., *In a Shade of Blue: Pragmatism and the Politics of Black America* (Chicago: University of Chicago Press, 2008).

7. Todd Levon Brown, "Racialized Architectural Space: A Critical Understanding of Its Production, Perception and Evaluation," *Architecture_MPS*, April 19, 2019, https://doi.org/10.14324/111.444.amps.2019v15i3.001.

Chapter 15. Studying Food, Race, and the South

1. Lisa Peters, *Heart of the City: Dying to Eat in Jackson*, Documentary (Black Entertainment Television, 2009).

2. Lombe et al., "Examining Effects of Food Insecurity and Food Choices on Health Outcomes in Households in Poverty," 440–60, https://doi.org/10.1080/00981389.2015 .1133469; Gavin Turrell, "Socioeconomic Differences in Food Preference and Their

Influence on Healthy Food Purchasing Choices," *Journal of Human Nutrition and Dietetics* 11, no. 2 (April 1, 1998): 135–49.

3. Michelle Jackson, *Manifesto for a Dream: Inequality, Constraint, and Radical Reform* (Stanford, CA: Stanford University Press, 2020).

Chapter 16. Afterword and Acknowledgments

1. Matthew Desmond, *Evicted: Poverty and Profit in the American City* (New York: Crown Publishers, 2016), 328.

Note: Page numbers in italic type indicate illustrations.

A NOTE ON THE TYPE

THIS BOOK has been composed in Miller, a Scotch Roman typeface designed by Matthew Carter and first released by Font Bureau in 1997. It resembles Monticello, the typeface developed for The Papers of Thomas Jefferson in the 1940s by C. H. Griffith and P. J. Conkwright and reinterpreted in digital form by Carter in 2003.

Pleasant Jefferson ("P. J.") Conkwright (1905–1986) was Typographer at Princeton University Press from 1939 to 1970. He was an acclaimed book designer and AIGA Medalist.

The ornament used throughout this book was designed by Pierre Simon Fournier (1712–1768) and was a favorite of Conkwright's, used in his design of the *Princeton University Library Chronicle*.